Edwin Arlington Robinson's

LETTERS TO

Edith Brower

Edwin Arlington Robinson's

LETTERS TO

Edith Brower

Edited by

RICHARD CARY

The Belknap Press of Harvard University Press

CAMBRIDGE · MASSACHUSETTS · 1968

Distributed in Great Britain by Oxford University Press
Library of Congress Catalog Card Number 68–17623
Printed in the United States of America

For H. Bacon Collamore and Mrs. William Nivison

who made it possible and pleasant

Acknowledgments

In 1938 Hermann Hagedorn, Robinson's first biographer, asserted in a footnote that he was not permitted to examine the letters of E.A.R. to Edith Brower. From that time, students of American literary history have desired access to them. Now, thirty years later, Miss Brower's accumulation is presented in its entirety, together with her "Memories of Edwin Arlington Robinson," and documentation of all relevant persons and allusions.

For aid in consummating this volume I wish to thank above all Mr. H. Bacon Collamore, who procured and made available the letters, and Mrs. William Nivison, niece and executrix of the poet, who gave permission to publish them without deletion or deviation.

I am also grateful to Kenneth P. Blake, Jr., Librarian of Colby College, for securing essential books, periodicals, and reproductions; Daniel R. MacGilvray, Director of the Wyoming Historical and Geological Society in Wilkes-Barre at the time of my researches there, for unstinted interest and courtesy; Frances Dorrance, Edith L. Reynolds, Modesta Ximena, Mrs. Alfred Schroeder, and Mrs. Franck G. Darte, who knew Edith Brower and generously shared their memories of her with me.

Finally, I defer to my wife and defenseless friends who, on request, stared at examples of Robinson's inscrutable penmanship and gravely rendered opinions.

RICHARD CARY

Colby College
Waterville, Maine

Contents

Edwin Arlington Robinson's

LETTERS TO

Edith Brower

Edwin Arlington Robinson, about 1897

Edith Brower, about 1880

(Courtesy of Colby College Library)

Introduction

"But this is poetry!" And again, "But this is poetry!" Thus, incredulously, Edith Brower proclaimed the genius of Edwin Arlington Robinson on first looking into his self-published collection of poems, *The Torrent and the Night Before.*

Having no prospect of sales, Robinson set about distributing the packet of 312 blue paperbound booklets when they arrived in Gardiner, Maine, in the first week of December 1896. He presented some to local friends and mailed others to book reviewers, who might conceivably bestow a notice, and to literary personages known to him only through the medium of their works. One of these was Dr. Titus M. Coan, a medical doctor turned manuscript doctor, who maintained a "Bureau of Criticism and Revision" for assumptive authors in New York City. Robinson had seen an engaging quatrain by Coan in the *Century* and concluded that he would acclaim the kind of poetry in *The Torrent.* Miss Edith Brower, one of Coan's staff of readers, commuted frequently from her home in Wilkes-Barre, Pennsylvania. During her visit to his office early in January 1897, the puckish doctor pushed a copy of the pamphlet toward her without comment (see Appendix I, her "Memories of Edwin Arlington Robinson" for a dramatic account of the proceedings).

The upshot of her reading was an impulsive note written on the spot. She recalls it as a curt demand, "Please send me at once a copy of your book, if you have to beg, borrow, or steal one. Should it be necessary, kill somebody to get it," whereas Robinson describes it as "a letter (4 pages)." On January 13 he sent her a retrieved copy of the poems with a response wholly antipodal in tone. Therewith was inaugurated a correspondence that extended across three and a third decades, to the year before her death in 1931. Robinson's protests to the contrary, Miss Brower preserved 189 of his messages. And, although he professed to have saved her first letter, only one postcard from 1926—fortuitously forgotten in one of his books—survives.

He was instantly intrigued by this "infernally bright" female who seemed to be "in a very bad way over my verses." Gradually, by transparent indirections and then through her photograph, he learned that she stood "five feet six in her stocking feet" and was "not at all ugly," with "dark sharp eyes" and "dark hair (gray on the forehead)." She was obviously older than he, and his fellow club member of The Quadruped, Arthur Blair, sniggered over Robinson's "great-aunt." She also rode a bicycle and was virtually a vegetarian. When Miss Brower embarked for Europe in the summer of 1897, Robinson importuned his friend Harry de Forest Smith, then in residence at a German university, to find out more about her. Smith did talk with some Wilkes-Barre acquaintances of Miss Brower in a Berlin pension but did not encounter her personally. After dodging repeated invitations for almost a year, Robinson finally detrained at Wilkes-Barre on Saturday afternoon, January 8, 1898, and they came face to face. Miss Brower rubricates this "little visit of two days and two nights" in her memoir. Approximately a month later Robinson said tersely to Smith (whom he had considered "working" into the same trip): "Had a good time and found a good friend." Edith Brower was all of that and more.

She was born in New Orleans on August 24, 1848, twenty-one years and four months before Robinson saw the light of day in Head Tide, Maine. Scion of venerable Puritan-Cavalier families—the Browers and the Gardiners of Long Island were established in the New World by 1637—she qualified as a member of the Holland Dames and the Daughters of the American Revolution. At the age of nine months she was brought to Wilkes-Barre, where she resided continuously until she died more than fourscore years later.

Unusually acute as a child, she was home-taught for five years before attending public school for the first time at the age of nine. This lasted only a few weeks; an attack of whooping cough necessitated withdrawal. She re-entered at ten, taking courses with girls three years her senior. At thirteen she registered at the Wilkes-Barre Female Seminary, a coeducational institution despite its title. Here she displayed brilliance, but in accord with the Victorian view of women's juniority she received no higher education.

By birth and training she was orthodox Presbyterian. She remained a faithful member of the First Presbyterian Church, dispensing Calvin's grim precepts in the Sunday School. But Edith Brower's mind was not one to be shackled long by dogma. In youth she comported herself "after the strictest sect of a Pharisee," but as a free-thinking adult she confessed to being "quite naughty" and ignoring the rigid, sanctimonious fiats. She worshiped often in Episcopal and Welsh Congregational churches, and became increasingly flexible, almost agnostic, in her beliefs.

She was equally broad in her social, civic, and political attitudes, pursuing progressive activities of the time while entertaining progressive (Socialist) friends and ideas. A feminist who nevertheless retained her feminine qualities, she articulately endorsed woman suffrage, advocated abolition of child labor, and pioneered in decent interracial relations with Negroes. A relentless writer of letters to the editor, she persevered while the town chuckled over her condemnation of "the man who spat on Franklin Street." In line with her campaign to clean up and beautify Wilkes-Barre, she organized the Town Improvement Society, which underwent mutations of title to Sociological Club, Civic Club, and finally Wyoming Valley Woman's Club. The amused aldermen, perceiving the handwriting on the wall, stopped laughing, and in short order they enacted statutes against the desecration of public thoroughfares and appropriated funds for the enhancement of the community landscape. At no time in the memory of her contemporaries did she relax vigilance over the administration of her beloved city.

This toughness was balanced in her nature by exceptional sensitivity to art, music, and literature. Armed with competence in all three, she embellished her life and the life of her friends with appreciation of them. A creditable pianist, she illustrated her popular lectures on music with selections on the instrument. This phase of her talent captivated Robinson, whose first enthusiasm after poetry was music. What held them together, however, was her aptitude as a writer and her discernment as a critic. When their correspondence started, Miss Brower had already published some twenty articles and stories in such periodicals as the *Atlantic Monthly*, *Harper's Weekly*, *Catholic World*, and *Lippincott's*—an imposing pantheon to a balked poet whose most prominent outlets up to then were the columns of a Boston evening newspaper and his own self-promoted booklet. He tramped miles in freezing weather to obtain copies of her publications, which he read eagerly and criticized sagely. She wrote romances in the manner of Scott, local color tales of the coal mining district, essays on art, music, local history, and literary critiques. She also composed poems, a scantling number of which came into print.

A germinal factor in the Robinson-Brower friendship was the streak of philanthropy in her makeup. Lacking adequate wealth, she exerted every influence at her disposal to assist gifted novices toward their goals. Sometimes, as in the case of teen-age Modesta Ximena, she arranged for piano lessons and put her in the way of prosperous sponsors. Given Robinson's age (late twenties) and temperament (fastidious reticence), this was neither possible nor desired. She offered instead mutuality of interests, intellectual interchange, and a sympathetic ear. On the practical side, she published a review of his poems (see Appendix II) and commended his work to professionals and devotees, perhaps most importantly to Mrs. Edward MacDowell, at whose Peterborough Colony Robinson was to enjoy the most serene and fertile seasons of his creative life.

Miss Brower's "Memories of Edwin Arlington Robinson," begun in March of her seventy-second year, sprawls over fifty-four sextodecimo pages. In it she reports the trepidations brought about by her unparalleled cache of letters and congratulates herself for not destroying or expurgating a single one. The fact is she did excise or efface passages in several instances. Now and again she is errant in the matter of names, dates, and places (those apprehended are rectified in the Notes). And although she recommends the magnifying glass to future readers of Robinson's "minute and compressed hand," she is guilty of misreading herself, for which he took her to task more than once. Beyond these minor solecisms the memoir is an invaluable index to her conception of him as a man and a poet.

Two highlights in Miss Brower's manuscript are the scene in Dr. Coan's office when she first sampled "the not unpleasing New England flavor of dry irony" in Robinson's verse, and his two-day visit with her in Wilkes-Barre. The latter is sparse in details but rich in insights to his sensibility as it touched hers. A tone of benign retrospection—bright with interspersions of stories about her cat and the jar of gooseberry conserve—pervades the essay. Distinguishable throughout is an accent of possessiveness—the protective, proprietary instinct of discoverer. Out of vanity, she depreciates other women who attempt to patronize and monopolize Robinson as his name grows. More meaningfully, she comprehends the basis of his frustration—*furor poeticus* stifling in a Philistine ambiance—and affords him stimulating, approbative, feminine release. By opening channels of communication and recognition acceptable to his disposition, she helped him transcend "that dismal, blank, misinterpreted life of his." She concludes, not without justice, that "the writing of these letters saved his life, so to speak."

Miss Brower ably conjectures upon the effect a happier youthful environment might have had on Robinson's evolution as a poet. From his minimal biographical disclosures and his personal habits she extracts the gist of his estimation of self, of other individuals, and of people generically. She is aware that vaporous praise is repugnant to him, yet his implacable modesty piques her because, finally, it impugns the sincerity of her favorable statements regarding him and his work. Thus she probes for the man in the letters, and in the end she decides to save all of them for the best of reasons: "Everything R. writes here throws some useful light on his mind and character."

It may be counted a gain for literary history that Miss Brower ignored Robinson's admonitions to tear up or burn these letters. He had small confidence in the quality of his letter-writing. When Esther Bates complimented him on the Morgan Le Fay letter in *Tristram*, he remarked artfully, "I wish I could write as good a one myself." Even though he wrote thousands of them, it was "always a grind," and he said flatly to Miss Brower, "I'm not literary when I write letters." Nevertheless, he was not totally unconscious of their possible merit. In 1931 Percy MacKaye proposed an edition of Robinson letters. Robinson responded characteristically that there could not be anything "very startling" or "very valuable" in such a volume, but then he supposed that "a book of selections from them might be readable and possibly mildly amusing."

We owe to Edith Brower's astuter judgment the opportunity to present here the complete collection of Robinson's letters to her. Shortly following the poet's death, Mr. H. Bacon Collamore saw a small group of them on temporary exhibit in a university library. He ascertained that they belonged to a physician living in New York, called on him, and learned that the letters had been bequeathed by Miss Brower to Miss Effie Parsons, a cousin, who had turned them over to the doctor in lieu of cash payment for medical services. Mr. Collamore purchased the letters and consigned them to Colby College for deposit in the Edwin Arlington Robinson Memorial Room.

Around the time Miss Brower set about writing her "Memories," in 1920, she also began to correlate Robinson's letters to her. Over the years she must have tucked them away in sundry recesses, not all of which she immediately remembered, and there are indications that she redeemed a few she had allowed friends to borrow. She arranged them in rather erratic chronological order. Some dated letters were out of alignment and the context of several undated letters belied their position. She numbered each letter at the top, arriving at a figure of 169. As she discovered additional letters, she numbered them—appending *a*, *b*, or *c*, as needed—and inserted them in the set. Two letters are unnumbered;

one (No. 73 in this volume) is a typed copy of the original; and the letter Miss Brower numbered 11, written between March 24 and April 2, 1897, is missing. At the outset she wrote explanatory or exclamatory comments in the margins. However, this practice petered out quickly, as though her septuagenarian stamina faltered in the face of Robinson's self-damned "nasty habit of microscopic writing." He repeated words or phrases, usually in moving from one page to another, and, when his mind outpaced his pen, he left out words. Miss Brower sometimes interpolated the omitted words and deciphered others, which as often as not she misconstrued. The present editor has eliminated Robinson's duplicated words and phrases, supplied missing elements within brackets, transformed ampersands, corrected occasional wayward spelling, formalized use of the dash, the hyphen, and the apostrophe; standardized punctuation, renditions of titles, and datelines. The same has been done in Miss Brower's "Memories" and notations on Robinson's letters. Dates appended to the letters in brackets were either penciled in by Miss Brower or determined by the editor on the basis of internal or other valid evidence.

During his early maturity Robinson had at least four friends to whom he could disclose his poetic hopes with the conviction that they understood and could help in a psycho-aesthetic way. All were residents of Gardiner: Harry de Forest Smith, Alanson T. Schumann, Laura E. Richards, and Caroline D. Swan. Over the men, Edith Brower commanded the advantage of sex; over the women, that of distance. Although he steadfastly avoided intimacy with women, Robinson felt that they responded more sensitively to his work; high among his aversions were men who regarded his poems as "dainty." From the start he observed that "the eternal feminine is much in evidence" in Miss Brower's letters, that she was "devilish bright," indeed "the most sagacious female that I ever ran across," and that he had to be "very careful how I express myself when writing to her." The fact that Miss Brower lived in Wilkes-Barre relieved Robinson's congenital diffidence. He did not have to face her day to day, as he did Mrs. Richards and Miss Swan. Therefore, he could with greater freedom and boldness discharge his surging ego on paper. As his "unknown female" she embodied possibly the most important unfettering influence of his emergent artistic life.

In tone and content Robinson's letters to Edith Brower follow a graph consistent with that of his growth as a poet. Three periods of vast interior change are determinable: 1897–1902, the irrepressible ferment that generated his first books; 1903–1913, the barren decade in which the urge for poetry was nearly buried; 1914–1930, the era of his great books and rise to fame.

The longest, most frequent, and most fervent of the letters were written between January 13, 1897—shortly following publication of *The Torrent and the Night Before*—and October 27, 1902, less than a month after the appearance of *Captain Craig*. In this interval Robinson dispatched 110 messages straight from the core of his parched and insatiable spirit. Here, at last, the chance to be expansive with one who knew "a great deal more than I do about books and things" had presented itself. And there is a touch of pathos in the way he leaped at it. Having verified that she was of an age beyond question of romantic attachment, and having prudently if clumsily impressed this upon her, he happily arrogated the role of Pygmalion to her superannuated Galatea. She induced him to believe that he had "straightened out some of her ideas," in fact "made her over." She infused him with confidence that he had "the power of helping others," and that he had spread "a little spiritual good in the world." While conceding to Harry Smith that this had "done wonders" for him, in his naivete and solipsism Robinson barely glimpsed the depth of Miss Brower's strategy.

Unquestionably the therapy was dual in its effects but, ultimately, more propitious for Robinson than for Miss Brower. At the moment in his development when he was most in need of a sounding board against which to let fly his uncontainable perceptions, she was there, steady and reflective, provocative and subordinate. Literally "a god-send," she furnished a timely anodyne—voluntary authentication by an intelligent stranger. She liberated his icebound *cri de cœur* and propelled him toward further quests of his profoundest self. In 1897, hampered by caution and inexperience, he vapidly described their association as "a very pleasant episode in a rather commonplace life." By 1920, with *The Man Against the Sky*, *Merlin*, and *Lancelot* behind him, he could tell her simply and surely: "Your persistent approval from the beginning has been of greater value to me than I have even so much as tried to tell you in language. But I have said it all in silence, much of which you have heard."

In the prolific first period of the correspondence, Robinson's concerns are those of the young, unsung poet scrambling among the foothills of Parnassus. He sends her early drafts of unpublished poems, requests assessments, and solicits suggestions for changes. He expounds phrases or themes in his poems misinterpreted by critics or friends, gratified that she is one of "the hopeless minority" who sometimes sees what he is driving at. Extremely thin-skinned about some of her reactions, he lashes back irritably, than repents for having hurt her feelings or making her cry. Altogether, he leaves no room for doubt that he "was doomed, or elected, or sentenced for life, to the writing of poetry."

He minutely analyzes her published essays and stories: first, because he is intoxicated by her achievement of print; second, because he is itching to display critical acuity to one who speaks his language. (In grateful recompense, Robinson grossly overrates her work.) Along the same vein he animatedly discusses Dickens, Browning, Hardy, Burns, Pater, Stevenson, Kipling, Emerson, James, Moody, Howells, Maupassant, Mérimée, and Zola, as well as others of lesser repute. He is drawn by the idiosyncrasies of "the race" to deliberate over world events, war, national and civic policies. But neither in this section nor through the entire range of the letters do his remarks jell into anything like a theory of literature or a universal philosophy. He habitually shies away from lofty cogitation, settling for a tart aphorism based on intuition.

Of greatest importance in the letters of this first period is his revelation of ingrained dissatisfaction with himself and his lot. Ordinarily, Robinson's dissections of his character and environment are guarded and usually camouflaged by quip or whimsy. Here (particularly in Letter 12), the stoicism and taciturnity which he wore as his mask to the world is pierced by unconscious appeals for understanding and commiseration. He depicts in quick strokes the states of mind ("spells") brought about by encroachments of family and community upon his commitment to poetry. He recognizes the absurd in his situation: pressed by outside forces to take a job and make a conventional success, impelled from inside to honor the claims of his aesthetic instinct. He shuffles uneasily between these gates of ivory and of horn. Was there greater virtue in being a "maker of three-dollar shoes" than he could see? His doubts are abstract and momentary. Predictably he yields to the "literary worm" in his head.

The signs of a destructive ambivalence are exposed in Robinson's reiterated impulse to escape to New Zealand, to Auckland—which turn out in the long run to be Boston and New York. In Letter 40 he offers perhaps the most incisive key to the motivation of his poems, the Tilbury and the Arthurian alike: "There are things to make me go to Maine, and there are things to keep me away from there."

Numerous warrants of his personality flash to the surface in these early letters: his addiction to Yankee saws and lore; his capacious love of music, from sportive folk tunes to operas and symphonies; the small vanity about his French and his weakness for limericks; his unfailing dry, sly Down East humor. Foremost, however, is the specter of his deep-seated reticence, what Chard Powers Smith has called "his appalling humility." It shows up in his insistence on destroying the letters, not only because he believes them worthless as literary expression but also because he senses that they contain clues to his introspective self. He is embarrassed by involvement in such a prosy activity as exchanging photographs. Time after time he apologizes when apology seems superfluous, vowing darkly that he is no gentleman. He sheepishly calls himself a "pote" and refers to his "pomes" and "wurruck." Continually he voices misgivings about his worth as a person. He "knows" that his friends consider him "the chief attraction for a dime museum," and cannot understand what they could possibly find "in a lopsided nature like mine" to interest them. He suffers extreme discomfort in crowds or among impressive strangers, preferring the homespun solidity of such comrades as Seth Pope and Arthur Blair. Robinson's psychic dependence upon a few highly selective individuals at this stage is unequivocally established.

The second period of Robinson's letters to Edith Brower includes the six he wrote between those of October 27, 1902, and December 21, 1913. After the amplitude of the years 1897–1902, six letters in ten years marks an astonishing attenuation. The explanation lies in Robinson's aimless, fruitless, disconsolate hand-to-mouth round of existence during this decade. He had gravitated to New York City. Brief tenure as a writer of advertisements in Boston had left him depressed, as did his work as a time-checker on a New York subway construction project. His appointment as a special agent in the Custom House rescued him from penury and conferred free time for writing, but his poems failed to catch the public mind. In this interlude only one new book and two reprints were issued, and only sixteen of his poems received periodical publication. His brother Herman died in a city hospital ward, and Robinson unsuccessfully tried to reorient himself in Gardiner. Back again in New York, he drank heavily and followed, after his fashion, *la vie Bohème*. He lusted after what proved for him to be false gods, consuming years in futile efforts to produce profitable novels and plays. He felt that he was "scraping bottom," and he held on by the merest string.

In this corrosive nighttime of his soul Robinson told Josephine Peabody that he could not "write letters anymore—for the present anyhow," and advised Laura Richards that he was terminating his correspondence with her. The first portent of a similar withdrawal from Miss Brower occurs in the middle of 1902: "I fear that I have no better reason for not writing than the ancient one called laziness." He was either evading or oversimplifying. In any case, the diminution thereafter was sudden and drastic. Beginning October 1903 at least one year and as much as four years elapsed between all but two of the letters he sent until October 1912.

The break in continuity is brought out as clearly in Robinson's salutations as in the datelines. In the first three months of 1897 he greeted her as "My dear Miss Brower," shifting to "Dear Friend" until the end of 1899. For the next eighteen months he launched directly into the message without formality of any sort. Only twice did he veer from these modes. The six letters of this second period show the widest variation of any consecutive group. The first three have no salutations; the fourth, after an hiatus of four years, opens bleakly "Dear Madam"; the fifth reverts to "Dear E.B."; the sixth, a fairly remote "Dear Lady." After two more irregular greetings Robinson goes back in the final period to a rhythmic alternation of "Dear E.B." and no salutation.

The mood and matter of the 1903–1912 letters are permeated by a weariness of spirit. After a year's void Robinson is prodded into writing a consolatory note to Miss Brower on the death of her aunt. As in other letters of this time, he asks forgiveness—somewhat wanly despite his epithets—for disregarding her. He represents himself as feeling "old" and "pumped dry" and "out of the game." His inspiration seems to have deserted him, and he is exploiting warmed-over ideas of past years, skeptical about the resultant poems and about his opinions of the poems. Countermanding his original ebullience, he decries the temerity of his "callow criticism" of her stories. He announces, in a monotone, the exhaustion of his hope to fulfill her high expectations of him as a poet. More than once he says that he wishes to see her when next she comes to town, but there is no warmth or urgency in the assertions.

From December 1913 to June 1930 Robinson's letters resume a steady flow, although palpably thinner than that of the first five years. In this third period of the correspondence no year is entirely skipped.

The resurgence of letters to Miss Brower coincides with the dissolution of Robinson's internal blight and the upward curve of his public reputation. If his turn of fortune may be ascribed to a single event, his first sojourn at the MacDowell Colony in 1911 merits the accolade. In successive summers there he seems to have regained his direction. From that date his work emanates a growing sense of peace, a new vibrancy of motivation. His inclusion in the menage of Mrs. Clara Davidge and in the domestic circles of the Ledoux and Isaacs families discounted the grinding loneliness of the impersonal metropolis, now his permanent home. Liquor was no longer a problem. After the publication of his two hard-won but negligible plays came *The Man Against the Sky* in 1916, then the crescendo of his most renowned books, the benediction of three Pulitzer Prizes, doctoral degrees from Yale and Bowdoin, and honorary medals struck by poetry societies.

The letters in this final period convey his restored self-reliance and the multiplied demands upon his time. They are shorter and less private. Robinson still discusses his compositions with Miss Brower; as before, he invites her comment and thanks her for suggestions. But the struggle now is of another stripe: he speaks of poems and books accomplished and of wounds inflicted by doltish critics and editors. Of her work no more is said. Her ailments, and those of their mutual friends, take precedence. Robinson's inerasable humility keeps cropping up, but between lines he can inform her complacently that his royalties have quadrupled. He reviews himself and the world, and grants that at this point "I'm not growling." He goes to England and remits none of his impressions to her; when she reproaches him he lightly cites his "reprehensible ways." In the searing travail of his black decade Robinson had matured. His vital psychic need of Edith Brower had disintegrated. Yet he never forgot her opportune ministry. His last letter epitomized the pattern of his gratitude. Its two prime topics: her health, his work.

Fifteen months later, on September 16, 1931, Miss Brower died of a heart attack. In obituaries and editorials the local press eulogized her as church worker, civic innovator, social and cultural leader, idealist, regional chronicler, champion of the young, and good neighbor. Two of Miss Brower's friends immediately notified Robinson of her death. To Modesta Ximena he wrote: "I have known her as the kindest of friends for more than thirty years, and shall remember her with much affection and gratitude"; to Katherine Schroeder: "I doubt if anyone ever lived who came nearer to giving her life to others." On January 12, 1932, several hundred people took part in a memorial service for Miss Brower held by the Wyoming Valley Woman's Club. The program was comprised of prayers, piano solos, and readings of several tributes. Among these was one from Robinson *in absentia*, but neither the two reporting newspapers nor any official of the club nor Robinson himself thought to preserve the text of his remarks on the occasion.

These letters will no doubt be perused via the Index by scholars with a thesis seeking corroboration, by critics for Robinson's views of his own work, by essayists with an eye for the provocative, by students for information, and by the merely curious for what he said about his contemporaries. A chronological reading of the letters, however, will yield an increment valuable beyond any such narrow acquisitions: the unfoldment of a poet from the hard, green, uncertain seed, through dry and infertile seasons, to the fullness of bloom, deep-hued and imperishable.

Robinson's Letters to Edith Brower

1

Gardiner, Maine
13 January 1897

My dear Miss Brower:

I send herewith a copy of *The Torrent*, which never found the person to whom it was originally addressed. So you have your book—even though it be a little worn by long journeying—without delay and happily without bloodshed.[1]

Your letter was surprisingly kind and appreciative, but I must confess that I'm wholly at a loss to find anything in my book to warrant your enthusiasm. The fact is, I cannot read it anymore without wondering if mortals are in any way responsible for what they do. The fact, however, that certain people can read it and take the trouble to write about it, gives me a little courage to think it something else than absolute drivel—which is considerable nowadays.

Thanking you again for your good words, I remain,

Very truly yours,
E. A. Robinson

To Miss Edith Brower,
Wilkes-Barre, Pa.

1. Above the dateline of this letter Miss Brower wrote: "See 'Memories' to make clear this allusion"—Appendix I of this volume. The original addressee's name on the title page of this copy is lined over in ink; above it Robinson wrote "To Miss Brower," and below it, "with compliments of E. A. Robinson." The date "16 December, 1896" is lined through, and Miss Brower wrote "Jan. 1897." She also set down an acerbic remark about Houghton Mifflin for taking money to print the poems, pasted a small photograph of Robinson and two of his Octaves in the book, and marked the text in a number of places.

2

Gardiner, Maine
26 January 1897

My dear Miss Brower:

I beg to assure you, sincerely and immediately, that you need have no further qualms of disappointment and distrust over my verses.[1] They are what they are, and they are done, I think, as well as I could do them. When I look back and consider the time and labor they have cost me, I feel rather guilty; that's all there is to my affected self-contempt. The fact that I published them at my own expense, and that as a last resort, is enough, it seems to me, to do away with any minute explanations.

At first I was rather sorry for the poems and for myself; but since they have met the approbation of almost everyone who has read them (publishers excepted)[2] I have concluded to let them go their own way and to fuss no more about them. It's another case of "Go, little book, etc."[3] How far it will go I have no means of knowing. I only know that I am not in a position to find fault with its reception, and that, for the present, is enough.

Dr. Coan's[4] manifested interest in the thing was a gratifying surprise to me, and goes, with your own sincere appreciation and that of many others, to make me feel that I have done nothing absolutely disgraceful. I may have to change my mind, but my philosophy tells me not to trouble myself about that.

You may consider the whole thing as a kind of self-defence against the abject materialism of a "down east" community whereof the whole purpose of life is to "get a job" and to vote a straight Republican ticket.

With repeated thanks, I remain,

Most sincerely yours,
E. A. Robinson

1. In the lower margin of the first page Miss Brower wrote: "I had written him that the tone of his reply to my enthusiasm over his 'verses' gave me the unpleasant feeling of having *enthused* amiss. I did not know the poor fellow then! He was simply morbid owing to uncontrollable circumstances."

2. See Hermann Hagedorn, *Edwin Arlington Robinson* (New York, 1938), pp. 105–106.

3. There are several verses beginning with these or slightly variant words, written by Chaucer, Bunyan, Byron, and Stevenson, but to judge from Robinson's mood he is alluding to Robert Southey's "L'Envoy," in *The Lay of the Laureate* (London, 1816):

Go, little Book; from this my solitude
I cast thee on the waters:—go thy ways!
And if, as I believe, thy vein be good,
The World will find thee after many days.
Be it with thee according to thy worth:—
Go, little Book! in faith I send thee forth.

4. Dr. Titus Munson Coan, whose letterhead proclaimed that his business was established in 1880, and that it consisted of "The Skilled Revision of Mss, Letters of Unbiased Criticism, Editing, Compiling." Robinson writes that in a letter to him, Coan said: "I call it unmistakable poetry . . . in many of the lines there is a deep and moving music. . . . Your gift seems to me quite a certain thing . . ." Denham Sutcliffe, editor, *Untriangulated Stars: Letters of Edwin Arlington Robinson to Harry DeForest Smith, 1890–1905* (Cambridge, Mass., 1947), p. 268.

3

Gardiner, Maine
3 February 1897

My dear Miss Brower:[1]

As a stranger-friend I would express my complete pleasure after reading a story in *Lippincott's* called "Old Friends."[2]

I can partly sympathize with Wheels, though I am not exactly musical. I used to blow a clarinet, however, gauging my progress by the impression I made on the cat. When he began to tolerate the "Miserere" I began to feel encouraged, and kept on feeling so till I discovered, on a woeful day, that the long-suffering brute was stone deaf. Since then I have lost my cunning with keys and reeds and stick to written words—an arrangement which is highly appreciated by my fellow townsmen. They don't have to read my stuff, but they couldn't get away from my fortissimo without moving into another village.

Most sincerely yours,
Edw. A. Robinson

1. Above the salutation Miss Brower wrote: "I had supposed R.'s second letter would close our correspondence and was much surprised the following week to get this."

2. Following this title Miss Brower wrote: "—my own invention." The story is "Old Friends," *Lippincott's*, LIX (February 1897), 274–286. "Wheels" is the nickname applied to Wyn, a child who rolled instead of walking on his little bowlegs. He grew up to be a successful composer of opera.

4

Gardiner, Maine
10 February 1897

My dear Miss Brower:

I don't like to reprimand you after all the kind things you have said about my *Torrent*, but you must be more accurate in the matter of your dates. I have just lugged a bound copy of the *Atlantic* (Vol. 71) over the ice for half a mile, with the natural expectation of reading the tale of your critical cat at the end of my journey. But the cat was not to be found; at any rate, I didn't find him. I have imagination enough, however, to take it for granted that he is in the January number of some other year than '93, and I shall endeavor to find him out.[1] In the meantime, I have to thank you for setting me on his trail.

If ever in the years to come you chance to resurrect your copy of my versicles, perhaps you will pick the cobwebs off rather tenderly and give a thought of charitable recollection to the unnecessary but well-meaning rhymester who once wished for you all sorts of success and happiness. Of the one, he feels assured; the other is, he hopes, included in the scheme of things.

Most sincerely yours,
E. A. Robinson

P.S. No, my cat was not a white one with blue eyes,[2]—if he had been I should have transported him,—but a black one with green eyes. He was very beautiful, but so incurably dignified, and finally so pessimistic, that I had to murder him. I did it with chloroform, however,—so it didn't hurt him any.

E.A.R.

1. Miss Brower's "My Musical Critic" appeared in the *Atlantic Monthly*, LXXIII (January 1894), 139–141.
2. Below his initials Miss Brower wrote: "Such are always deaf."

5

Gardiner, Maine
19 February 1897

My dear Miss Brower:

I have read everything you have prescribed, and now I want some more. Oliver has been cruelly overworked, but I want some more.[1] Where am I going to find it?

Your "Remainder-Man"[2] is very well done, and is exceedingly clever (that's the worst I can say of it) but I must confess that pernickity old maids and fastidious tomcats are not exactly my ideals of literary subject matter. As far as fiction goes, I like you much better in "Old Friends." There I find a kind of spiritual appreciation of the commonplace (so-called) and an insight into the emotional complexities which none of us are yet wise enough to name with words. When words begin to be something more than material figments and shadows, men and women will begin to see things. Until then, these things must be felt and suggested; and what I have read of your work convinces me that you are gifted with the spiritual charity, as well as the appreciation, which goes to make this sensation and suggestion (sometimes they seem to be the same thing) a possibility. The "clubs,"[3] though short, have this same quality. This is particularly true of "Appreciation."[4] In that, and in the more ambitious musical essay,[5] I find enough to make me glad for having said the little I did about your future success. "Old Friends" alone was enough to keep me from feeling sorry.

I do not ignore George Washington, and your sensitive friend who resents the belated emendation of great writers.[6] I only mean that these are not worth so much to me as the others. The difference is, perhaps, rather of degree than of quality. If I were to assume the right to give you any advice, or to make any suggestion, I would say this: Don't ever permit a transient pessimism to blind you to the elemental fact that human life is a compensatory struggle toward the realization of the universal mind; don't let your characters go to ballrooms and afternoon teas (don't give them tea[7] at all unless you give them a square meal with it); don't go to these places yourself any more than you have to,[8] and keep out of the *Ladies' Home Journal.* The thing for you to do is to go right down into the middle of life and compel the world to feel, as you feel it for others, the tension of endeavor, the pathos of failure and success (there is no pathos in a good failure), and the pulse of human realism, of human passion that drives itself through all strong work like blood through a strong man—or a strong woman. I must give the "strong-minded" woman a place by herself and ask her to stay there.

The musical essay[9] is of course the best thing you have given me to read, but I still think you were born to write fiction. I find in "Old Friends" the same thing that I find in every book of imaginative prose that stands today for what is real. No difference of degree can ever kill the truth. *Mother Goose* is just as surely a work of genius as *Hamlet* is, and just as immortal.

If you sacrifice yourself to the conventional frivolity that gives the mortal smell to almost everything now written in America, you will throw away your chances. I don't think, however, that you can do that. The rabbit climbed the tree because he "had to," and it seems to me that you are going to put some life into American prose for pretty much the same good reason. I do not need to say anything that seems to be a formal expression of thanks for your own past kindness and I hope I have not done so. I say nothing that I do not mean. I say that you are on the right track. I say that you have done good work and that you are going to do a good deal better. You can't help doing it.

At the possible risk of making a mistake I must ask you to remember that literature is more than music. You know it already, but there may be troublesome moments when you are inclined to doubt it. I would also say that woman is more than man. Feminine strength is mostly the secret of masculine power (brute force is another thing) and though a man may write bigger novels and compose bigger symphonies, the woman's intuitive utility reveals and acknowledges itself in the greater works that are never written, but simply *are*.

You will probably get more of amusement than anything else from this letter; and if you are forty years old with glasses and gray hair you may show it to your friends and have more fun with it. Otherwise, I would infinitely rather have you tear it up, believing me respectful and sincere, and always very grateful for your friendliness.

Most sincerely yours,
E. A. Robinson

1. Dickens' Oliver Twist and his pitiful plea for a second helping.
2. "The Remainder-Man," appeared in *Two Tales*, II (September 3, 1892), 298–316, a periodical issued each Saturday by the Two Tales Publishing Company of Boston. The story concerns Peter Economy, "a huge striped pussy, who weighed fifteen pounds if he weighed an ounce," who becomes the residuary legatee of an indulgent widow.
3. Several of Miss Brower's essays were published in "The Contributors' Club" department of the *Atlantic Monthly*.
4. "Appreciation Through Enjoyment," *Atlantic Monthly*, LXXII (July 1893), 141–143.
5. "Is the Musical Idea Masculine," *Atlantic Monthly*, LXXIII (March 1894), 332–339.
6. George Washington is the critical cat referred to in the preceding letter. "My Musical Critic," *Atlantic Monthly*, LXXIII (January 1894), 139–141, relates his hatred of vocal music. "Appreciation Through Enjoyment" (see note 4) contains some literary evaluations of an eight-year-old girl.
7. To the right of this Miss Brower wrote: "I never did!"
8. To the left of this Miss Brower wrote: "I don't."
9. See note 5.

6

[February–March 1897]

My dear Miss Brower:

I would not for the world say anything to discourage you or to dishearten you in the smallest degree; but I have come to the conclusion, regretfully and reluctantly, that I don't care very much about Eisteddfods.[1] I once knew a Welshman—a parson—who was very interesting in many ways; he was a good fellow and a good singer, but he never said anything about Eisteddfods. By the way, he died of a broken heart. As a writer of fiction, you may be interested to know that such things happen. The rest of the story is too commonplace to be worth telling.

As for your poor little stories, I do not think you need lose any of your affection for them. I have read them—together with your very brilliant essay on MacDowell [2]—with much pleasure, and I have no hesitation in advising you to go on writing them—even though I do not feel in any way qualified to criticize your work. But as long as you "court criticism," and have such poor success in getting it, I'll be as hard on you as I can and take the liberty to point out a few things which do not seem to me to be in accordance with the true scheme of literature. To begin, I cannot resist the temptation—even might I hurt your feelings—to express my absolute dislike for dialect and local color. I am not foolish enough to fancy it will make any particular difference to you whether I like them or not; but as long as I am three or four hundred miles away, where you can't get at me, I will assume the pomposity to say, as my own opinion of the matter, that you will do better to forget all about mules—four-legged ones—and miners [3] for a while and keep on with the pure, unrestrained humanity of "Old Friends." There is something in that story to make a man feel glad that it was written. There are places in it that might be improved—so there are in *Hamlet* [4]—and there are a few forced colloquialisms that do not seem to ring quite true; but the story is a good thing and—this is infinitely more to the point—it is worth writing. This I can hardly say of the others—no matter how well they may be done. From an objective point of view—(and you are inclined too much to be objective) perhaps "His Dry Sunday" is the best of all. There are no weak spots in it, nor much that I can see to find fault with. There may be some ambiguity in the description of Susi "sitting and sewing on Heini's shirt," but it would be unkind to call your attention to it; and I can't afford to be unkind to anybody, and least of all to one who has been so generous in her appreciation of my own work. Do not misunderstand me when I say that these stories are "not worth writing." What I mean is, they are not worth repeating. With a little deeper sense of life you will see that surface work doesn't pay—no matter how much money you may get for it. You may possibly be interested to know that it was that same musical essay of yours which convinced me that you were "born to write fiction." As an essay alone, it is very fine, and wonderfully attractive. It is attractive because it is *alive*. It is fine because it is feminine.

And I honestly believe that you, with so much life and so much of that "ewig weibliche,"—which you seem to be half ashamed of because you have never thought of it in the light of ideal truth,—can do something that will make your pulse shake and quiver so much that you won't have any appetite for luncheon till you have given yourself a good half hour's relaxation, and rid your mind of the fact that you are cumbered with a body and its attendant complexities. When you come to recognize the Divine through your own spiritual reasoning and discovery you will begin to lose faith in local color. If you "belong" to any creed,[5] shake yourself away from it and give your mind a chance to get acquainted with itself. There are many men and women in the world who can help you, and all of us, with an occasional suggestion; but there is no man or woman who can do your thinking for you. There is a popular delusion that Christian idealism is easy, but the truth is it is only simple—so simple that our great scholars (who are for the most part spiritual ignoramuses) don't like it. Artificial complexity is the easiest thing in the world. Simplicity is hard, because belief is its one and only resource. But a little leaven has a most surprising effect—has a surprising effect sometimes—more than a dozen decades of Orthodox intimidation. There is only one religion, one faith, one substance; you may find it in the Gospels, in Emerson, in *Sartor Resartus*, and, if you will take the trouble to look for it—in a temple. You will also find it in Davies' essay on "The Upanishads" and "Tao" in the *Atlantic* Vol. 72–73—particularly in "Tao."[6]

If you think there is no connection between all this and your fiction-work, I shall be very much disappointed, but I do not think that disappointment will come. Keep your thoughts ahead of the world and the world will follow them. You can do this in a mining story as well as in anything else, but I hope you will write a dozen ideal, purely ideal, sketches before you try it. By ideal, I mean, of course, real—not material; spiritual, not mortal. You did this in "Old Friends," but only in a way to make me feel that the real thing is coming. The fact that I write this implies, perhaps, more appreciation than I seem to express.

I just mentioned *Sartor Resartus*. Of course you are more or less familiar with the book, but if I may keep on "advising" you, I would suggest that you soak yourself in it for a time instead of in Dante.[7] As for direct fiction, there is perhaps no novel that will take the place of Rosny's *L'Impérieuse Bonté*[8] as an external illustration of what I am driving at in this letter. I think a careful reading of the book would help you—in fact, I know it would, but Ruth Ashmore might prick up her ears a little if she knew I was recommending it to an unknown female who knows much better than I what she wants to read. The book, however, is a wonderful piece of work. So is *Esther Waters*, though I don't imagine you will agree with me when I say so. You see I am limited in my criticism for the fact that I do not recognize art in the objective as an end of real literature. The Doyle-Weyman school[9] are to me intolerable. I never could read Scott; Bulwer is for the most part a humorist—particularly when he raves as in *The Disowned*—which, by the way, is a good steppingstone to that funniest of all books, *Contarini Fleming*.[10] Thackeray in the last third of *The Newcomes* has achieved what seems to be the culmination of the human in fiction. Here you will probably agree with me. I certainly agree with you in your judgment of George Eliot. I wonder if you think with me that Hardy has never surpassed his *Mayor of Casterbridge* as a study of masculine life. Constructively I don't like it. *Jude* is a mechanical wonder to me, but the philosophy of it is false. The same will hold true of its author—for all his genius.

I am writing to you as if you were a little child, but I do not think you are one. If I have infused more brotherly enthusiasm than is in accordance with the tenets of your *Ladies' Home Journal*,[11] kindly excuse me on the ground of my sincere interest in your work. I don't know whether to keep on and give you some technical advice or not. It isn't every day that I have so good a chance to pose as a literary master, so perhaps I may as well tell you that you have an unpleasant way of putting in brief passages as separate paragraphs which gives now and then a sense of difficulty on the part of the author. I also think that three more writings of each thing you do would make you better satisfied. Don't think of printing a story until you have done it five or six times; don't show it to your friends—not even to your own people—until you have done it twice. Try to leave pictures—tone-pictures, eye-pictures, thought-pictures, according to the context—that no reader can forget. That night scene on Chatteris Bridge[12] hasn't very much in it, but it has enough to make it immortal. Here is a bit from Zola,[13] which I do not think you will be likely to forget: "Elle, la tête levée, cherchait d'où venait un filet de voix, qu'elle écoutait depuis la première marche, clair et perçant dominant les autres bruits. C'était, sous les toits, une petite vieille qui chantait en habillant des poupées, à treize sous."—"Chaque arbre fut une forêt, surtout à mesure qu'une buée l'environnait, pareille à une toison vaporisée"—Rosny.[14] As far as the formation of a story goes you are all right. All you have to do is to pitch your ambitions a little higher and cultivate a desire to surprise yourself. You have everything to encourage you, but I hope you won't persist in saying "gotten."[15] Dr. Worcester once threw a dictionary at a schoolboy's head for saying it—at least, I have been told that he did.[16]

It is not necessary for me to say anything about your essay-work. There you are sure of your ground, but you must never be satisfied with staying on it. Do not think of shutting up your fiction shop until you begin to find out what there is in it. Thus far, you have only glanced at the things right before you. You do not know what there may be stored away in boxes waiting to be brought to light.

If this letter gives you a momentary feeling of disappointment and disgust,[17] take it as a good sign. All that I have written is an attempt of mine, in my blundering clumsy way, to help you a little and to make you feel a little stronger for the undertaking of more serious and satisfactory work. I don't know how much of it you will read, or how much of it you will care for; but if I succeed in giving you two or three suggestions that will be of some service to you, I shall be satisfied that my blue-covered book was not altogether a mistake. You need have no fear that I am writing now for the fun of it, for letter writing is always a grind for me. You may also be sure that I am not flattering you, I don't believe in that sort of thing—particularly when there is no occasion for it. If your work did not not convince me that you are going to do something infinitely finer and stronger, it would be very easy for me to write a formal note of thanks and never think of it again.

I am very glad to know that you will send me one of your photographs. I am, for no particular reason, beginning to wonder if you look at all like that peculiar person on the cover of the current issue of Mr Bok's joke-book.[18] This, however is not my only reason for wanting one. There is something in your frankness that makes me feel that you would be a good friend to me if I had the pleasure of knowing you. I am not a sentimentalist—(I am too big-boned and angular to make it worth while) but I was lucky enough to be born with a desire to see others[19] succeed and to feel an earnest pleasure in doing or saying any little thing that will send a ray of brightness into anybody's life—if only for a moment. So, if you will send me one of your pictures, I'll keep it as a remembrance of a very pleasant episode in a rather commonplace life. No, I don't think

I should have a nice time at one of your sequestered teas. I was not intended for that sort of thing, and I find it expedient to stay at home. I should probably tip everything over the first time I tried to say something pleasant.

I am glad, too, that you have the right idea of relations. I once told a fat uncle of mine[20] that relations were the finest things a man could have; and he agreed with me. It was surely very good of you to trust so much to my integrity, and I hope you will believe my gratitude to be genuine.

Most sincerely yours,
E. A. Robinson

I have a friend who speaks occasionally of Wilkes-Barre and his old Boston roommate, Allan Dixon.[21] He, or his wife's father, I don't remember which, had something to do with the mines. Possibly you have heard of them.

I only made that little allusion to your age to see if it would make you mad. I am glad that it did not. Do not think me so weak-minded as to have supposed you would feel it. I am pretty green, but not so bad as that.

E. A. Robinson

Do not form too strong an attachment for the five chapters of your novel.[22] Find out where you are before you try another, and remember that it is a very long story indeed that can't be told in 75,000 words.

1. Apropos Miss Brower's "The Meaning of an Eisteddfod," *Atlantic Monthly*, LXXV (January 1895), 45–61.

2. "New Figures in Literature and Art: IV. E. A. MacDowell," *Atlantic Monthly*, LXXVII (March 1896), 394–402.

3. "His Dry Sunday," *Catholic World*, LXII (March 1896), 780–790. Miss Brower also wrote about mines and miners in "Bonny Hugh of Ironbrook," "Treshornish," "Chunky," and "The Big Boss's Parade."

4. To the right of this Miss Brower wrote: "All this criticism is most just. But I wasn't as big as he tho't me."

5. To the left of this Miss Brower wrote: "I didn't."

6. William Davies, "The Teaching of the Upanishads," LXXII (August 1893), 178–190; "Tao," LXXIII (February 1894), 182–198.

7. To the right of this Miss Brower wrote: "I had taken my 'soak' while R was yet a boy!"

8. J.-H. Rosny was the collective pseudonym of the brothers Joseph Henri and Séraphin Justin Boëx.

9. A. Conan Doyle and Stanley J. Weyman, producers of popular historical romances.

10. Benjamin Disraeli's novel (London, 1832), subtitled *A Psychological Romance*. The protagonist suffers much, writes poetry, and dedicates himself to the amelioration of his kind.

11. Miss Brower underscored *your* twice and wrote to the right of it: "*My*? But I now know—and knew long since—that he, tho' sincere in what he says, is talking because he is dying to talk to someone who *may* understand him." To the left she added an oversize exclamation point.

12. In Thackeray's *Pendennis*, end of chapter 14.

13. In chapter II of *L'Assomoir*.

14. From page 359, part three, XVIII, of *L'Impérieuse Bonté* (Paris, 1894).

15. To the left of this Miss Brower wrote: "Save in the sense of *acquired*."

16. Joseph E. Worcester (1784–1865), American philologist and lexicographer, whose chief work was *A Dictionary of the English Language* (Boston, 1860).

17. To the right of this Miss Brower wrote: "No, it only *amoozed* me. It's tone, I mean. It's all perfectly true criticism."

18. Edward W. Bok (1863–1930) became editor of the *Ladies' Home Journal* in 1889 and remained in the post for thirty years.

19. Miss Brower misread this word as *writers*, which she wrote in the right margin, adding parenthetically, "Poor chap!"

20. Edward Proby Fox who worked at the Riverside Press and helped to get *The Torrent and the Night Before* published. On October 15, 1896, Robinson wrote to Harry de Forest Smith that "It was only through the friendly intercession of my Uncle Fox, the fat man, that they would undertake the job at all before December" (Sutcliffe, *Untriangulated Stars*, p. 257).

21. Allan Hamilton Dickson, son of a preacher, attended Yale and later took up the practice of law in Wilkes-Barre. His wife's father, Payne Pettebone, had extensive mining interests in that area.

22. Miss Brower worked intermittently on a novel about the Pennsylvania mining locale. Modesta Ximena asserts that it was never published, in fact, never finished.

7

Gardiner, Maine
14 March 1897

My dear Miss Brower:

I thank you for telling me the truth. When I read your first two letters in reply to my experimental criticism of your work, I was conscious of a great pleasure—one of the greatest pleasures of my life; but if the words were not sincere, if you were really disappointed and angry at what I said,—it is best for me to know it,—as I do—now. I can say, however, and with all frankness, I did not quite like your almost complete acceptance of my criticism; it did not seem to me in accordance with the "feminine strength" which is so characteristic of your work, and I wondered at it. But I was pleased, and I was very glad.

Now you have put things in another light. I suppose you are wondering what I shall say. Let me say, first of all, that you need not feel in any way disheartened or discouraged. My faith in your ability to do remarkable work is not weakened in the least by your rather impetuous confession; on the contrary, it is strengthened. You are, or seem to be, undergoing a kind of transitional upheaval which I know is not very pleasant, but which I know to be the best possible thing for you. As to your age, of course I can only imagine it from the evidence of your work; but I write, and have been writing all along, on the supposition that you are a woman somewhere about thirty-five years old. Do not, for heaven's sake, think me asinine enough to take this time to throw out "feelers"; I only want you to know that I have not for a moment dreamed that I have been writing to a "girl." No girl could have written those two papers in the *Atlantic*; no girl, unless she were a dangerously precocious one, could have written "Old Friends."

What I did think, and still think, is just this:—that you have considered story writing too much from the popular point of view, though you may have done so without knowing it. Even after all you have said, I will say now that you might write for a hundred years after the manner of Mrs. Harrison, Miss French, Mrs. Magruder,[1] and the rest of them, with no better chances than theirs of doing anything that would really count in literature. In your "Old Friends" and in your musical essay, I find a tendency to work in a new field and a knowledge of life to make that work a possibility. If I had not found these two things, I should never have written what I did. I appreciated, more deeply than you suspect, your kind recognition of my own work; but I have suffered too much in the past from the meaningless and indiscriminate praise of friends (?) to inflict the same thing on you. All I wrote was sincere; I hoped it would help you, and I still believe it will. In fact, I think it has already—I know it has. I am glad for having written it.

As for the popular American story writers, who command such prices and are so ridiculously overrated, I advise you to steer clear of them. As long as they are well advertised they will make an impression on the public, but when they die, their work will die with them. Two or three stories by Miss Jewett, two or three by Miss Wilkins, one by F. J. Stimson ("Mrs. Knollys")[2] and a few other scattered sketches, will live; but they will only live for the spirit that is in them. None of them can live for the sheer art of their making. That sort of thing does not exist outside of France, and France is dying. If you wish to study the power of sheer art, buy a copy of Coppée's *Vingt Contes Nouveaux* and read, and re-read, "La Sœur de Lait." This is, to me, the greatest short story in the world—considered as a short story. Aside from his wonderful art (when he chooses to make the most of it) Coppée is the only French author—excepting perhaps Daudet—who gives me any spiritual pleasure. Maupassant can draw an object lesson, as in *Une Vie* (you needn't read it), but the only truth in his work is that which is compelled by Truth itself—in spite of the author's pitiable pessimism. Sin and ignorance destroys itself; Maupassant destroys Maupassant;—and it does it every time. Art for art's sake is a confession of moral weakness. Art for the real *Art's* sake is the meaning and the truth of life. This is just beginning to be understood, and it is on this understanding that the greatness of future literature depends. If Mr. Howells[3] could realize this, he might write novels that would shake the world; as it is, his novels shake nothing but his own faith. I have the greatest admiration for the man, but I pity him. Zola is a parallel case, but his objective power is so enormous that his work must eventually have a purifying effect.

You tell me that you realize all this when you labor for weeks and weeks over clever trifles like "His Dry Sunday," etc., but I wonder if you really mean it. It seems to me almost a crime for you to sacrifice your wonderfully attractive and elastic style to these little temporal themes, and I make free to tell you so; and you get "mad."[4] I would not be impertinent (I can hardly afford to be) but the "madder" you get, the better it will be for you. By and by an idea will come into your head and you will trace it to this very fit of anger. Then you will see that I am a friend, after all, and that the very thing you needed most was this same stirring-up of your latent consciousness. At present you can do nothing? —then don't try to. Go to your piano and play the "Pilgrims' Chorus," and then play "Yankee Doodle." Then try to figure out why it is that neither of these can ever die. At a first thought this may not seem to have much to do with literature but it has a good deal.

You ask me if your weakness lies in a lack of faith in yourself or in the lack of a definite ideal; and I am very glad you ask me, for I think I know. The answer is—*both.* If you had a really definite ideal, you would have the faith to admit its possible attainment and the courage to undertake the struggle. "When your views of life deepen" [*In the margin, with a line pointing to the first word in this sentence, Robinson writes:* I'll try to say something about this further on.]—When you are willing and glad to look on your past work as practice work and on your future work as a certain realization of your best ambition, your ideal will reveal itself and your faith will never waver. When you work for a forenoon over a single sentence and then throw it away, you will simply deny the impossibility of failure and laugh at the idea that you cannot do the work you have undertaken. If you really desire to do it, you will do it; but you must ask yourself—before you go ahead, "Is this thing really worth doing?" Beware of *cleverness*; think of nothing but greatness. Make up your mind to write the greatest short stories in the world, and do not permit yourself even to dream that you cannot write them. You may not do it; but the attempt will be there, and the attempt will count. If you keep this up for twenty years, you will surprise yourself, and have lots of fun. This is misleading. I mean that *in the course of* twenty years you will surprise yourself a great many times. I think you will do it between now and Jan. 1, 1898 (that's going to be a good deal easier to make than 1897 and I'm glad of it.)

In your remarks on motherhood and fame, I see the subject of a most remarkable tale—a tale of two female characters, the story tells itself and is worthy of infinite strengthening and elaboration. I do not agree with you—you have practically confessed that you do not agree with yourself—but there is an argument for both sides. See *The Story of an African Farm.*[5] But I forget—you don't read modern novels. In the main, you do wisely.

Now you give me permission to "smoke and mope" in your study, and relieve me from all tea-drinking obligations. I think I shall be tempted [to] call when I am in Wilkes-Barre. I shall probably get there just about the time Nansen reaches the North Pole.[6] No, it [is] not likely that I shall ever see you in person—unless it by some strange chance, so I would suggest that you send that picture along as a peace-offering. I want something to make me feel that I am not looked on as a monster. I know I have hurt your feelings, but I did it "only to be kind."

Please remember that I have nothing but the most friendly interest in you and in your work, and that I have perfect faith in your power to do work that you will feel proud of—proud of in the right way—and believe me,

Most sincerely yours,
E. A. Robinson

P.S.—My remarks on the "forced colloquialisms" in "Old Friends" were, I fear, rather hasty and unfair. I was thinking only of Mrs. Teeter. I cannot quite see the efficacy of her bad English.

I regret that I played such havoc with Mr. Dickson's name. I had nothing to guide me but my ear.

This letter will disappoint you as an evasion of the question that is now causing you so much trouble. I am very sorry to have offended you, but you must remember that things written down thoughtlessly, or at least hastily, are likely to be interpreted with far more seriousness than the writer intended. I cannot see wherein the matter is worthy of any more worry on your part. It was unfortunate, and I own it. What more can I say? When I wrote the words that "rankle" in you, I was forgetful of anything but your lightest work. I was too anxious to be of a little use in the world, and so, as to my custom, made a mess of it.[7] There's a big place paved with good intentions, and most of us—all of us, I think, are in it now.

E.A.R.

I take the liberty to throw in a clipping from the Boston *Transcript* which reveals a rather startling typographical "error."[8] There is at least an advantage in private printing.

1. Constance Cary Harrison (1843–1920) depicted American social ideals comically and seriously in *The Anglo-Americans* and *A Son of the Old Dominion* during the 1890's. Under the pseudonym of Octave Thanet, Alice French (1850–1934) published numerous short stories of local color in Arkansas and Iowa. Julia Magruder (1854–1907) wrote her most successful book, *Princess Sonia*, in eighteen days, three hours per day.

2. Sarah Orne Jewett (1849–1909), author of *The Country of the Pointed Firs*, was an outstanding local colorist of Maine scenes and character. Mary E. Wilkins Freeman (1852–1930) wrote more sharply about New England types and experiences. Frederic J. Stimson (1855–1943), Massachusetts lawyer, United States ambassador, and Harvard professor, also wrote fiction, notably *Mrs. Knollys and Other Stories* (New York, 1897).

3. William Dean Howells (1837–1920), influential editor and literary critic of the *Atlantic Monthly* and *Harper's*, was a forerunner of realism in American fiction. His most important novels on social and ethical themes up to this time are *A Modern Instance*, *The Rise of Silas Lapham*, *A Hazard of New Fortunes*, and *A Traveler from Altruria*. He expounds his literary credo in *Criticism and Fiction*.

4. To the right of this Miss Brower wrote: "I wasn't as 'mad' as he thought me."

5. In this novel, published in London, 1883, Olive Schreiner (1855–1920) gives a rationalist feminist view of woman's place in a world which restricts her social movements, moral convictions, and political opportunities.

6. Fridtjof Nansen (1851–1930), Norwegian scientist and explorer, headed several extended expeditions to the polar regions, one lasting over three years.

7. To the left of this Miss Brower wrote: "Poor dear fellow!"

8. This is apparently the clipping of "Octave" (Boston *Evening Transcript*, February 26, 1897, p. 6) which Miss Brower pasted to page 44 of her copy of *The Torrent and the Night Before* (see Letter 1, note 1). The phrase "all the tomes" in the final line is crossed out and "any tons" written below. This Octave is reprinted in its original version in Charles Beecher Hogan, *A Bibliography of Edwin Arlington Robinson* (New Haven, 1936), pp. 174–175.

8

Gardiner, Maine
18 March 1897

My dear Miss Brower:

Owing to the very tragic tenor of your last letter, I forgot to tell you that I shall not be able to get hold of the *Atlantics* you referred to until I get to Boston—some time next week.

I may go to New York. If I do I shall call on Dr. Coan,[1] and find out all about you.

Sincerely,
E. A. Robinson

Evidently your idealism and mine are two different things. Idealism that can't go through a coal mine, or a town caucus, and come out undismayed, is a misnomer.

E.A.R.

1. Robinson did get to New York City by way of Cambridge in December and soon met Dr. Coan, with whom he was not unfavorably impressed.

9

Gardiner, Maine
21 March 1897

My dear Miss Brower:

I would not have you think that I intend to inflict semi-weekly letters on you for the rest of your life, but surely I ought to thank you for the two photographs you were good enough to give me. I am very glad to have them and I congratulate you upon your physiognomy—if you will pardon my freedom. I like the firmness and the fineness of the face (excuse the alliteration, please) and I am glad to note the absence of a certain touch of masculinity which, in spite of your "weak heart" and your dramatic ideals, I was a little afraid of. My candor has made enemies for me in the past, but I hope it will not have that effect in this case. You are evidently a woman (about thirty-five years old[1] and very good-natured) and that [is] the main point for you.

I thank you for telling me that I may read those letters again as I read them first. As for my unhappy allusion to your "views of life," perhaps I made a mistake. When I think of your more serious work, I am inclined to think I did, but I did it honestly and with all good purpose. According to my figuring, I am considerably younger than you, so you need not take my preaching too seriously. I have nothing to take back in the matter of your stories. However, I cannot but feel that you have been on the wrong track. You will never find out what you can do in this line until you strengthen and deepen your *motif* (I don't like the word, but there doesn't seem to be any other).

Hoping this will find you well out of your illness, I remain

Most sincerely yours,
E. A. Robinson

I am not at all certain about the hat—but then, I ought not to find fault, so I won't.

1. To the right of this Miss Brower wrote: "I was 41!" She was in fact forty-eight at this time, but may be referring to the year the photographs were taken.

10

Gardiner, Maine
22 March 1897

My dear Miss Brower:

I'm sorry I made you cry, but still it is your "idiotic womanishness" that makes me have so much confidence and interest in your future. You started me a little when you implied that I looked on dreaming as the end of life. That's all that made me speak as I did. True idealism is not mooning. You know that well enough, but you didn't stop to think.

I'm getting reconciled to that hat. I never thought it was too young for you, but I was not quite sure, at first, that it was an architectural success. Now I think I was wrong.

Please do not forget that the realization that I have been of some little service to you makes a big difference in my life. It makes me feel that I may be of a little use in the world after all, though I shall always feel that I assumed rather too much authority. I don't know just why I did; but I did it and I am glad. You may be sorry some time, but I don't believe it.

Sincerely yours,
E. A. Robinson

II

79 Perkins
Cambridge, Mass.
24 March 1897

My dear Miss Brower:

As my written French is mostly a thing to be sorry for, I'll tell you in plain English that I am very glad to know that you have confidence enough in my sincerity to ask me to come and talk with you—a thing I would do, and gladly, if it were not impossible. It does not look now as if I should get to New York.

I have just read your "Songs With Variations" and "Certain Insubordinations" [1] and I have enjoyed them very much, though I can't think your final maxim in the last named is valid. It seems to me to be contrary to the scheme of fiction, though my own experience (it took me six years to find out that I could not write a story) compels me to sympathize with you to a certain extent.

I thought I could remember the names of the other "clubs" but I only remember "A Sunrise Service," [2] which I cannot find. The volume is out.

I am here at Harvard for a few days to look over the old place and to breathe again the multifarious odors of Memorial Hall, where sophomores throw apple cores at heads across the way and where black waiters wash their thumbs in luke-warm *consommé*. [3]

I am writing this almost in the dark and with a very fine pen. If you cannot read it, try to believe that it is an expression of good will and gratitude on my part, and that you need not have the slightest fear but that I shall "stand by you." The obligation is all on my part. You have given me the courage to work and to feel that I am good for something.

Very sincerely,
E. A. Robinson

1. "Songs With Variations," *Atlantic Monthly*, LXXIV (November 1894), 715–717; "On a Certain Insubordination in Fictitious Characters," *Atlantic*

Monthly, LXIII (January 1889), 134–135. In the latter Miss Brower declares that in order to achieve "a sustained artistic effect . . . the best way is to resign yourself wholly, go into a sort of literary trance, and let your 'monsters' have things all their own way."

2. "A Sunrise Service," *Atlantic Monthly*, LXXI (April 1893), 565–566.

3. Robinson spent the academic years of 1891 and 1892 at Harvard College as a non-matriculating student.

12

[2 April 1897]

Dear Friend:

I am at home again now and am very glad for a chance to write something in reply to your two letters. You ask me to tell you something about my life and about myself, but when you do that, you put me in a very hard place. If I were to tell the whole story, it would make sorry reading indeed—so I won't tell it. Perhaps it will be enough for me to say that the word "home" is a kind of mockery to me, and that I look back on the twenty-seven years of my life as a thing that is best to be forgotten and put away. My surroundings have been a little too much for me and even now I doubt sometimes if I shall be able to more than half realize my ideals. I know next to nothing of what the world calls pleasure; my pleasure is entirely of another sort and is purchased sometimes on spiritual credit. I don't know whether my accounts are even now or not; but I do know that all there is to life—to my life, at least—is the recognition and realization (part realization) of the infinite ideal, which is All.

My father died four years ago with a quite natural impression that I was a failure, and four months ago my mother followed him [1]—though with a little better opinion of me. I am glad for both of them that they are out of this life, because I know well enough that nothing awaited them here but more suffering and sorrow—and heaven knows they had enough of both. What strength I have is the result of tedious and almost intolerable isolation. I still have that isolation, but it is no longer the complete curse that it used to be. I can reason around it and through it and find in it a meaning and a compensation that keeps me alive. There are other matters—family matters—of which I cannot write, and of which the knowledge would only disturb you. You have been too kind to me—too much to me—to warrant my paying you back with a detailed account of my personal affairs.

Your recognition of something in me that makes you glad for finding it is, I think, the greatest pleasure of my life. It is my first absolute proof that I am working in the right direction and I am very glad to tell you so. If you are still unable to see wherein you have helped me, I shall be surprised, though not discouraged. Nothing discourages me any more. I have been disappointed so many times and in so many ways that I am used to that sort of thing. The worst part of my interviewing publishers last week, for example, was the monotony of the thing. Sometimes it made me grin to hear them talk so seriously, and sometimes it made me glad to feel that I was "fired" once more. I rather like to be rejected now. I am so used to it. If ever I achieve worldly success, I'm half afraid it will finish me.[2]

Two years at Harvard opened my eyes in many ways. I went there to save myself from going to pieces, and I did it. I got nothing in particular from my books, but I got a good deal from the place and from two or three good friends. The whole was a kind of blur to me at the time—it was then that things were going at the worst—but now I can look back and see what those years did for me. Last week I went back and was received like a lord by men who never knew me—never had a chance to know me—as a student, but the whole thing made me uncomfortable. I felt out of place and the sight of that blue-covered experiment of mine on Barrett Wendell's[3] desk made me almost sick. I don't know why, but I felt ashamed of myself. I felt that I had better go back to Maine and stay there. And here I am—for the devil knows how long and for what purpose. I can't get away, and if I could, I should not know where to go. Sometimes I am tempted to take Dr. Coan's facetious advice and "go to London and stay there." But starvation is so unattractive and inconvenient that I hardly dare try the experiment. I think also of going to New Zealand, but I may never get there. I do not believe in time and place, but I like to draw long, long lines from the years 1880—1897—no, I'll say 1896—and from Gardiner, Maine (Kennebec County). The Kennebec, by the way, is a very beautiful river.

I should be pleased to meet your Boston friend, but I fear I should disappoint him. I am a very poor talker (so my friends tell me) and am very long and awkward—as you know already. To quote from *The Seven Seas*, I'm "no special chrysanthemum"[4] in any way, but I'll send you a photograph if you want it. I haven't had one taken in nine years, but I can hardly refuse so small a favor to one who has done so much for me.

I'm afraid this letter will tire you, and I'm half afraid it will make you think less of me—less of me as a "strong man." But you must remember that I do not pretend to be very strong—only strong enough to keep on my feet and to see something through my cypress trees that isn't eternally suggestive of thunderstorms. I am doing what I can for myself and a little for others; and I am very glad to know that I have been of some slight service to them. There are two or three fellows whom I have really helped. I know it; they have told me so; and their actions prove the truth of what they say. And now you—a total stranger—tell me that I have helped you. What more can I ask?

I shall be very glad to hear from you at any time and to have you feel that I am more than ready to do whatever may be in my power to prove the complete sincerity of my friendship—if any proof is necessary. I have very few friends, but the fault is, I think, my own. In spite of all my good feeling for everybody and everything, it is only once in a great while that a man or woman attracts me. I dislike solitude, but I prefer it to that peculiar thing called "sociability." I'm not sociable, but I could talk with you by the hour.

Most sincerely,
E. A. Robinson [5]

Here is another Octave:—[6]

1. Edward Robinson, June 19, 1818–July 15, 1892; Mary Palmer Robinson, July 28, 1833–November 22, 1896.

2. To the right of this Miss Brower wrote: "(It didn't! 1920)."

3. Barrett Wendell (1855–1921), professor of English at Harvard and historian of American literature, wrote an encouraging note to Robinson on receipt of his blue-wrappered *The Torrent and the Night Before*.

4. From the last line of the fourth stanza of Rudyard Kipling's "Soldier an' Sailor Too."

5. Below Robinson's signature Miss Brower wrote: "April 2." Context establishes the year 1897.

6. The sheet is cut off below this line. The fragment containing this Octave is pasted into Robinson's gift copy of *The Torrent* to Brower (see Letter 1, note 1). The text of the Octave, which has been published only in the *Colby Library Quarterly*, II (February 1947), 13, follows:

Idealist?—Oh yes, or what you will.
I do not wrangle any more with names—
I only want the Truth. Give me the Truth,
And let the system go; give me the Truth,
And I stand satisfied. Fame, glory, gold,—
Take them, and keep them. They were never mine—
I do not ask for them. I only ask
That I, and you, and you, may get the Truth!

13

Gardiner, Maine
10 April 1897

Dear Friend:

I enclose two products of amateur photography which will give you a chance to form some idea as to what I look like. I am holding my hat (my big, bewildered hands must have something to do) and I look very weak and sleepy. I always do in pictures; perhaps I do in life, though I hope not. I'll send you a legitimate photograph before long.

You ask me to tell you more about myself, but I cannot think of anything that would be satisfactory. If ever I get a chance to talk with you, I think perhaps I can clear up a few things, though I should hardly be doing justice to others if I were to give you, or any one else, my life history—that is, the history of events that have influenced my life, and maybe made it what it is. If I had not been shut out from material pleasures I should never have written *The Torrent*, and if I had never written that I should not feel that I had done anything. I don't feel that I have done very much as it is, and I doubt very much, sometimes, if ever I shall do anything better. I have done forty Octaves—there are to be about sixty in all—but I do not think they will be very well received. They are wicked things to make—infinitely harder than sonnets—and I have not yet succeeded in making one that even suggests completion. The one from the *Transcript*[1] is altogether too rickety to be considered for a moment as a finished poem, though I don't know just what I can do with it. No, the other was not written for you—the repetition of "and you" gives it to anybody,[2] but I'll write one for you if you want me to—sometime when I feel like it.

It is very good of you to want to help me, and the wish is help in itself. But I don't want you to lie awake o'nights, for I agree with Nikola Tesla[3] when he says that sleep is a very good thing for men and women. I don't get very much of it myself, but I manage to get enough to keep me going. I do not agree with the nine-hour people, however, for that seems to me to be throwing life away. The same, of course, will hold true (to my mind) of sleeping during the day. That's not what we are here for.

But this is wandering. What I was going to say was that you are magnifying my importance. There are thousands of people in the country who could do infinitely more for you than I have done, or ever can do; and whom you, in turn, could help and encourage in the same way that you have helped and encouraged me. The trouble is, you have never met them. But they exist all the same, and are waiting and hungering for some proof to tell them that they are not nonentities—no I don't mean that, either. They know better than that; but they don't know, as they would (and as they should) that they are not alone. Time and place have nothing to do with one's isolation. A friend in Wooloomooloo or Wilkes-Barre is just as much to me as one in Gardiner; and such a condition is—even though I say it at the expense of my logic—distinctly an advantage for the friend. Others will tell you that Gardiner is one of the most attractive places in the United States. *Perhaps* it is. *Perhaps* I don't know. *Perhaps* I don't know what I want, but I have a notion that I want to bury myself in London or Auckland, or New York, for about five years—up three flights—and see what I can do. I shall never find out here, where I am looked upon as an unpromising freak and a queer cuss without any ambition—when the whole purpose of my life is to do a little to make others half as well contented as myself. "Queer cuss" might be in quotation marks.

I hope you do not think that I ignored your reference to a possible meeting in Boston. If you do, you are very much mistaken. Nothing would please me more or give me more conclusive proof that there is something in me or in my work (which is the same thing) that has a touch of life. When a few words bring about an invitation like that from a total stranger, I feel, in spite of my doubts and misgivings, that there must be something in them.

I do not "resent" anything you have said, nor do I think you need feel sorry for anything. I am not exactly a fool—though perhaps I show my vanity in saying so.

Most sincerely,
E. A. Robinson[4]

1. "Octave," Boston *Evening Transcript* (February 26, 1897), p. 6. True to his feeling about this verse, Robinson never collected it. Miss Brower pasted a clipping of this on page 44 of her copy of *The Torrent and the Night Before*.

2. See last line of this Octave, Letter 12, note 6.

3. Nikola Tesla (1856–1943), inventor of practical electrical apparatus, promulgated the principles of the rotary magnetic field and alternating current.

4. A section of the sheet below the signature is cut off, possibly the Octave Robinson refers to in Letter 29 (see note 1).

14

Gardiner, Maine
21 April 1897

Dear Friend:

If you think it strange that I should care so much for your appreciation of my work, it may be of interest to you to know that you are the only person who seems fully to realize what I am driving at.[1] It never occurred to me that the poems would be considered obscure, but obscurity seems to be the strong point of my critics. In a thing like "Luke Havergal," of course the meaning is all suggested, and is not capable of a definite working-out by anyone who doesn't happen to sympathize with the writer's fancy; but it is not the criticism of this poem that disappoints me;—it is the total inability of almost everybody who reads the book to find out what I mean by the last two lines of "The Torrent" and their unconscious agreement not to say anything about the "Two Sonnets." You know me well enough by this time to know that I am not after their praise—if the work deserves praise it must get it sometime—and I hope you know me well enough to believe that I am always glad for intelligent "damnation." I have been lucky enough to get a little of it—enough to make me ready to cancel the Hardy sonnet and to feel very shaky about "For Calderon"[2]—which always seemed to me a little childish. I should like your honest opinion of it.

Your comments on my friends were most interesting, but I am sorry to be compelled to say that you were rather unjust to the "animal." Pope[3] is in love, and is one of the most harmless creatures in existence. He worries about the grossness of his features and makes epigrams. The fighty man with the pouted frown is not a bad lot. The worst thing I have against him is that he sings in a church choir. You may sing in one yourself, but a woman can stand it. A man can't. Blair[4] (you see we have poetical names down here) also plays the fiddle and writes rondeaux. Once he tried to write a baby song for an air I was reckless enough to "compose" once on a time;[5] but he got stuck on the second verse, so the thing never materialized. When I look back on my methods—I used to manufacture tunes on the black keys of a piano—I never could do anything with the white ones—then reproduce it, by ear, with a clarinet that wheezed and shrieked most wonderfully, and finally get it down on paper, one or two notes at a time. I had none of the facility of your "Wheels." Sometimes I make a sonnet in an hour, but I don't make any more songs.

I cannot but feel that you overrate my influence in clearing up your thoughts; I can't believe that I was born ever to be of so much direct assistance to anybody;—but if it is true, I am very glad—or shall be very glad—indeed. Whether you are mistaken or not, you have given me a great deal of courage and confidençe that I should not otherwise have had, and these things I shall keep whether you go back on me or not. The fact that I am strong enough to set another person thinking is enough to make me work.

You give me great pleasure when you give me permission to live in Wilkes-Barre. I fear that it will be a long time before I get there, however, and that I might have a hard time getting a job. In the meantime, you might try to get me one in the mines. I think I could drive a mule (I could call him Pegasus) and be very happy. The trouble is not so much with Gardiner as with its population—that is, the size of it. A man is not supposed to think here; he is supposed to get a job; then he has acquired absolute respectability.

As to that touch of masculinity, I do not think you need worry over it. I cannot tell you just what made me look for anything of the kind, but I fancy the big freedom of your handwriting had something to do with it. That, however, is no guide. Big hands make small letters (I can swear to that) and the contrary is often true—I mean, small hands make big letters. That is all I have to say on the subject, all I can say. The rest, if there was anything, was a false impression.

I'll spare you the octave this time. The things are not half done, and I doubt some if ever they will be. When they are, to my mind, tolerably passable I may print them to see how they look, or I may not. I may tear them all up, as I have torn up bushels of stuff in the past and go to work on something else.

I suppose your robins are with you by this time and you are contented again. I don't know very much about birds, but I think my favorite is the crow. His song isn't very valuable but his plumage—to say nothing of his personality—is most fascinating and satisfactory. And then there are swallows.

Most sincerely yours,
E. A. Robinson

1. To the right of this Miss Brower wrote: "He generally *suggests* rather than *tells out* his meaning."

2. Robinson included "For a Book by Thomas Hardy" in the 1928 edition of *The Torrent and the Night Before* and in *The Children of the Night* (1897,

1905) before dropping it; "For Calderon" reappeared only in *The Torrent and the Night Before* (1928), an autographed edition limited to 110 copies.

3. Seth Ellis Pope taught school in Gardiner. He was one of The Quadruped, a coterie of artistically minded young men who met in a room over a drygoods store to talk over their ideals. Twenty years later Robinson shared an apartment with Pope at 810 Washington Avenue in Brooklyn.

4. Arthur Blair, another member of The Quadruped, worked in a Gardiner bank. The fourth member of the group was Linville Robbins, a geologist.

5. This tune, entitled "Slumber Song," was published after Robinson's death by Bruce Humphries, Inc., in October 1935, with words by Louis V. Ledoux and piano accompaniment by Lewis M. Isaacs. Robinson originally set to music James Whitcomb Riley's "A Life-Lesson," three seven-line stanzas, which begins: "There! little girl; don't cry! / They have broken your doll, I know." See *Edwin Arlington Robinson: A Collection of His Works From the Library of Bacon Collamore* (Hartford, 1936), pp. 59–60; Hogan, *Bibliography*, p. 52; Sutcliffe, *Untriangulated Stars*, pp. 196, 200, 233.

15

Gardiner, Maine
25 April 1897

Dear Friend:

You are a most remarkable person. Not content with calling me "a poet—a real one" (those words will embarrass you some day) you must send me another book. I shall be very glad to get it, though I don't feel that I deserve it.

I know Pater only as the author of *Plato and Platonism*, written for "young students." I like the idea of having his last work[1] and I shall read the book with great pleasure, though I fear I cannot do so right away. I am having a bad time with my eyes just now and my hours, or rather minutes, of reading are limited. It is wonderfully good of you to send it.

This is a sunny day, but the sunlight doesn't fall white off the backs of sheep. It just glares on dead dirty brown turf and tries to persuade me that things are going to be green by and by.

I prize the young one's criticism exceedingly—as I do that of an old white-whiskered farmer who reads my stuff—like Edward Eggleston—"because he cannot help it."[2] He says it sounds "jest as if an ol' man done it." This criticism coming from all quarters makes me wonder if I shall ever do anything better. If I don't, my career is ended.

Very sincerely,
E. A. Robinson

P.S.—No matter about propriety. My stationery ought to make you easy on that point.—E.A.R.

1. Walter Pater's posthumous volume, *Gaston de Latour* (London, 1896).

2. The Indiana author of *The Hoosier Schoolmaster* said in "Edward Eggleston: An Interview," *Outlook*, LV (February 6, 1897), 436: "A man in Gardiner, Maine, has written lately some delightfully original little bits of poetry and printed them in a little blue pamphlet . . . His name is Edwin Arlington Robinson. I never heard of him till he sent me this booklet. They send me books of poetry until I cannot get around for them, but he has sent me a book that I cannot help reading."

16

Gardiner, Maine
9 May 1897

Dear Friend:

Vous allez à la campagne, bien;—c'est-a-dire que vous aurez tout le temps d'écrire etc. No, I'm not going to write this in French; I'm only quoting Mérimée[1] (I don't think very much of him) to show off. Perhaps you think the Large Birds of Prey have carried me away, but they haven't. I've been lazy—that's all.

You are right in saying that I am a poor correspondent. I'm not very much on letter writing, but I hope that won't influence you. If I'm one of the "few" whom you afflict in this way, so much the better for me. Your letters are very welcome to me, and your last one—I mean the last long one—was particularly so in that it took a thousand-pound weight right off my shoulders. When you tell me that you interpret "The Torrent" by the "Two Sonnets," you say everything that is necessary and make me feel that I am not helplessly dense—as so many of my critics (?) would imply, when they go so far as to imply anything at all.

You may be interested to know that Professor Trent of Tennessee[2] has sent me a copy of his *Sewanee Review* in which he says that the "Broken Flutes" ballade is a failure and that the impassioned effort of "The House on the Hill" is not worth striving after. Perhaps Marjory[3] knew what she was talking about, after all. The Proff—oh, the deuce!—Professor's criticism was on the whole most friendly, however, and he won my lifelong affection by speaking a good word for "The Night Before." There is a man in Oregon who likes it, and another in Cleveland; but most people give it the "damnation of silence."[4] You, for example.

Don't think from this that I am in any way dissatisfied with you. I could hardly be that with the only person in America who has said what I have been waiting for someone to say. I'm getting sick of surface praise, and very sick of the sight of "Oh! for a Poet." If that is the best thing I have done, the sooner I stop the better. When I put the book together I had half a mind to throw it out.

To break away from myself, let me ask you how much longer you intend to keep up your incidental pathos in regard to your never writing anymore. Do you think I am so young and inexperienced that you can play on my—what would the German be for "remorse-harp?"—in such a way as that? You could not stop writing if you wanted to, and I am very sure that you don't want to. If you do, you are temporarily crazy. It is only on that ground that you can make me sorry for you. The imaginative sympathy displayed in your best work ought to be enough to make you strong, and I think it is, though you don't like to say so. Don't be afraid to tackle a big subject and don't be afraid of a little passion—mental or spiritual.

Just now I'm reading Pater's *The Child in the House* and am finding a great deal in it. Like the Plato book, it is a little too suggestive of gods in evening dress, but still I like it better than anything I have happened to read for a long time. I do not worry about *Gaston.* I know I shall get him sometime—perhaps about the time you get that photograph. I haven't had it taken yet, but I'm going to have it before long.

I don't believe I can write any more now. I want to have a smoke. Please write whenever you feel like it.

Very sincerely,
E. A. Robinson

Quatrain—

We were all boys, and three of us were friends;
And we were more than friends, it seemed to me:—
Yes, we were more than brothers then, we three . . .
Brothers? . . . But we were boys, and there it ends.[5]

E.A.R.

1. Prosper Mérimée, *Lettres à Une Inconnue* (Paris, 1874), p. 1.

2. William Peterfield Trent, "A New Poetic Venture," *Sewanee Review*, V (April 1897), 243–246.

3. Miss Marjorie Hanson was the daughter of Mrs. Ernest S. Hanson, one of Miss Brower's close friends. The English-born Hansons conducted private instructions for young students in their home. Marjorie is presumably the "girl

whom Edith Brower placed in [Robinson's] path," and whom "he dodged alertly" (Hagedorn, *Robinson*, p. 171).

4. For further comments on Oregon and Cleveland, see Sutcliffe, *Untriangulated Stars*, pp. 269, 278. Contrary to Robinson's remark, there was a plethora of newspaper and magazine commentary on the book (*ibid.*, pp. 267–278).

5. This quatrain appeared in *The Children of the Night* (1897), p. 118; section I, "Boys," of the poem "Romance."

17

Gardiner, Maine
15 May 1897

Dear Friend:

What kind of a letter did I send to you the other day? I know that I quoted something from the first page of *Lettres à Une Inconnue* and said something about the pathos of your uncertainty in regard to the outcome of your literary compositions; but I did not mean to write anything to insinuate that you were a Baby. I don't think you are anything of the kind.

The trouble, if there is any, is just here: when I wrote that letter I hardly knew what I was doing. I think I have trained myself to the point where I can overcome an ordinary snarl, but when things get too badly tangled and the future looks too dirty, sometimes I go to pieces; and for the past week or two I have been mostly a matter of fragments. I would not say this, only I feel that I ought to make some sort of apology for any seeming rudeness or incongruity that may show itself from time to time in my letters. I don't intend to be a brute, but now and then I fear I am one, or something very like one. So please think back in all that I have said to you, and be generous enough to forgive anything that seems uncalled for in the way of familiarity. I prize your friendship too much to let myself, consciously, do anything that would put myself in an unpleasant or unsatisfactory light. I am not what they call a "polished gentleman" anyway; but I mean to be decent in my own way.

As I read farther into the *Lettres* I like them better—that is, I like the man better. Up to this time, I have known him only as the author of that tedious little masterpiece, *Colomba*—which I shall never read again—so I now have been able to judge him at his best. I appreciate *Colomba* as a work of art, but art alone is not enough—for me. I don't think that I shall ever have the courage to tackle *Carmen*. Bizet's muse is good enough for me.

To use your own words, "you make me laugh" when you speak of my "reeling off" quatrains. It may or may not interest you to know that the three in *The Torrent* cost me, I should say, something like forty or fifty hours each of diabolical brain labor. The "Brothers" [1] was another wicked grind. A year ago it was a sonnet; now I'm not sure that it is anything. "J. Wetherell" [2] was an "inspiration"; and is about on the level I think with the bulk of inspirational work. The first draught comes easily, then comes the struggle. I wish you could have seen me growing lean over "The Master and the Slave." I'm glad you still see something in my "House on the Hill," but I'm sorry to see that you misinterpreted my words when I spoke of "The Night Before." No, I was not fishing for praise. Praise that comes in that way doesn't interest me, so perhaps it will be better if you say nothing more about that poem. If it is good for anything, it will stand; if it isn't, it won't.

You will not find me very ferocious when you meet me. On the contrary I fancy I shall be disappointingly docile. I may hurt your feelings now and then with my talk, but you have my warning and need not mind that. I'm not exactly jolly today, but still I'm nothing like what I was last week. I can look back now and feel ashamed of myself—which shows that there is very much of the human in me and that I have a great deal to learn. There is no danger of my going back, but once in a while I catch myself standing still.

Very sincerely,
E. A. Robinson

Did I, or did I not, tell you of the missing line in "The Ballade of a Ship." [3] I think I did. I don't care much for the poem, but I would rather have it printed as it was written. It was bad enough then.

E.A.R.

1. "Boys." See Letter 16, note 5.
2. "James Wetherell" is section II of "Romance."
3. In *The Torrent and the Night Before* (1896), pp. 6–7, the fifth line of the second stanza—"But they danced and they drank and their souls grew gay"—was omitted.

18

20 May 1897

Dear Friend:

The first thing I saw in opening *Gaston* [1] was a marked passage in which the gist of idealism was admirably expressed. If that is a sample of the book (I shall not be able to read it right away) you have done me a great kindness in sending it to me. In a week or two I hope I shall have read enough of it to tell you what I think of it.

I am glad to know your altitude, and do not think five feet six any too much. Like Byron, "I hate a dumpy woman"; but on the other hand I don't like her to be six feet four (like an acquaintance of mine) and still growing. Now you'd better keep on and send me your avoirdupois and the color of your hair and eyes, and may God forgive me if the first is gray. I don't think it is, though; I think it is brown. The eyes seem to be dark and sharp,—sharp, at any rate, though not unpleasantly so. In fact I like the looks of you very much in your pictures and do not hesitate to tell you so because I know you aren't foolish.

You did not quite understand my apology. I was only a little afraid that I hurt your feelings when I meant only to be complimentary. My compliments are sometimes obscure and are often taken for something else. So, in spite of your friendly remarks, I am still uncertain as to whether or not I had made a mistake. The letter was written, as I saw, when I hardly knew what I was doing. I still have the New Zealand fever. I know how to get there but I don't know how to get back. They say that if one goes to Auckland, he never wants to come back, but I'm not quite ready to make an exile of myself—that is, not for more than three or four years. If I could be free for that length of time, I have a suspicion that I could do something. But I may be all wrong, and better off where I am. The only long journey I ever took was one from Boston to Springfield to see a football game. If you don't think that is a long journey, try it—especially the ride back.

I've been wheeling in wood all day and my fingers are stiff and shaky. For this reason my handwriting may not be as good as usual; and if so, I hope you will be kind enough to excuse me. I don't suppose you ever wheeled in any wood, so you can't exactly appreciate the effect the process has on one's hands and on one's happiness. It is not a pleasant effect but it gives one a splendid opportunity to philosophize. The mental expenditure is slight. If this information leads you to think me a clodhopper, it will not be leading you far astray. I suspect I'm one of the "common people" and I'm mighty glad to think so. When I get to New Zealand I shall hire a small room and say what I have to say about spiritual equality. I fear, however, that I am writing too many sonnets.

If you happen to be acquainted with Mrs. Dickson—Mrs. Allan Dickson, you might tell her that her husband's old friend Jones [2] of Chicago is no longer a high roller, but a quiet working man, a philosopher, and a wonderfully good fellow. He always speaks of Mr. Dickson as an exceptional man. He has a child named after him, I think.

I suppose you know about J. K. Paine's[3] grand opera. I have not heard any of it; but someone who has heard some of it, or who has heard someone say so who has heard some of it, says that it is good.

Very sincerely,
E. A. Robinson

I have just been reading Augusta Webster's *Portraits*.[4] Do you know them? They are not great, but they are exceptionally good. The nineteenth century dream is in them, but they are not morbid. They are too human, I should say, but they are wonderful for all that. Some of them come home to me strongly—until I pull myself together.

I am trying to place *The Seven Seas*. Do you know where it belongs, and do you know just how much of it is brass band and how much of it is the real thing? "Brass band" is not original with me, but it is very much to the point when it comes to "The Last Chantey" and "The Song of the English." And what is it that happens when "the lean, locked ranks go roaring down to die?"[5] Is that the high water mark of descriptive genius, or is it something else?

E.A.R.

1. Walter Pater, *Gaston de Latour*.
2. Jones (first name unknown) was a middle-aged resident of Gardiner with whom Robinson became acquainted early in 1896. A Christian Scientist, socialist, and philosophic idealist, his forthright opinions impressed Robinson, who formed a deep respect for him. "Jones is rather visionary, but he is a mighty good fellow and his friendship helps me out amazingly. Of course he cannot be just like a fellow of my own age, but on the other hand the difference has an advantage" (Sutcliffe, *Untriangulated Stars*, p. 262). They read together and, importantly for Robinson, discussed Carlyle, Emerson, and Zola.
3. John Knowles Paine (1839–1906), professor of music at Harvard, was also an influential composer of symphonic and choral music. His opera, *Azara*—for which he wrote both words and music—was published in 1901.
4. *Portraits* (London, 1870), a book of verse.
5. From the penultimate stanza of "The Song of the Banjo" in Kipling's *The Seven Seas*.

19

Gardiner, Maine
6 June 1897

Dear Friend:

I tried to write you a letter last week but gave it up. Things have been going so many different ways lately that I haven't succeeded in doing anything—not even in keeping my shoes clean. As for writing, the business seems out of the question; not for lack of thoughts, but for lack of a chance to loosen the strings. I do not say this by way of complaint—that would be foolish—but to keep you from being too greatly disappointed with whatever I may produce in the next year or so. I can't very well help writing the stuff but on the other hand I can't help feeling—no matter how much I may work over it (or at it)—that it is not half done. This may sound more or less contradictory to what I have said in the past in regard to art, but I only want to say that art alone was not enough. The thought alone is enough sometimes, but not when the thinker pretends or attempts to write poetry. I often wonder why it is that poems are so long. Why should a man write thirty or forty stanzas when the whole story could be better told in a dozen, or fewer? I say I wonder, but I think I know. The reason is that it is infinitely harder to tell a story or to express a thought in a dozen lines than it is in fifty. A man hasn't the courage to spend as much time over four lines of a short poem as he would over forty of a long one, and the result is that ninety-nine one-hundredths of the poetry written nowadays isn't good for anything.

Don't think I am saying this out of anything like jealousy, for I do not think, considering my one feeble output, and its reception, that I have any good cause for any such feeling. I know the publishers have "no use" for me, but I have long since given up worrying over them. Editors likewise. My literary income for the past twenty-seven years has been just seven dollars—paid to me three years ago by the editor of *Lippincott's* for a sonnet not yet printed. Two years ago its appearance would have tickled me, but I have grown old since then and would not give five cents to see it now. In fact, I am not entirely sure that I would not rather have him keep it pigeonholed for good; there are places in it that don't suit me at all, though I fancy the sestet is tolerable. It is a sonnet called "For a Book of Poe's Poems."[1] I may have told you all about it. If I have, please excuse me. I like your change of *but* to *yet* in "The Torrent," but I'm afraid I cannot agree with you in your suggestion that I change *gleams* to *glows* in the other sonnet on p. 8. *Know, glow, glows*—are you sure you like the sound of it?[2]

I am alternating *Gaston* and *The Bothie of Tober-na-Vuolich.*[3] *Gaston* is more satisfying, though the *Bothie* is undoubtedly amusing and occasionally great. I fancy you have read it; if you haven't, do so on my recommendation. Some of the hexameters are criminal, but some of them are wonderful; so the thing is pretty well evened up. As for *Gaston*, I cannot really tell you what I think of it yet. I haven't [read] enough of it. Thus far it is mostly a fuse of verbal magic with an undercurrent of something that I cannot name,—something like a consciousness on the part of the author that he is trying something stronger than he ever tried before, and that his art must have a deeper mission than in the past. This may make you laugh—it may make me laugh when I have finished the book—but this is my impression just now. I can't believe that Swinburne was so much to the author of *Gaston* as he was to the author of its predecessors—*Plato and Platonism* included. As long as I have not read *Marius*, however, I ought not to say much about Pater, for I cannot know much about him.

If I go to New York (Brooklyn) instead of New Zealand I may get a chance to talk with you—by telephone at any rate. Please write when you feel like it.

Very sincerely,
E. A. Robinson

I enclose a German "joke" which may or may not appeal to you.[4]

1. The editors held the poem for another nine years, then published it as "For A Copy of Poe's Poems," *Lippincott's*, LXXVIII (August 1906), 243.

2. In line 8 Robinson had written: "But a gladness now and then"; he changed *But* to *Yet* in subsequent editions.

In line 8 of "When we can all so excellently give," Robinson wrote "God's wholeness gleams"; he retained "gleams" in subsequent editions.

3. Arthur H. Clough's poem of 4000 hexameters, subtitled "A Long-vacation Pastoral," was published in London, 1848.

4. The clipping is no longer with the letter.

20

Gardiner
12 June 1897

Dear Friend:

The western world will be very dull and uninteresting without you, but I'm glad you are going to have a good time. I'm also glad that you are coming back in the Fall,[1] for then I can get your judgment on the new book—i.e., partly new—that I shall get out in November.[2] At least, I think I shall get it out. Don't say anything for certain; can't look two days ahead—have no particular desire to do so.

My thoughts nowadays are of all sorts and colors—sometimes rather cerulean, though I don't mean to have them so. This is why my letters are so irregular and empty of sound thought. I can think for myself without the medium of words (which, by the way is a poor way to think) but when it comes to arranging those thoughts in language, I find myself stuck. True, I have written poetry, or something that has the appearance of poetry, but I haven't the slightest notion as to what it is good for. I only know one thing about it, and that is: it is good for something or nothing. Rather different, I fancy, from what you will expect, if you expect at all. Whatever you do, don't expect too much; then, perhaps, you won't be disappointed.

I sincerely hope you will send me some letters from Europe and that you will not say anything in them about the places you travel through or the cathedrals you admire; no, nor the sunsets that most travelers rave about. Tell me what you think and read and let the scenery go. If a fellow wants to know what Mont Blanc or the Cologne Cathedral looks like he must buy his ticket and find out. No book can tell him. Personally, I don't care very much what either of these look like. Are either of them as interesting as good anthills with ants crawling over them? I don't think so. Cathedrals, I think, would be particularly uninteresting to me: they suggest everything I oppose and the mere external beauty of them would lose half its excellence in its degenerate appeal to spiritual cowardice. This may shock you a little, but I don't think it will very much. Even Trinity Church in Boston makes me uncomfortable. What effect Notre Dame would have I can only half conjecture, but I'm pretty confident that I shouldn't bring home any photographs of it. That makes me think. Don't please, send me any photographs from abroad unless it be of some man or woman. I should like another of you, with your hat off, perhaps. I can't stand hats in pictures, particularly a plug hat on a poet or a critic. Foreigners seem to like them but I'm not a foreigner. I'm an American all through, but I don't care overmuch for American institutions as they stand today. I like to look into the future and congratulate the world on what they are going to be. Patriotism, I'm afraid, is not a thing for me to enthuse over. American patriotism is illogical; British is unchartable; French is funny. The whole thing is a farce, except as the word is applied to character. America, to me, is a grist mill, through which the whole world is to be ground. The mill needs a good deal of improvement, but the improvement will come. I do not say that schoolbook patriotism is a mistake. I can only say that it never appealed to me.

I'm getting more and more out of *Gaston.* You did me a good turn when you sent it to me, but I won't thank you for it any more. You are lucky in having so good a companion on your trip and I trust you will not take it in the wrong spirit if I say the same of her. I don't much think now that I shall go to New Zealand. Don't see how I can. I don't imagine I shall even get wholly over the fever, but that will be no great matter. I have had fevers all my life and always expect to have them.

It looks now as if you would be likely to wait till you return before you get the other picture of me. I dread a photographer's shop as I do a dentist's—rather more, I think. It makes me feel foolish, as I said before.

Perhaps you will write again before you emigrate. I hope so, at any rate.

Very sincerely,
E. A. Robinson[3]

1. Miss Brower and Mrs. Ernest S. Hanson, mother of Marjorie, embarked for Europe on July 6 and returned the last week in August. Miss Brower sent back a series of weekly letters to the Wilkes-Barre *Times* on her experiences and impressions in Paris, Lausanne, Geneva, and Zurich. Despite Robinson's satiric injunction about landscape and imposing edifices, she dwelt on these aspects, although also observing native costumes, customs, and character. Mrs. Hanson later moved to New York City and kept in touch with Robinson.

2. *The Children of the Night* (Richard G. Badger & Co., Boston) appeared on December 6, 1897. It included forty-one of the poems in *The Torrent and the Night Before,* omitting only "For Calderon" and "A Poem for Max Nordau," and offered a selection of new ones.

3. In the right margin of page 3, *Modesta Ximena* is written heavily in ink. Miss Ximena (1892), a teacher of piano in Wilkes-Barre, was first introduced to Miss Brower at thirteen years of age by her own music teacher. Moved by Miss Ximena's musical talent, Miss Brower roused community interest in her through lectures and personal persuasion, with the result that she was sent to Scranton for lessons. Later, Miss Brower took her to New York and induced Mrs. Edward MacDowell to instruct her three afternoons a week and to provide a scholarship for her at the Peterborough Colony in 1908 and 1909.

Miss Ximena describes Miss Brower as an "all-round, extraordinary woman, many years ahead of her time," skilled in art, literary criticism, and music. (She recalls Miss Brower playing Scarlatti's "Cat" fugue for her.) During her stay in New York, Miss Ximena lived in a Greenwich Village boarding house, where Miss Brower came to visit her. During one of these visits Robinson called. Miss Ximena says that Miss Brower talked, Robinson listened, and she did nothing at all. At the time she considered Robinson "a bore," but now says she was "rather immature" then.

Her name is written thickly on three other letters: 21 (June 27, 1897), 185 (June 24, 1929), and 189 (June 1, 1930). She has no knowledge of how this came about or who may have done the writing.

21

Gardiner, Maine
27 June 1897

Dear Friend:

The Jefferies book [1] reached me all right, and I have read it with great pleasure. As a rule, I do not care overmuch for "nature books" but this is different. I ought to be better acquainted with the author but, as it is, I only know that he lived a most wretched life and did not find out what he was really outfitted to do till he was almost dead. The truth is, I haven't read much of anything during the past four years, so I only know what other people say, which is not much better than nothing at all. I am pretty well along in *Gaston* and think more and more of it with every page. It is a wonderful piece of writing.

The other day I received a very friendly but rather mysterious letter from one Mr. Carroll Brent Chilton [2] who tells me that you have been quoting me in your letters. He asks me to hunt him up when I go to New York but he doesn't give me any clue as to where he lives. A New York postmark is all I have to go by. He tells me that he is a musical person, but not so hopelessly musical but that he can enjoy literature, for which I congratulate him. The only thing in his letter I do not like is an incidental statement that he took my stuff for Browning's. I have had this thing happen too many times. Not that I dislike Browning, but cannot help feeling that my own little efforts must leave, with the intellectual reader, an impression at least of unconscious imitation. I did not desire to be big, but I did hope to be tolerably original. You say I am, but still you let the Browning element creep in. Evidently you can't help it. But this sounds too much like faultfinding, and that, after all your kindness, would be boorish indeed, so please don't take it that way. Only tell me, if you can, what there is in my book that makes so many people say the same thing. Is the resemblance in the style or in the thought? If it is in the style, I'm afraid there is no hope for me; if it is in the thought, I can only say that I write what is in me and let it go for what it is. As far as I know, "James Wetherell" [3] is the best thing I have done. Is that like Browning? (By the best thing, I mean from the point of view of mere art: the thought, to use Pope's description of a muscular relation of his, "isn't exactly transcendental." By Pope, I mean the Pope in the picture.)

This letter is all about myself, but still I am not wholly a selfish person. The pen is very bad, but I have no other at hand. I can't write with a steel pen anyway—never could. What do you think of E. R. Sill?[4] I'm going through him now, but cannot wholly admire him.

Very sincerely,
E. A. Robinson

1. Richard Jefferies (1848–1887) wrote poetically and philosophically about nature in *The Gamekeeper at Home* (London, 1878), *Wild Life in a Southern County* (London, 1879), *Wood Magic* (London, 1881), and others.

2. Editor of the *Aeolian Quarterly* and publisher of his own booklets with elaborate subtitles such as *The De-Assification of Music,* a propagandist magazine of one number, containing news of importance to all music lovers, especially to all owners of player pianos (New York, 1922); *World Town-Meeting On the Air,* a festival pageant of music with world-culture olympics designed for applying the power of the soul and the might of culture to the cure of war (New York, 1940); *East-West Wisdom Digest,* for the resurrection of the soul from the death-in-life of a materialized humanity towards a philosophy and a religion for the world citizenry (New York, n.d.). He became progressively distasteful to Robinson, who finally vented his accumulated resentment on Miss Brower (see particularly Letters 22, 38, 51, 59, 88, 121, 138, 140, and Miss Brower's "Memories").

3. Section II of "Romance," first published in *The Children of the Night* (1897).

4. Edward Rowland Sill (1841–1887), studied law, medicine, and theology but became a professor of English. He published many essays and poems in magazines, although issuing only one volume of verse during his lifetime, *The Hermitage and Other Poems* (New York, 1868).

22

Gardiner, Maine
31 July 1897

Dear Friend:

Your card from Dijon came yesterday and emphasized the fact that I had not answered your letter. As for the matter of bullfights and morning mass I do not know that there is much to choose between them—when it comes to the question of spiritual advancement. I cannot speak for the bullfight, however, as I have never seen one.

So your friend likes my "Two Sonnets?"[1] Well, I'm glad to hear that. Most of the people I know are inclined to keep judiciously silent about them. One or two are open enough to call them "damned queer"—whatever that may signify, but that is all. Blair (the fighty-man) takes them, with the "Chorus"[2] in *Aegeus* (*Aegeus* was never finished), for the gist of the book. I do not find any fault with his choice, but his crotchety personality is open to criticism. He'll fiddle for me if he feels just like it; otherwise he won't. He read *Pendennis* when he was too young and has never quite got over it. You may or may not see the relation between the two things, but I think you will. I have great faith in your mental perspicacity, but I suppose I ought not to tell you so. But you do see things sometimes in a way that is gratifying.

By the way, does your friend Chilton (I had a penitential note from him the other day, inferring that you blew him up—your own language) play the fiddle? If he does, I fear we shall not get along very well together—unless he is one of those long-suffering enthusiasts who will do anything as long as it's music. I have a friend at Harvard who plays the viola [3] on this principle. He says he likes to play as long as anyone will listen intelligently. That's a compliment to me, so I keep him at work. Once, a little after midnight, he kicked; but that was the only time.

Why don't you send me that poem you wrote up there among the bears? I didn't suppose it would be necessary for me to ask for it, or I should have done so long before this. I've written a nice little thing called "Richard Cory"—"Whenever Richard Cory went down town, we people on the pavement looked at him . . . And Richard Cory, one calm summer night, went home and put a bullet through his head." There isn't any idealism in it, but there's lots of something else—humanity, maybe. I opine that it will go.

Did you ever read *Evan Harrington*? [4] In it I am told that a man who has nothing in this world has a right to claim a part of the heavens. This, I fancy, explains my writing poetry when I ought to be doing something else more lucrative. I shall have to get a little money sometime, I suppose, but I'm going to do the other thing first. I've gone contrary to reason all my life, and I may be an idiot sometimes, but for the present I'm going to gamble two or three of the best years of my life and see what comes of it. Oh no—not on the Richard Cory plan: he was merely a kind of recreation—and an object lesson at the same time. The new book will have in it about a dozen of the Octaves—that is, if [I] succeed in getting them ground down to where I want them—and several other things. I'm struggling with a sonnet on "Calvary" but the bigness of the subject kills my confidence at times. I know just what I want to say, but I'm never sure of the way I say it.

Please do not think I fail to appreciate your kindness in introducing Mr. Chilton. It is a great favor to me and I only wish I could feel that you have done as much for him. I'll try to be decent, however.

Very sincerely yours,
E. A. Robinson

1. "Just as I wonder" and "Never until our souls" in *The Torrent and the Night Before*, pp. 30–31.

2. Robinson was proud of his accomplishment in "The Chorus of Old Men in 'Aegeus,'" which was not a translation but his own commentary on the fate of the Greek king. He transferred it from *The Torrent and the Night Before* to *The Children of the Night* and to successive editions of his *Collected Poems* without a change.

3. Fullerton Waldo (see Letter 91). On January 1, 1901, Robinson wrote to Josephine Preston Peabody: "Moody thinks Waldo's viola makes too many demands on one's nervous system" (Ridgely Torrence, ed., *Selected Letters of Edwin Arlington Robinson* [New York, 1940], p. 36).

4. Novel by George Meredith, published in London, 1861.

23

Gardiner, Maine
7 September 1897

Dear Friend:

I can't for the life of me understand what you mean by accusing me of obscurity in "When we can all etc."[1] When a kind mother wallops her only child does she not do so for the supposed wisdom of the thing? And when the Eternal Wisdom of the Universe makes life hell for us poor devils cannot the spiritual eye perceive a living principle of Compensation—not exactly like Emerson's—that is inevitable? This comparison may or may not be a happy one, but it is the best I can give today.

I feel as if my shoulders had been relieved of something like five hundred pounds. I packed the manuscript off yesterday morning and camped out for the rest of the day—with Blair and Pope. Blair did the cooking—i.e., fried the onions, and Pope and I washed the dishes. The only proper way to wash a spider is to take it down to the banks of a stream and rub it with sand and gravel. Certainly Pope and Blair are not the people in the quatrain.[2]

Speaking of quatrains makes me think of octaves. I have written sixty-four of them, but, partly by my own persuasion and partly by the merciless scavenging of Pope, I have cut them down to about 25—I don't remember just how many there are, but I know there are enough. I rather fancy some of them are pretty good but can't feel at all sure of them as they have not yet been tested by disinterested readers. The praise of friends is pleasant, but it is not to be taken too seriously. If I were to believe my friends I should feel justified in wearing golf-trousers, no matter what the people might say about my legs. I have a spindle-shanked friend who wears them—blue ones, at that, and I have but to look at him to renew my faith in the permanence of comedy. Blair can wear them all right—he has good legs, but Pope knows better. So do I.

Did I tell you that the title of the new book is to be *The Children of the Night*? Well, it is, and "James Wetherell" is going to be one of them. Why don't you like "Richard Cory?" You say it makes you feel cold, but that statement doesn't seem to agree with my impression of your character. It can't be you are squeamish after all. If you are, don't read "Reuben Bright" or he will knock you down. I used to read about clearness, force, and elegance in the rhetoric books, but I'm afraid I go in chiefly for force. So you will not be offended if I'm not always elegant. There are too many elegant men in the world just now, and they seem to be increasing.

I have thrown out "For Calderon" and "Max Nordau." I have also thrown away the "Saints of all Times" octave. Couldn't make it go to suit me. Sometime I may straighten it out, but rather doubt it. "The Idealist" won't suit it. There wasn't enough to the thing to make it worth printing.[3] The other day I wrote something for you and threw that away too. I was going to let you know how much I prized your criticism and appreciation but the lines were not good for anything. I have been tinkering all summer and I see that I must do something else for a while. I have a prodigious woodpile to manufacture and then I may go to New York. I rather think that I should prefer Mr. Chilton's fiddle to his symphony. A fiddle is a part of a man and too often the best part of him. I do not fear for your friend, though. You would not recommend him so highly if [he] were not worthy of it. I hope he is not too ethereally compounded to get proper satisfaction out of a pipe. If he is, he will have to make up the discrepancy with extra fiddling. Can he play "Oyster River?" If he cannot, he must learn. "Oyster River," "The Pigtown Hornpipe" and "I have lost my Eurydice" are the things fiddles are made for. Handel's "Largo" is good but not as good as "Oyster River."

Very sincerely yours,
E. A. Robinson

1. Sonnet in *The Torrent and the Night Before*.

2. Robinson is referring to The League of Three, composed of himself and two Gardiner friends, Edward G. Moore and Arthur Gledhill (see Letter 16, note 5).

3. "Saints of all times" is the beginning of the octave published in the Boston *Evening Transcript* on February 26, 1897, a clipping of which Miss Brower pasted in her copy of *The Torrent and the Night Before* (see Letter 1, note 1). Robinson never collected it, but it may be found in Hogan, *Bibliography*, pp. 174–175. for "The Idealist," see Letter 12, note 6.

24

Gardiner, Maine
15 September 1897

Dear Friend:

I'll stop chopping wood now a little while to let you know that I shall be very glad to see you in New York, Wilkes-Barre or anywhere else. If you like, I'll come down—or do you say *up*?—and talk with you some Sunday. I'm not a very good talker but I can listen. When I do talk, I am likely to say too much and so hurt people's feelings. Feelings are a mistake: we ought not to be bothered with them. Mrs. Richards (*Capt. January*, etc.)[1] had me out to her camp on Cobbossecontee Pond (you don't have such names as that in Pennsylvania?) and there I was compelled to make [myself] agreeable and interesting to five females, one Episcopal Dean, one scientific Professor, one Harvard instructor and one small dog that snored so that he had to be sent back. I washed dishes, lugged wood, stirred porridge and made breaks—some of them pretty bad, I'm afraid. I don't know why it is, but I've done this sort of thing all my life. It is only for the innate godliness of humankind that permits people to stand me at all, and I am not altogether sure that I am not a beast. I'm not a gentleman—never can be one—don't want to be one. I've lived alone so much that I have lost all desire to conform with the ways of decent people. All I am good for is to live by myself and write. What the writing amounts to—or will amount to—I don't know. You have been very kind to me. I have never tried adequately to thank you and don't much think the trial would do any good.

Of course I am glad to see you [back] again. Why do you ask me that? And why did you throw *Esther Waters*[2] overboard? Didn't she pass through enough on earth to be spared that ultimate ducking? I should say so, and I am rather surprised at your actions. If you had read the book to the end you would have felt the tremendous power of it, and so would have felt better and stronger all your life. Mental medicine, to be any good, must be of a pretty strong quality—stronger than people like. *The*

Prisoner of Zenda[3] is nothing but literary pop-beer, and I shouldn't advise you to imbibe too much of that sort of thing. I read it half through once, but had to give it up. I'd rather sit still and count my fingers.

So I am very funny, am I? Well, I didn't know it. I don't feel very funny nowadays—particularly when I think of some of the things that seem to be coming. But they'll come, and [I'll] get through them, I suppose. If I don't, I shan't be morbid or unhappy. That is all nonsense —if people could but realize life, they would not bother themselves so much about death. Death, like Mulvaney's sleep, is "a shuperfluous necessity."[4] I do not see anything in it to scare anyone, though there may be times when it is rather exasperating. After I have worked for five or six years longer, I can tell you better whether I hanker for any more. No, this is not contradictory to my philosophy.

I'll get Blair to copy "Oyster River," but it will not be good for anything or any instrument but a fiddle. You won't care much for it, anyway. I don't know who composed it.

Very sincerely,
E.A.R.

1. Laura E. Richards (1850–1943), daughter of Julia Ward Howe and author of many childhood favorites, came to Gardiner in 1876 and lived there until her death. She was among the first to encourage Robinson in his literary aspirations.
2. Novel by George Moore published in London, 1894.
3. Novel by Anthony Hope published in Bristol, 1894.
4. Terence Mulvaney is one of the three privates in Kipling's *Soldiers Three.*

25

Gardiner, Maine
29 September 1897

Dear Friend:

Your last letter was a rather queer performance, but I think it was also a good thing for me. It brought me to realize that I have been too careless in expressing myself in the past and that that I have naturally made myself misunderstood. For this I am glad and sorry:—glad for the chance it gives me to answer you that I am not a beast, sorry for the demand it makes upon my human dignity—(or whatever you call it) in trying to praise myself. If I told you that I had lost all desire to conform to the ways of decent people—why, my pen must have slipped. For *desire* I meant *hope*, and for the whole thing I meant that I realize my inborn and incurable clumsiness to an unfortunate extent. In short, I am a kind of well-meaning swine in some ways. I wallow in the trough sometimes, but I don't enjoy it. Other people may enjoy seeing me but the fun is all for them. Possibly the figure is not beautiful—I don't know; but it seems to be a fair illustration. As for the gentleman part of your difficulty, I would say that I referred to the external side of the question. Instinctively, I fancy I am something of the kind, but my instincts and my actions, sometimes my words, belie each other. I am forever getting in my own way—if you know what that means. I hurt people's feelings too, but never intentionally. At the same time I always hurt my own and wonder why it is that I have to keep on in this way. Living too much by myself is the reason, I think, for much of it.

This may sound rather serious, but I fancy there is a tone of suspicious disappointment in that last letter of yours. You seem to fear that you have made friends with a stranger and that your stranger may not be the person you took him for. This, I hope, will not prove true. I have already told you that I am not a chrysanthemum; now let me tell you that I am not of the sort that includes clot burrs, beggar's lice, and that sort of thing. I don't know very much about botany, but I do know that I am the easiest person in the world to get rid of. You need not be afraid of my bothering you if you find that I have painted myself in too seductive colors. Anything touching on insincerity makes everything fly to pieces with me—particularly in the matter of friendship—and I think I may say without egotism that I am sincere. I may be "several other things" not so commendable, but I try to be myself. The fact that I have some very good friends means a great deal more to me than those same friends suspect. I also assume it to mean that I have some good in me that makes me tolerable. I do not feel that I shall have very much difficulty with Mr. Chilton—that is, if I don't make him fiddle beyond the point of human endurance.

You tell me that you have written an octave, and I am sorry to hear it. Not because I do not think you can write one, but because I know you will never write one that will begin to satisfy you. I speak now from experience. I have made over sixty of them and have come to the conclusion that the form is impracticable and needlessly severe. True, I have printed some of my own but I more than half wish that I had spent the time and labor on something else. And yet, the thoughts would not go any other way—so perhaps it is all right. At any rate, the things are "writ" and set up, I suppose, by this time. I'm looking for the proof any day. I enclose a circular which was issued without my knowledge. I may be "a yearning spirit" but I don't like to tell people so.[1]

Very sincerely,
E. A. Robinson

P.S.—Blair is very slow, so I can't send "Oyster River" this time.

1. Robinson is referring to the phrase in Harry Thurston Peck's review of *The Torrent and the Night Before* in *Bookman*, IV (February 1897), 509–510: "But here and there in a sonnet he lets himself go, and the cry of a yearning spirit enters the lute of Orpheus and sounds a sweet and wondrous note."

26

Gardiner, Maine
7 October 1897

Dear Friend:

I'm glad to hear that I misinterpreted your last letter, for I really feared that you were getting suspicious of me. I think, as far as "common decency" goes, that I am all right though I feel that I lack certain external attributes which count for a great deal in the eyes of people at large. You may be glad to know, however, that I do not smoke cigarettes —a performance which I take to be the unpardonable sin.

Nothing would give me greater pleasure than to have you criticize my new book, though I should feel very bad to have you perish in the effort. I do not think the poems are to be taken so seriously as that, and I am half afraid that you may have some difficulty in finding an editor who will agree with you in thinking them worthy of any elaborate criticism at all.[1] McDowell's[2] position in the world and my own are two different things to consider. That of one is accepted, that of the other is not even considered; so I think you may not be quite politic enough in your project. Whatever you do, don't feel obliged to write something because you have mentioned doing so. If you conclude to do it I shall be glad but I shall demand your sworn assurance that you are doing it for the fun of the thing and not to please me. I will also ask you not to feel afraid that I am laboring under any childish delusion that you are satisfied with anything in the book or that I shall be downhearted or in any way offended if you "wipe" me now and then. In fact I should be disappointed if you did not. I know as well as anyone that the book is full of flaws and that the touch of the novice is everywhere, or almost everywhere, apparent. So don't be afraid to say what you think.

I am preparing to leave this region about the first of November, rather later than I first intended, and I expect to be in New York about the first of December. I shall stay there till June and possibly through the summer. It will depend entirely on how things go and how I feel. My final settlement in any place will depend a good deal I think on the location and general attractiveness of its almshouse. You see I have not yet quite conquered the human influence of place. I'm beginning to be half afraid that I shan't get to New Zealand though I shall always have a hankering for Auckland, the isolation, and the New Zealand bigness of things. When I get there, I should probably want to get back again; but three or four years of that kind of exile might bring something out of me —that is, if there is anything in me. *The Children of the Night* is a feeler. I don't expect very much from it but I hope it may be [the] means of my feeling a little more certain in regard to what I am here for. I like to think the new work is rather better than that in the blue book,[3] and Pope says it is, and I have a good deal of faith in Pope. Smith[4] says it is, too, and I have a good deal of faith in Smith; but Smith and Pope are friends of mine and therefore are not wholly to be trusted in a matter like this. With you it is different, as I have never seen you; but even your words are occasionally suggestive of a little too much enthusiasm.

Sincerely hoping that your trouble has left you by this time, I am, etc.

E. A. Robinson

1. See Letter 30, note 3.
2. The American composer, Edward A. MacDowell (1861–1908), about whom Miss Brower had written in the *Atlantic Monthly*, LXXVII (March 1896), 394–402.
3. *The Torrent and the Night Before.*
4. Harry de Forest Smith, a Gardiner friend of Robinson, became a professor of Greek at Amherst College. See Sutcliffe's volume of Robinson letters to Smith.

27

Gardiner, Maine
1 November 1897

Dear Friend:

I am sorry to find out that I put myself in a wrong light by misconstruing your random remark in regard to criticizing my verses.[1] You must think me an idiot, or something very like one, and I cannot be surprised if you do. All I have to say is that I am not childishly ravenous for press notices, but that I wanted you to feel that I appreciated your interest in my work. The fact that I blundered in doing so will not, I hope, be fatal to friendship. As your last letter, though rather brief, was not at all fierce, I venture to hope that you will permit me to land in Wilkes-Barre for a day sometime about the first of December.

No, I am not going to fast and pray. I'm going to stay in Boston for a couple of weeks and then go to New York. I shall leave here about the 10th of this month, if all goes well, and the book [2] will be out at about the same time. I thank the ruling powers that I am still philosophical over that book. If I don't sell five hundred copies in a year I shall be somewhat surprised but not discouraged. There is another book of a different sort that I must work out of my system during the next year and after that a lot of sonnets and things. I still want to go to New Zealand, and shall get there sometime if the thing is possible, but for the present it will be impossible. I shall be brought up with quick rein someday, I suppose, and have to solve the bread-and-butter problem with some kind of work that pays, but for the next two or three years I intend, like Kipling's fool, to follow my "natural bent" [3] and see what comes of it. If I were offered a ten thousand dollar position today I should be "fired" inside of three months for the reason that I should forget what I was supposed to do.

I forgot to tell you that I am a wretched talker. You will have to do the talking, or most of it, and keep me good-natured or I shall feel unhappy and get out. Also, I must ask you again not to make any tea. I went on a potato-roast with some young persons the other afternoon and was unhappy all the time because they persisted in spoiling the pastoral effect by making tea in a two-quart dipper. Can you tell me what anyone wants of tea when there is a fire in the woods to look at? I don't believe you can. Nor do I believe I can tell you "just how I feel." I think I feel very well just now, but I should feel better if things were to straighten out a little.

I have just read *Kidnapped*, *David Balfour* and a lot of bad poetry. *David* is a good book but not satisfactory from a human point of view. Barbara is the best person in it. They say she is Stevenson himself. Too dark to write any more.

Sincerely,
E.A.R.

I enclose a "review" from the Chicago *Record* [4]

1. Above the dateline Miss Brower wrote: "This refers to my article in Wilkes-Barre *Times*."

2. At the bottom of page 1 Miss Brower wrote: "His first *published* book, *The Children of the Night*." See her "Memories" for the distinction she made between privately and commercially published books. This book was first issued on December 6.

3. From the third stanza of "The Vampire": "But a fool must follow his natural bent."

4. Anon., "The Torrent and the Night Before," Chicago *Record* (January 23, 1897), p. 11.

28

5 Thayer Hall
Cambridge, Mass.
20 November 1897

Dear Friend:

You think, no doubt, that I am either dead or very ill, but the truth is that I am feeling tolerably well. I hear from Mr. Badger[1] that the book will be ready in about a week; so, if you are really agitated over its non-appearance you will not have to wait much longer. Personally, I am not at all excited. I don't see any reason to expect anything in particular, therefore I am not expecting it.

I shall be in New York, as I said, about the first of December, and shall take a trip to Wilkes-Barre sometime before New Year's—that is, if you are still possessed of the notion that you want to talk with me. I tell you very frankly that I shall disappoint you. I disappoint everybody and almost everybody disappoints me. I make free to say this, knowing that you will do nothing of the kind. You will have to do more or less piano work, and you will have to refrain from asking me what I mean to do for a living; but I know you are considerate enough to do these things and I know I shall have a good time, if I behave myself; and I'll try to do that.

Oh, I forgot all about the margins.[2] Kindly excuse me this time for I can hardly be expected to remember everything when I have two calls to make in town on people I do not know and who have no earthly interest in me. If there were any possible way to get out of them, I should take [it], but there isn't, and I must go and make myself agreeable and impressive—lit.—impressive and agreeable, of course. I'm not literary when I write letters, as you have observed. I don't think I am very literary when I write sonnets, but I leave others to be the judge of that.

This is a cold snowy day, and everything is white and sticky. The college yard is deserted, and the future, when I think of it, seems strangely dense. Pope says life is not a dream but a damned nightmare—a statement which contains (with the proper interpretation of *life*) the very essence of Christianity. Pope doesn't see that, however, and I'm afraid he never will. He partly sees it, or he could not interpret my octaves as he does; but he doesn't see it in a way that will convince him that there are two females in the world, or that will help him any when his dinner hurts him. My future doesn't really appall me, but I own that it keeps me mentally active at times when I would rather be oblivious to clocks and almanacs. This, of course, is my weakness.

Do you know why one of Haydn's symphonies—I forget the number—is called "The Bear?" I heard it Friday evening in Saunders[3] and it made me laugh—that is, it made me feel like laughing. Why, I cannot say, but there's the fact. Maybe the simplicity of the thing, after Brahms, made me glad. If you don't know, I must ask Mr. Chilton why it is called "The Bear."

Very sincerely,
E. A. Robinson

1. Richard G. Badger, publisher of *The Children of the Night*.
2. Miss Brower evidently complained about the width of his margins. Beginning with this paragraph he wrote a longer line in this and several subsequent letters, but soon he reverted to his old practice.
3. A theater in Cambridge, site of concerts, plays, lectures, and other cultural events. Built in 1876, largely through the bequest of Charles Sanders, it is situated at the east end of Memorial Hall, Harvard University, at the corner of Quincy and Cambridge streets.

29

129 West 64th St.
New York
14 December 1897

Dear Friend:

I hunted up your Mr. Chilton last evening and found him in every way worthy of your eulogy. He didn't fiddle to me but he drew all sorts of effects from his Aeolian and gave me two bottles of beer. I gave him a

Free Cuba cigar of the long nine variety and we became friends—at least I hope we did.

Why do you think I meant to say "clear seers."[1] Certainly not. "Clear" would spoil the whole thing, it seems to me. At any rate, I never thought of it. The trouble must have been in my handwriting.

Am I to understand from your reference to your work that you have taken up writing again? Surely I hope so and feel confident that you will find that your period of "helplessness" has been a good thing for you. Sometimes we think we are doing nothing, but that is all wrong. Development goes on though the intellect seems to decay. My own seems to be decaying more than half of the time, but still I manage to see the light most of the time.

Won't you write me a letter and tell me something about yourself?

Very sincerely,
E. A. Robinson

1. Robinson is referring to the last two words in line 2 of "Octave XXIV" which appears on page 114 of *The Children of the Night* (1897): "Forebodings are the fiends of Recreance; / The master of the moment, the clean seer . . ." Miss Brower evidently excised his prepublication manuscript version from the last sheet of Letter 13. In her copy of this book the lower half of page 114 shows evidence of a clipping once pasted there and subsequently removed. Notwithstanding Robinson's somewhat irritable explanation, Miss Brower quoted the words as "clear seer" in her Wilkes-Barre *Times* critique (see Appendix II, where it is corrected by the present editor in order to prevent continued misquotation).

30

129 West 64th St.
17 December 1897

Dear Friend:

I'm very sorry to say it, but I cannot possibly go to Wilkes-Barre tomorrow. Sometime about the first of next month I shall be able to come, and very glad to—if you want me then; but just now it will be out of the question.

Last evening I went around to the Authors' Club[1] at the request of your friend Dr. Coan and found in the Doctor himself the only one of the crowd whom I would care to go very far to meet again. There was a general suggestion of swelled head for which I could see no good reason. All this is, of course, unnecessary—I mean my writing this—but I am given to certain periods of indifference to all things but the real thing, and I trust this may account for my lack of enthusiasm last evening. The Club is all right—the trouble is with me. I am curious to see the Century [2] fellows, but shan't be able to get around to them just yet. Told the Doctor to put me down—or up, about the middle of January—his invitation—for a month. I like this man, the Doctor, though not for his favors to me;—rather for something else—something in his personality.

I thank [you] most sincerely for your friendliness in asking me to your place, but can—for the present—only repeat that I am absolutely unable to leave this village tomorrow or next week. Please write very soon and tell me what you want me to do. Also send me a copy of your "appreciation" [3] and let me see what you have been doing with me.

Very sincerely,
E. A. Robinson

1. A New York City society organized in 1882. Its membership was limited to less than two hundred, the prime requisite for admission being that the candidate "have published at least one book pertaining to literature." On its roster at this time were Rudyard Kipling, Frank R. Stockton, Brander Matthews, Richard Watson Gilder, Edward Eggleston, Richard Henry Stoddard, Edmund Clarence Stedman, and Hamlin Garland.

2. The Century Association, a New York City society of "authors, artists, and amateurs of letters and the fine arts," was founded in 1847. It included among its members Rudyard Kipling, William Dean Howells, Theodore Roosevelt, Henry Van Dyke, Admiral Alfred T. Mahan, clergymen, lawyers, doctors, and diplomats.

3. Miss Brower's "Edward [*sic*] Arlington Robinson" appeared on page 15 of the Wilkes-Barre *Times*, December 20, 1897, a three-column, page-length review of his work. See Appendix II.

31

135 West 64th St.
Christmas 1897
Notice change of address

Dear Friend:

I am just inconsistent enough to let Christmas give me the blues. I don't know whether you are affected in this way or not, but I fancy that almost everybody is glad when the day is gone by and things right themselves again. Of course I exclude the children—they know no better. Or do they know too much? Sometimes I look at a child and feel sorry for myself; and then sorry for the child again to think it has to grow up. As far as I am concerned I am quite willing to live it out and see what I can bring to pass for myself and (though indirectly, I fear) for others; but when I look about me and see the people at large with their hopeless lack of resource and even the conception of any that cannot be shut up in a foolish book, I own to seasons when I feel sour. I feel as if I wanted to start things and then feel sick for my own relative inability to start myself. Some day, as I have ventured to tell one or two courteously incredulous friends, I think I shall disappear, though of course I may turn up again. There is no tragedy in all this, but just an indescribable conviction that pride will overcome policy—justifiable policy, maybe—and compel me to get out. If you are the sagacious person I take you to be, I think you can partly appreciate this feeling.

I called on Dr. Coan the other afternoon and had quite a talk with him. I understand what you mean by some things you have said and appreciate your feelings. I don't think his critical ideas are large enough to suit me—from a general point of view, though I have no doubt he might go through my *Children* and make infinite verbal improvements. He did not find much fault, however, with anything but the last two lines in "The Torrent," which are getting to be a subject over which I can no longer talk with much enthusiasm. I feel that they are as good as I can do them.[1] I should really like to see your article, but do not wish to pester you. So I'll say no more about it.

Very sincerely,
E.A.R.

I enclose editorial from the N.Y. *Sun* which will please you. It pleases me, at any rate.[2]

1. The controversial lines to which Robinson has referred several times—"The jealous visionings that I had had / Were steps to the great place where trees and torrents go"—prevented him from selling the poem. The editor to whom it had been submitted rejected it because Robinson refused to alter them. He persevered in his conviction; they remained unaltered through eight of his books from 1896 to 1929.

Typical of the comments about "The Torrent" that exasperated him was this one from the *Christian Register*, LXXVI (January 21, 1897), 43: "'The Torrent,' which begins grandly in the octave (it is a sonnet) does not run itself clear in the sestette. A fifth or sixth reading does not make the meaning clear."

2. This may be the anonymous editorial by Frank P. Church, which appeared for the first time this year and has been reprinted widely ever since. Entitled "Is There a Santa Claus?" it is the answer to a letter by eight-year-old Virginia O'Hanlon who requested the unvarnished truth. Church's response included the oft-parodied statement, "Yes, Virginia, there is a Santa Claus."

32

29 December 1897

Dear Friend:

I did not intend to pull your heartstrings in my last letter though I must confess that I was a little out of sorts at the time of writing. There is a good deal more of the human in me than you think and I am subject, occasionally, to all sorts of foolish moods. I don't really have the blues but there are times when I get twisted—if you know what that means.

I read your criticism with a great deal of pleasure—not for the praise that was in it (I forgot myself—you told me there wasn't any) but for the intelligent sympathy of the thing. No doubt you are right in what you say regarding my tendency to forget singing for preaching,[1] but what the deuce am I going to do when scholarly people tell me they don't understand "John Evereldown?"—and that there is no connection between the first and second parts of the quatrain "Drink to the splendor, etc?"[2] Such criticisms as these make me wonder what kind of stuff I have been writing and if it is worth while for me to keep on. Then you come along and find no difficulty in seeing what I am driving at and I feel encouraged again. I do not mean that you are alone, but still you are one of an apparently hopeless minority. To be honest, I must say that I was completely dazed when I was compelled to see that that blue book of mine was generally misinterpreted, for I thought it was as plain as daylight. There was praise enough—evidently more than you thought—when you wrote that article—but praise without sympathy is like butter without bread, and just about as appetizing. I might have made my own bread and buttered it on both sides but fortunately did not have to. You took upon yourself the double duty of bread maker and churn-minder and relieved me from the possibility of starvation. In short, you are responsible to a large extent, I think, for the publication of *The Children*, though there were six or eight others who helped things along.[3] Don't think from this that I am inert, and wholly dependent on the opinions of others, for I am really something better than that: I merely recognize the influence, conscious or unconscious, of outside encouragement and give that influence its due. Sometimes am called obstinate and "bull-headed," but that is mostly an error. I bend, like the rest of people. The thing is, not to break.

Yes, I'll go to Wilkes-Barre on the 8th if you won't ask me to go to church. You will have to play the "Wallenstein" sonata[4]—the second part of it, at any rate, and a lot of other things—including "The Arkansas Traveler," which, though the fact may never have occurred to you, is a work of genius. So is "Oyster River," but I didn't have the heart to send it to you after your remark about your musical education. Of course I knew you had one from what you had written but I didn't think of it at the time. Associations were too much for me then: Blair and his fiddle, Pope, pipes, and all sorts of worldly things which you do not care for. Mr. Chilton gave me *Death—and Afterwards*[5] and my landlady borrowed it.

Very sincerely,
E. A. Robinson

1. See Appendix II for Miss Brower's review.
2. The second of "Three Quatrains" in *The Torrent and the Night Before*.
3. William Edward Butler, one of his Harvard friends, offered to pay the costs of publication. Laura E. Richards and John Hays Gardiner gave frequent aid in these early days.
4. Robinson is confusing two frequently performed concert pieces: Vincent D'Indy's dramatic symphony based on Friedrich von Schiller's play, *Wallenstein*, and Beethoven's opus 53, a pianoforte sonata in C major which he dedicated to Count Ferdinand Waldstein. See Letter 33.
5. Edwin Arnold, *Death—and Afterwards* (London, 1887), an essay from the *Fortnightly Review*, with a supplement; probably the 1897 issue by the New Amsterdam Book Company of New York, reprinted from the 14th English edition.

33

135 West 64th
6 January 1898

Dear Friend:

I'm sorry I blundered on "Waldstein"—thought it was "Wallenstein"—my error again—never saw it printed.

I'll see you Saturday afternoon—if nothing happens to prevent my getting to Wilkes-Barre. The cat and I are going to get along first-rate[1] and I'll try to get a sight of your beautiful city from the car-window.

Very sincerely,
E. A. Robinson

1. See Miss Brower's "Memories" for an account of their meeting.

34

135 West 64th St.
15 January 1898

Dear Friend:

I don't know what notion got into my head when I spoke of sending the photographs of my father and mother for you to look at, and as I think of it now I try in vain to wonder what you thought of me. Still, as long as I said I would send them, I am going to do it and ask you to excuse me for making you go to the trouble of sending them back. The whole thing was done on impulse, and was hardly characteristic of my general way of doing things, and I think you must understand why it makes me feel a trifle foolish.

Just at present—that is to say for the past week—ever since I came back from Wilkes-Barre I have been trying to get started on a piece of blank verse which, if it is ever done will be a book by itself—not a very big one, but still a book.[1] If it goes on as it has been going it will be out some time in the middle of the next century; but I hope and rather feel that I am slowly getting it under control and that I shall be able to do it somehow. I doubt if many people will care to read it but that doesn't seem to make any difference; I've got to do it. And let me add—to relieve you of a possible uneasiness—that it is not "preachy." It isn't much of a story either—in fact, I don't know just what it is. Perhaps you will be able to tell me.

I wonder if it would make you feel any better if I were to tell you that my visit to Wilkes-Barre was one of the greatest pleasures of my life. I didn't say very much, I may have been rather wooden for the most part; but now, as I look back on it I can't but have a feeling of honest gratitude for you and for your aunt.[2] You said it was strange that I should be there, but to me it was the most natural thing in the world. Before I had received half a dozen letters from you I knew I should see you before a great while. You may think I have been taking a good deal for granted, but I cannot help that.

Last evening I "made a call" of some excellent and unpretentious people, but it was no go. You don't understand these things—you never can; so please don't try to. Tell me more about Dallas.[3]

Very sincerely,
E. A. Robinson

I'll send *Vampires*[4] in a few days. Don't like it very much.

1. "The Book of Annandale," over 500 lines, first appeared in *Captain Craig* (Boston, 1902).

2. Miss Brower lived on South Franklin Street with her aunt, Laura Gardiner Brower, a highly regarded member of the community, devoted to church work and encouragement of the young.

3. At this time "a pleasant little country town" near Wilkes-Barre with one hotel, the Rhoades, which accommodated vacationers. Miss Brower stayed at various boardinghouses there from time to time, usually in the summer, often accompanied by Modesta Ximena.

4. Novel by Julia G. Cruger, published under her nom de plume of Julien Gordon by Lippincott (Philadelphia, 1891).

35

New York
26 January 1898

Dear Friend:

The pictures came back all right and I am glad to know (you see I believe pretty much everything you say) that they did not bother you. I still think, though, that I did a queer thing in sending them.

Yes, I was glad for your story about Ginn's poetical agent. Whenever I hear that a new man or woman has found something in my book—particularly a new woman—I feel encouraged and there is no reason why I should feel otherwise. I do not pretend to be indifferent to recognition: the truth is, I want all I can get of it provided it is of an intelligent sort. When men tell me, as one did the other day, that my poems are "dainty"—then I begin to feel uncomfortable.

I have been laid up for the past week with a cough—something very unusual with me—and have made the discovery that I care positively nothing for Browning outside of his lyrics. They are the greatest we have, to my mind, but the longer things I cannot read. At least I cannot read them when I have a cough. If the *Parleyings*, for instance, were written in decent prose I fancy they might make rather good reading. I gave up the plays long ago and as for *The Ring and the Book*, I like Calverly's version of it much better.[1] Of course I may live to change my mind but I don't [think] that poetry without even the music of good prose in it will ever appeal to me.

I had some astounding news the other day. Badger writes me that he has got rid of three hundred copies of *The Children*. I can partly account for 150 of them but the rest have gone off into the unknown and the unknowable. That's where I like to have them go.

If you have any regard whatever for my feelings, don't say anything more about "booklets." The blank verse affair is to be a book even if I print it on bag-paper and without covers. "Pamphlet" if you like, or "small book," or anything—anything but "booklet." The word suggests to me the essence of everything that is little and really makes me feel uncomfortable inside.

I'll return *Vampires* as soon as I accumulate energy enough to do it up. If I were to criticize it I should say that it was very well conceived and very badly written. But then, I'm still coughing.

Very sincerely yours,
E. A. Robinson

1. This parody by Charles S. Calverley is "The Cock and the Bull," in Walter J. Sendall, editor, *The Complete Works of C. S. Calverley* (London, 1901), pp. 110–114.

36

6 February 1898

Dear Friend:

I ought to have written to you right away but somehow I didn't. I'm feeling much better now and think you need have no further fears as to the question of my existence. I am still a little out of tune and my teeth are teaching me lessons in idealism every day, but still I manage to do something. I don't know what you will think of the new thing in blank verse; I don't know what to think of it myself. I only know that it comes hard and that I have but 220 lines or so. The plan of the thing is rather new, as far as I know, and offers every opportunity for a man to make a total failure of it. I am so constituted, though, that I'd rather fail at something large than succeed at something small; so I shall see it through and do what I can to make it worthwhile.

I am forgetting all about margins again, I see. Don't take it as a sign that I am ignoring your request for that is not so. I return *Vampires*, even though you don't want it, and also send a section of the *Journal* containing an announcement of a new book which may or may not be of interest to you. I haven't seen Mr. Chilton for some time—two or three weeks—but shall drop in on him again very soon now and get him to grind something out of that lovely instrument of his.

Very sincerely yours,
E. A. Robinson

37

14 February 1898

Dear Friend:

I have been a long time sending this book of Coppeé,[1] and even now do not feel sure that you want it. I think, though, that you cannot help liking some of the things in it—"La Sœur de Lait," "L'Ouvreuse," "L'Enfant-Bibelot" and three or four others. To me they are wonderful as illustrations of compressed narrative—perhaps too much compressed to be permanent, although I cannot yet think so. Keep the book as long as you want it. If I want it back I'll write for it.

Mr. Chilton gave me a very pleasant call the other evening but I was so thoroughly twisted from one cause and another that I fear I may have been a trifle dull to him. He is a remarkably interesting man, but not one, I think, with whom I could ever be altogether at ease—"brotherly ease" I mean. The fault however, is mine, not his. My limitations are too many—more even than I used to suspect. I left Wilkes-Barre with a feeling that I had proved a total disappointment to you but you tell me that this is not true and I suppose I shall have to believe you. If you think this feeling incompatible with my statement that I got great pleasure from the visit, all I can do is to ask you to study the matter a little.

I'm not doing much of anything now—can't do anything; but I can see how things are forming themselves and how this blank verse affair must eventually materialize (not the best word, perhaps) and be printed in a book for such men and women to read as may care for it. My ideas of poetry are growing more and more verbacious every day—so much that I am positive that our excellent friend Dr. Coan will be more anxious than ever to pack me off to England after reading this thing I am doing now. My life has been prosaic as hay for the most part but that hay has been so full of thistles and things that I have managed to get some feeling out of it.

The notion of my *Children* being put into the nurses department of Pulitzer's newspaper is novel and very attractive but somehow I don't conceive of its coming to pass.[2] I thank you again for all your missionary work, and remain

Very sincerely,
E. A. Robinson

1. François Coppée, *Vingt Contes Nouveaux* (Paris, 1883).

2. Miss Brower must have made a small jest based on the daily SITUATIONS WANTED—FEMALE advertisements in the New York *World*, to which Robinson was answering in kind. One section, titled "Nurses, Ladies' Maids, &c," contained numerous offers to take care of children.

38

New York
2 March 1898

Dear Friend:

I am forming a very bad habit of writing long letters to you and to my friend Mrs. Richards, and then tearing them up. A day or two ago I wrote a long one to you that would have made you ferocious for a week, had I been maniac enough to send [it], and tonight I am writing another which may produce the same effect, though I hope not. You see, in my other letter I tried to explain my difficulty in getting close to Mr. Chilton, and did it so viciously (and, I think, a trifle falsely) at my own expense that I concluded to throw the whole thing away and try it over again when I felt a little better satisfied with myself. I am not at all sure that such a time has come to me now, but still I shall try to say what I mean and leave you to understand. In the discarded letter I applied to myself the rather verbose term of "aesthetic inferiority," and by that I meant that Mr. Chilton has something that I have not and—I may as well say it—something I do not wish to have. I cannot give it a name but I think you can feel for yourself about what it is. Whether or not he is better off with it I do not pretend to say; but as long as he has it, and as long as I shall (mind you I don't say "will") never have it, there must always be an impediment in the way. On the other hand I care a great deal for him—infinitely more, from the nature of things—than he can possibly care for me, and this fact gives me a great deal of pleasure—pleasure of a kind that I am confident you can appreciate. All this is rather vague talk but I won't venture anything more explicit for I really want this letter to go. I feel that it is about time for me to acknowledge and return that astonishing hymn to Ceres, which I cannot criticize or laugh at: —I cannot possibly laugh at it—and this fact will have to go for criticism.

Mrs. Richards tells me that she has written to you in regard to some sort of musical business and I suppose she has, out of the goodness of her heart, advised you to find out whether I eat anything and if I go down Broadway in my stocking feet—with my toes out. She is one of the best and kindest women in the world but the motherly instinct is so rampant in her nature that [it] is rather given to worry about everybody—young or old—who is not under her immediate care. If ever you meet her you will like her, and I hope the meeting may come about in some way.

I have thrown my blank verse effusion aside for a time and am slowly writing—in my head—another of an entirely different sort.[1] When the two are done, as I hope they may be by next December, I shall feel that I have given myself a trial. This new book is going to be a wicked dose for Dr. Coan, and possibly the same thing for you; but I hope you may be able to stand certain parts of it. As for sending advance sheets, I can only say that they are at present in no condition to be sent to anyone, not even to Pope—who is working on the ice.[2]

Very sincerely yours,
E. A. Robinson

1. The poem which he tentatively called "The Pauper" and published as "Captain Craig."

2. Ice harvesting on the Kennebec River by the Knickerbocker Ice Company of Philadelphia was a gainful industry for Gardiner men, many of whom helped to scrape the ice after every snowstorm.

39

[March–April 1898]

Dear Friend:

I am perfectly willing to go to Pennsylvania to see you but sometimes it gives me great qualms to call on anybody here in this wicked city. Still, if you will tell me where you are, I'll try to find you (I positively refused to go across the city with Mrs. Richards the other day). I'll find you. I don't think, however, it will be possible for me to do so until after Thursday.

Mr. Chilton has asked me to assist at an Aeolian function Sunday afternoon and implies that you are to make up the rest of the audience. Don't for heaven's sake make the man unhappy by telling him that I told you that he had no aesthetics. I merely used him as a means to say that I haven't them and am strongly aware of the fact—painfully so, sometimes.

It looks now as if I should leave this place for Winthrop, Maine, in a few weeks. I may come back in the course of years, but that is a matter of conjecture.

Very sincerely,
E. A. Robinson

40

14 April 1898

I don't have trances, furors or ecstacies. My poetic spells are of the most prosaic sort. I just sit down and grind it out and use a trifle more tobacco than is good for me.

I haven't yet quite settled as to where I shall go this summer but I shall go somewhere before very long. There are things to make me go to Maine, and there are things to keep me away from there. Probably I shall go, however.

I understand your feelings in this war business, but I shall not add to the talk that is going on. There is (at least I think there is) a good deal to say on both sides and the *Post* is to me as unconvincing as the *Sun* is unreasonable. I cite these papers as typical of the two extremes. Personally I have my opinion of Spain and the Spanish. They are a little lower than the Cubans and the Cubans are what one might call humanity in the abstract. Mr. Chilton's indifference is all right but I fear the thing that makes it possible is likely to weaken the spine of his Aesthetics. My Americanism is not at all rampant—in fact the crudeness and general cussedness of things American makes me sick until I stop to think; then it makes me sorry, and finally glad. There may be a collapse before long but it will be to get a new start.

I have been intending to write to your friend Alexander,[1] but my letters have been very few since I came here. I can't write or do much of anything but let the strings get slackened out to where they belong. I'll wait now till he comes back and then look him up.

You may call me anything you like—anything but Eddie. I had an aunt who called me Eddie and now she doesn't call me at all.

Very sincerely yours,
E. A. Robinson

1. Miss Brower's pet name for Chilton, who in turn called her "Sibyl."

41

Gardiner, Maine
9 June 1898

Dear Friend:

I have been letting you go with a loose string for some time past, but I have had hold of the other end all the while and haven't had the smallest idea of letting you get away. You ask me to say strong things but I'm afraid just now that I can't say very much. I must say, though, to begin, that nothing would have given me greater pleasure than to have gone to Dallas for the summer—which was, unfortunately, entirely out of the question. I'm not quite sure that I can stay here, but I'm going to try it for a few months. After that I expect to go into the night-watching business and find out what I am good for with a broom.[1] Five or six hours of sweeping every night will, I think, be an excellent thing for me, though I suppose such work would be intolerable under any different circumstance. Looking at it as a miserable means to a worthy end, a man can go through almost anything. There are friends(?) of mine who will think less of me if I do this, but I'm not in a position to consider their feelings as much as my own. If I can stand it, I feel that they ought to get along with it somehow.

Yes, the future is very misty—but I have a great deal to be glad for—the fact that you still stand by me and that I fell in with Dr. Coan and poor old Louis.[2] Without them my winter in New York would have been very different from what it was; without you to keep me alive to the fact that I do not work for nothing, things would be woefully rough just at present. However, I go along, and still believe that I am going in the right direction, even though the eyes and actions, if not the words, of nearly everyone but Pope, would tell me that I am going wrong. They don't see where the money is to come in; Pope doesn't care—so long as something "gets itself uttered." So you mustn't ever go back on Pope, even if you have to go back on me.

Your letter made me strangely uncomfortable, but when it comes to helping others, I am afraid I can't do very much more than to tell them that I am on their side and that I am infinitely better off for knowing them. There are so few to whom I can honestly say this, that I am compelled honestly to think that the possibility of my doing so points to an unsuspected reserve fund of spiritual strength which is bound to carry them through. You told me nothing of late about your writing, but somehow I think you are doing something that doesn't come very fast or quite to your liking. In this case, all I can say is, keep at it and put away every idea of possible failure. (I said this once before, but it will do no harm to say it again.) Then there is the war which is having its effect on you—a war which is to me so obviously working out of an eternal principle through the agency of men who hardly suspect what they are doing—I include even the politicians and financiers, who are all doing their work—that I do not worry about it. It is a war that will, I believe, be of tremendous historical importance, though I may be wrong in my estimate of it. At any rate, I have lost whatever little sympathy I ever had with the shortsighted whimpering of the *Post*, and, on the contrary, I cannot tolerate the equally shortsighted enthusiasm of the other papers who see nothing but a "glorious war for humanity" and the like. Cuba is a very small part of it.

Well, I'll stop here and go on some other day. I'm to see Pope at 2.30. Please write as often as you are in the mood, and believe me

Most sincerely yours,
E. A. Robinson

Observe that I have given you particularly narrow margins—which means that I am particularly good-natured and self-sacrificing this afternoon. Don't think of expecting it every time.

E.A.R.

1. William Edward Butler, whose father owned a Boston department store, offered Robinson a job as night watchman there, but he took a position as confidential clerk in the President's office at Harvard in January.

2. Alfred Hyman Louis, a philosophic and disreputable New York friend whom Robinson adopted as the main model for Captain Craig. See Denham Sutcliffe, "The Original of Robinson's Captain Craig," *New England Quarterly*, XVI (September 1943), 407–431.

42

Gardiner, Maine
24 June 1898

Dear Friend:

This is a sharp steel pen—and I can't seem to do very much with it. Still, I think I can manage to let you know that I am alive. I've really been at work since I came back to this place, but just now there is pause. Think I can get down to it again tomorrow—on something new. The man and woman thing in blank verse[1] is still unfinished but I think I have it where it can't get away from me. Once I was half afraid I had lost it, though I didn't want you to think so. Probably I shall go to sweeping in the fall. It is bad to prove such a miserable disappointment to one's friends—there is no need of expecting them, or even you, to put the world away altogether—but I don't seem to see my way to anything better unless it be so murderously at the expense of the other thing—the real thing—as to make it worse than penal servitude. Sometime in the future I may get out of the dark and into the light again; but even if I don't, I shall always have the satisfaction of having tried to do something. I cannot feel that I have done very much yet.

I don't hear anything from our contented friend Mr. Chilton, but expect to in the course of time. The Doctor is also silent, but he will write by and by. So will Louis. If they don't, I shall begin to think that Gardiner is the only immovable place in the world. It is very beautiful here now. The Common (we have a Common) is kept clipped like a prisoner's head and not a blessed young one is allowed to play on it. The head figure doesn't work out but the fact remains that this asinine city government compels its school children to go into the streets in order that the Common may look pretty. It looks very pretty to a fellow with any notion of human nature.

I appreciate anything in the *Post*[2]—nearly forgot to say anything about it. I appreciate anything now—even straw-colored cats. We have one about nine inches long and an inch thick. He eats enough, but he doesn't grow. Probably he is a pessimist and a walking image of his thoughts.

The next thing I do is going to be humorous. It's about two old men.[3] If I have no particular setbacks the new book will be out in a year and a half.

Yours sincerely,
E. A. Robinson

1. "The Book of Annandale."
2. A review of *The Children of the Night* in the New York *Evening Post* (June 4, 1898), p. 17, reprinted from the *Nation*, LXVI (June 2, 1898), 426.
3. "Isaac and Archibald."

43

Gardiner, Maine
22 July 1898

Dear Friend:

I have been neglecting you again but I trust you have [not] troubled[1] yourself too much about [it]. I have thought much of you and your mud turtle, and whether or not I ought to write personally to Mr. March[2] in acknowledgement of his very friendly sonnet. The reason why I have not done so is that I have feared I might seem to be making too much of it. I sent a note to Miss Hanson, however, thinking that [it] would be quite enough to show that I appreciated the man's recognition of my attempts to write. Do I, or do I not give the impression that I have sour milk in my veins instead of blood? Tell me without any circumlocution and I will try to mould my future actions in accordance with your opinions. I have great faith in you and think you know a good deal. So tell me anything you think of that [will] do me any good. I have no particular feelings to hurt unless they are fooled with by people who do not impress me as knowing what they are about. I am quite ready to have Mr. Higginson[3] call me crude but I don't want the *Outlook*[4] man, or woman, to write about any "misplaced emphasis." The man in *The Musical Courier*[5] changes "alnage" to "selvage" and "removed afar" to "removèd far," all of which is unpleasant, but he praises me most outrageously, so I suppose I ought not to growl.

I am still hard at work, and I really believe that I am doing something. It is too early in the game to tell, though, and I may have to throw it all away. I have enough, in first (or twenty-first) draft to make a good-sized book, but I do not think it can possibly be made ready for publication inside of eighteen months at the least and then I doubt very much if I can find a publisher. But I shall print the stuff anyhow and trust to its making its own way sometime.

Dr. Coan is in Mystic, Connecticut, surrounded by seven beautiful females, four of which are sylphides. He says they float about the roads on wheels in light clothes, which seems to me to be a most bewildering thing for them to do. I don't think the Doctor ought to stay there much longer. He doesn't even mention Louis. The poor old man must be having a dull time of it this summer: he told me some time ago, on one of his characteristic postal cards, that he had lost his most important colleague in business, and that he was feeling far from well. I have a notion that his business enterprises are largely in his visions, but of course have no good right to say so.

Pope has lost his "girl" and has had a bonfire. He tells me that some of the things almost refused to burn, particularly an embroidered picture frame which sputtered and sizzled a long time before it showed any signs of mixing with the elements. I don't think he enjoyed it very much, but it is much better for him. He suspects she has married, or is about to marry, a young preacher of the Gospel who gets two thousand dollars a year. The whole thing is amusing, but P. doesn't entirely see the joke. He will have to see it some day, though, and congratulate himself. I saw the girl once and drew my own conclusions.

Please write more about the mud-turtle, and tell me if [you] think I ought to put Paris green on cabbages and cauliflowers. I don't want to kill anybody, but still I want the things [to] grow since I have the care of them. They are not mine.

Most sincerely,
E. A. Robinson

1. This letter is an emphatic example of Robinson's mind outstripping his pen. The obvious omission of *not* here is only one of five such instances of skipping words in the following text.

2. Charles March was a teacher of English at the Wyoming Seminary in Wilkes-Barre.

3. [Thomas Wentworth Higginson], "Recent American Poetry," *Nation*, LXVI (June 2, 1898), 426.

4. In a thirteen-line review of *The Children of the Night*, in *Outlook*, LVII (December 25, 1897), 1013, the anonymous critic wrote: "Mr. Robinson's verses are of unequal merit; some lines have misplaced emphasis; many have a genuine song-swing; all have an underlying seriousness."

5. Vance Thompson, "A New Poet," *Musical Courier*, XXXVII (July 13, 1898), p. v of the "Books and Bookmen" department. He said: "Robinson reveals himself as a poet of rare sincerity, force and delicacy. Years have brought us nothing so good."

44

Gardiner, Maine
25 August 1898

Dear Friend:

I hasten to answer your good letter and to apologize, as usual, for not writing before. I am living a strange sort of life this summer and am not, I fear, giving due attention to my friends, though I think as much of them as ever—more, if possible. Of course you know me well enough to know that my silence means nothing, but I mention it out of habit.

Just now I am reading Pater, Kipling, and Emerson, and like Emerson rather the best. He is so strangely great and human that I can't let go of him; and it is something the same with Pater (*Appreciations*), Kipling is really big, but not so big as he might be if he were to give himself a chance. There is a remarkable performance, however, in the last

McClure's, called "In Ambush"[1]—a story of boys in school—real boys, full of blood and deviltry. Read it and tell me what you think of it.

Mr. Chilton told me something of his woes and left me to fancy that under all his lightness there was something like to real misery. He'll get over it, though. They always do, if you give them time enough. And you are quite right in thinking it will be good soul-tonic for him. He needs a little stirring-up and my personal feeling is that he is getting it. Don't dream that he will be cured when this attack leaves him, for love is not the measles. It is more like malaria—liable to show itself at any time when the amorous microbe finds itself in the presence of the right kind of food. Nor is it always the right kind, either; for the parasite may fill himself and get sick and do everything but die. There are some fairy tales to the effect that he dies, but I never put much faith in them.

The book[2] is getting on slowly. I write and read and let the thing soak during the day, and in the evening console myself with Pope and the fiddle. I have about made up my mind to go to Winthrop this winter and shut myself up. By next June I hope to have the book pretty well straightened out, though it will [not] be in any condition to print.

Sincerely yours,
E. A. Robinson

Did I ever answer your question in regard to Rossetti? If I did not, I have only to say that I cannot bring myself to call him really great, though some of the sonnets are marvels of technique. The "Last Confession" partly suggested "The Night Before,"[3] but I was not conscious of it at the time of writing six or eight years ago.[4] It was partly a "job" done entirely with cold blood and consciously for literary practice. This may account for some rather inflammatory passages in it, which I had hardly written had the thing been done more spontaneously. This may sound paradoxical, but it is quite in accordance with my methods. It is about the only thing in the book that is absolutely impersonal, but still I have never been altogether glad that I have printed it. I have something the same objection to it that I had for "Calderon" which was off the same piece and done in the same mechanical way.

Write from Boston if you get a chance and feel like doing so. I am sorry I cannot come up to see you, but I positively can't.

E.A.R.

1. Rudyard Kipling, "'In Ambush,'" *McClure's*, XI (August 1898), 307–325.
2. *Captain Craig.*

3. Dante Gabriel Rossetti's "A Last Confession," his dramatic *chef-d'œuvre*, has been cited for its Browning influences. Robinson does not mention another possible derivation—his "Ballade of a Ship," originally published as "Ballade of the White Ship," from Rossetti's ballad, "The White Ship." A copy of Rossetti's *Ballads and Sonnets* (Boston, 1882) in Colby College is inscribed "Edwin A. Robinson" and dated by him "November 19, 1891."

4. To the right of this Miss Brower wrote: "He must have been about 20."

45

Gardiner, Maine
26 September 1898

Dear Friend:

You aren't going to get a letter this time (I don't know that I shall ever write another to anybody) but just a few lines to easy my conscience and incidentally to keep you good-natured. I can't afford to lose you now, of all times in my life, for I am soon going, I expect, into winter exile—that is, to Winthrop. There I expect to do some work and to find out whether or not there is anything in my new book. Just now it is in a most chaotic uncertain state and I am very far from feeling sure of it.[1] It is a little too big for me, and I shall have to grow a good deal in the next six months. The fact that you still think I am good for something is going to do great things—at least in the way of keeping me at it. There are times when I feel strangely in danger of stagnation, which is the one thing that will not do at all.

Remember me to Mrs. Hanson, and believe my little apologies for letters to be just as sincere as if they were as long as some of Richardson's.[2]

1. Robinson originally planned to publish two books: *Captain Craig* alone, and a collection of shorter poems separately as *Isaac and Archibald*. Both were eventually combined as *Captain Craig, A Book of Poems* (Boston, 1902).

2. Allusion to Samuel Richardson's epistolary novels. Two inches of the sheet has been cut off below this line, apparently only for the autograph.

46

[September–October 1898][1]

Dear Friend:

I did not mean that you should take me quite so seriously. By "letters," I meant long ones:—in short, that I might not send anything but brief notes. Either my temperament is changing or I am drying up

—I don't know which—but somehow a page or two pumps me quite dry nowadays. Still, like Dr. Johnson, "I hope to mend."

Where is the Doctor? I hear nothing from any of them, or from Mr. Chilton. (Why *Mr.*, I wonder?) I want to go back to New York as a cat wants to go home but I am in this locality for the winter and am schooling myself to make the best of it. The mere fact of place is not the thing —though of course it is part of it. There's another element—several of them in fact.

Has it occurred to you that a great story might be written on the theme of your *Atlantic* essay?[2] I may have mentioned this before—I have thought of it a good deal. As far as I know the field is absolutely unworked.

[Signature excised]

Also read the Dickens letters.

1. Dateline and signature have both been excised from this letter, which is written on stationery similar to the three preceding and one following letter.

2. "Is the Musical Idea Masculine," *Atlantic Monthly*, LXXIII (March 1894), 332–339.

47

Gardiner, Maine
22 October 1898

Dear Friend:

I do not know that I got so far as to think out a plot for the musical novel, but it seems to me that with the woman who would compose great music but can't and a man who can but doesn't until he meets her, we might conjure up a dozen plots in as many hours. A "happy" ending would be rather unnatural, but a mental or even a moral tragedy need not give an effect of weakness or despair. Of course such a work would be a great undertaking but I am inclined to think you could do it if you really gave yourself up to it. Personally, I should lay the scene in New York, but you may prefer to go to Europe, so sacrificing a good deal of originality and inviting a good deal of unnecessary rivalry. For myself, I feel that I am at work again and that my late period of inactivity was in reality a season of internal development. At any rate, I have grown and am beginning to see that while I thought I was losing time I was really building at work,—half consciously, but still at work. It took the place of my usual trip to Boston.

Maine is getting to be a barren state now. The maple trees are mostly skeletons and the others are going the same way, and the late October "feel" is in the air making me hungry for a big hearth-fire and all sorts of semi-sentimental accompaniments—pipes and cider, and a fiddle; also some very good [things] to eat. Materialism and idealism get strangely mixed with me at this season, but the ideal is always uppermost. Certainly you will send along the gooseberry jam.

Very sincerely,
E. A. Robinson

48

Winthrop, Maine
2 December 1898

Dear Friend:

I have dug this paper out of Blair's banking apparatus,[1] and will tell you, while he is shaking down the furnace, that the jam is to come to Winthrop, in his care. (A. H. Blair). This rather gives the impression that I care more for the jam than I do for your friendship, but that is not the case. Only I have no chance to write anything just now and perhaps would not improve the chance if I did have it.

I have been here since Tuesday and am beginning to feel at home. I am reading *Sandra Belloni*[2] as a preparation for work. Of course you know it.

Very sincerely,
E. A. Robinson

1. The bottom half of a large, white, unruled sheet without the printed letterhead. The watermark is a double oval within which is the legend REAL IRISH LINEN and an heraldic device of coronet and flowers.
2. Novel by George Meredith, published in London, 1864.

49

Winthrop, Maine
10 December 1898[1]

Dear Friend:

The jam came yesterday afternoon and you will be gratified to know that one jar of it is already gone. I did the best I could with Blair but he persisted in going for it in spite of my remonstrance. It was very considerate and altruistic of you to send it, and I already feel the beginnings of an inspiration.

The work is going on, but there is a possibility that it may be interrupted. I am threatened with compulsory prosperity in the shape of a job. If I get it of course I shall have to take it; but I am sorry that I cannot feel a little more enthusiastic over the prospect. I realize now more than ever my one-sidedness. This need not prevent me from doing good work but one-sidedness doesn't often go with the production of anything great. It is mostly my friends—a very few of them—who look to me for anything of that kind, however—that is, unless I am setting up my standard of greatness too[2] The thought that I shall ever do anything even approaching it sometimes makes me laugh.

If the job comes, the book will probably be delayed a year, but that will make no particular difference. For the present I prefer to say no more about it, but will give you the particulars later.

Sincerely,
E.A.R.

1. This letter is written on a smaller, white, ruled sheet, the letterhead of which identifies A. H. Blair as Manager of the Winthrop Agency of the Augusta Safe Deposit & Trust Company.

2. The lower left corner of this letter has worn away. It may have contained the word *high*.

50

Winthrop, Maine
29 December 1898

Dear Friend:

You may be glad or sorry, as you choose, to know that my literary plans have been smashed. Instead of staying here with the natives—they are not a bad lot—I am going to Cambridge, where I have a "job" in the College office—a sort of assistant secretary and metaphorical bottle washer to the whole concern. The place offers some advantages and some possibilities in the way of advancement, but it is not, somehow, the thing I am hungering for just now. Still, it is better than sweeping out Butler's store and I suppose the atmosphere must inevitably count for something. Just where my opportunity for writing is to come in, I don't quite know: after eight or nine hours of hard work, I doubt if I find myself in the mood, or condition, to do much original versifying. And yet, when I am honest with myself, I feel that the whole thing is for the best. It may be that the stimulation of regular employment is the very thing I need and that after a year of it I shall be better able than I am now to localize the stuff that is now running riot in my much-befuddled brain. It is true that I have the book written in a way, but that way is not to my liking. The whole thing must be readjusted and I think it will be much better to put it all in the closet for a year or so. This takes some patience and some philosophy, and so does everything else that is worth while.

The Children are keeping very quiet now but once in a while there is a call for one of them—perhaps once in two or three weeks. It is hardly probable that a second edition will be called for.[1] The jam was very gratifying and had a humanizing effect on my feelings. So I do not think you need feel sorry for having sent it—though of course it was a bother to you. I have not heard from you lately, but I take it for granted that all is going well with you. When you have nothing else to do, you may meditate on the unexpected material rewards of the "pote," as illustrated in my own case. The job is directly due to the book; so if I never write anything more (which, however, is not the future I have in view) I cannot feel that I have worked utterly for nothing.

Sincerely,
E. A. Robinson

Of course you understand that I am not in a position to choose in regard to financial matters. I have to take what comes, and the Harvard job, from every rational point of view, is not to be despised. There is yet a question though as to whether I can fill it. Success will be largely a question of personality and practical imagination. My Cambridge address will be No. 1716 Cambridge St.—not the College.

E.A.R.

1. A second edition of *The Children of the Night* was issued in October 1905, and reprints in 1910, 1914, 1919, 1921.

51

14 Oxford Street
Cambridge
20 February 1899

Dear Friend:

I'll be frank enough to say at the outset, that I don't feel like writing to you, or to anyone else; but as I do feel that I am not treating you very well nowadays, I think I ought at least to let you know that I am conscious of my shortcomings. I am going through one of my spells, during which it takes all of my spiritual force to keep myself together. When I get out of it I shall be all right again but for the present I am not to be counted. I had a chance the other day to go to Kansas City and become, or try to become, a newspaper man, and turned it down—two thousand a year and all. Now I am wondering if I did not make a fool of myself. I shall be interested to know what you think. You see, it has made me feel as I never felt before what it is to be in the power of an ideal and how utterly impossible it is to make up one's mind as to the advantage or disadvantage of mixing the false with the true. And there is another question as to whether I could ever force myself into doing a thing that was positively repulsive to me and succeed in making myself of any value to my employer. There is still a chance that I may go out there but I hardly [think] I shall get there. I am beginning to feel, almost with satisfaction, sometimes, that I have done the little there was in me to do in a literary way and that the rest of my life is to consist "merely" in making the most of myself under whatever circumstances may arise. The thought is good for the man, but it is rough on the artist that is in him. However, as I said, I am now going through some sort of process and I cannot even guess just what is coming of it.

I saw Chilton not long ago and was glad to see him so well contented. I am afraid though that contentment, when rooted in a kind of negative selfishness, is likely to breed some sort of microbe in the course of years. I really like the man very much, and I want you to know it, but I cannot possibly be quite at ease with him. There are certain people who make me feel, whenever they look at me, that I am socially impossible,—which is quite true—and he happens to be one of them. The fault is not with him, but wholly with me—the result of the way I grew up.

Mr. Macy[1] was over to see me about three weeks ago but I regret to say that I have not yet been over to see him. I am going tomorrow evening if I can work myself up to it. Evidently you are quite right in your judgment of him. He is the real thing.

Very sincerely,
E.A.R.

1. Possibly John A. Macy (1877–1932), at this time a senior at Harvard, then a graduate student and instructor in English, who became associate editor of *Youth's Companion* and literary editor of the Boston *Herald*. *The Spirit of American Literature* (Garden City, N.Y., 1913) is his best-known work.

52

[March 1899]

Dear Friend:

I am going to be happy all the rest of this week. I was referred to the other evening, here in Cambridge, as a fellow who wrote "a corking good thing on a man who shot himself, and a rotten sonnet on Boston."[1] This is not polite parlance, but of course I am not to be held responsible for that.

The reason why I sent my last letter to Wilkes-Barre was that I posted it about ten minutes before I received your own from West Virginia. So there is one Coanism you will have to strike out of your estimate of me. By the way, where is the Doctor now and what is he doing to his book?[2] I hear nothing from him, though I wrote some two months ago. Also, where is that sonnet to Bach.[3] I wrote to Chilton for it, but have not yet extracted it from him. It seems to be like Donatello's wine, which would not stand exportation. Suppose you send it along.

Sometime I am going to write you a letter, but not tonight. This is merely a certificate of my existence and, incidentally, of my incurable optimism. I am going to work right away on a thing about a pauper—I have a soft feeling for all paupers—which will consist of something like a thousand lines of blank verse and will be a sort of human development of the octaves. It will disgust and frighten some people, and, I hope, please others. I have just heard Mrs. H. A. A. Beach[4] pound one of the new "Steinertone" pianos[5] in Sanders Theatre, but have no criticism to offer. She played her own stuff and I have no doubt she played it well.

Very sincerely,
E. A. Robinson

1. Robinson dropped the sestet in the next edition of *The Children of the Night* (1905) and all subsequent collections, presenting "Boston" as a poem of eight lines.

2. Titus Munson Coan was the author of some dozen books. Robinson may be referring to one of the two studies of Hawaiian climate and natives which he published in 1901.

3. For a copy of this sonnet, see Letter 61, note 1.

4. Mrs. Beach (1867–1944), a child prodigy as a pianist, wrote songs and chamber music, developing into one of America's first important composers of symphony.

5. An invention of Morris Steinert (1831–1912), a Boston cellist and piano dealer, renowned as a collector of antique clavichords, harpsichords, and other precursors of the pianoforte. In an attempt to recapture the expressive tone

qualities of the clavichord, he "constructed a mechanism which resembles greatly the natural formation of the human arm and hand, which could influence the hammer and control the strokes when meeting the string, the same as the violinist holds and controls his bow." This was attached to the pianoforte. See Jane Marlin, editor, *Reminiscences of Morris Steinert* (New York, 1900), pp. 251–256.

In her article, "Cristofori Redivivus," *Music*, XVI (May 1899), 1–5, Mrs. Beach reviews the history of the piano, explains Steinert's mechanical innovation approvingly, and describes the occasion of its first public demonstration: a concert at Sanders Theatre on March 14, 1899, given by the Kneisel Quartet under the direction of Professor John K. Paine, at which she played her "Sonata for Piano and Violin" with Franz Kneisel.

53

HARVARD UNIVERSITY
CAMBRIDGE, MASS.
6 April 1899

Dear Friend:

I don't like to fall back again on the ancient and rather distressing excuse that I have nothing to write about, but that seems to be very near to the truth. I also owe a letter to Miss Marjory Hanson, who must think me rather unappreciative of her attentions. Please be good enough to tell her that I shall write it sometime.

I find I am not a Wagnerite, after all. The *Walküre* is merely a musical debauch to me, studiously contrived to make a direct attack on people's nerves. The third act of *Tristan*, however, is quite another thing, and I in my musical ignorance (which is complete) do not see why the "Kurwenal" music might not have been written a hundred years ago. I have no doubt but that some of it was. As for Isolde's final spasm, I have the same respect for it that I have for anything that is done supremely well. Sometimes it seems to me that Wagner was really a great musician but that the devil got hold of him and made him insane with a desire to do something new. I cannot feel that his annihilation of —something,—I don't know just what—is along the lines of true art; nor can I help feeling, when I think of the last act, that some of his pet themes come very near to going back on him. This, however, is all out of my field and need not be taken very seriously. I accomplished *Faust* last evening and was miserably disappointed in everything but the trio and perhaps the little chorus of old men. And yet, there is something in the devil music—particularly when the great Edouard[1] gives it to us.

Saturday afternoon they give *Don Giovanni* and [I] shall take it for a tonic. By the way, Professor Paine's *Azala*[2] is soon to be brought out in Germany. He has been at work on it for sixteen years, I am told. It ought to be pretty bad. Tonight we have the third "Leonora"[3] and Brahms and Liszt's "Loreley" on a flute. Next week I am going to sober down and see if I can do some work. How are you getting on with the natives?

Very sincerely,
E.A.R.

1. Edouard deReszke (1853–1917), Polish basso and brother of the tenor Jean, sang in some thirty operas at the Metropolitan Opera House from 1891 to 1903. His most famous role was that of Mephistopheles in Gounod's *Faust*.
2. Robinson means *Azara* (see Letter 18, note 3).
3. Beethoven's "Leonora No. 3 in C" (Opus 72), is the second of four overtures he wrote for his opera *Fidelio*.

54

[April–May 1899]

Dear Friend:

A week or two ago I wrote to the editor of the *Aeolian Quarterly* that I liked your Bach sonnet, but thought it a little over-thunderous, or something of the kind. And I wrote it after a hasty glance at the poem before rushing out to breakfast at a quarter before nine. Afterwards I saw that I was all wrong and felt correspondingly foolish. You see, I missed the whole point and gained some valuable experience, which I hope to profit by. The sonnet is fine—much finer, to be honest, than I thought it would be; for I had a notion that your business was wholly with prose. I see my mistake and gladly rectify it. If you have any more sonnets, send them along. I could not resist giving Chilton a mild blowing up for the last of some of his editorials; nor, on a second reading of these, can I change my mind. He is in danger, it seems to me, of going a little too far with his public.

Please tell Miss Marjory Hanson that I have her letter still on my desk and that I am suffering great pangs of conscience for my slowness in answering it. The fact is I am out of all mood for any kind of civility. When I get myself together I'll try to be decent again (?). The office work goes on day after day, though I can't say there is much work to it, and at night sometimes I try to write something. The result of course, under such conditions, is worthless. I feel that there is going to be a change sometime, however, and that I shall eventually succeed in turning night into day. At any rate, I don't mean to growl, for I have, relatively, nothing to growl at.

Very sincerely,
E.A.R.

55

HARVARD UNIVERSITY
CAMBRIDGE, MASS.
16 May 1899

Dear Friend:

I like the sonnets,[1] but I like "The Enthusiast" much better than the other. It seems to me that in writing of MacDo well, or any other man, you would do much better to avoid the cataloguing process altogether—though I [am] aware that this is pretty largely a matter of taste. At any rate, the MacDowell doesn't give me half the pleasure that the other does. I appreciate the poetry of it, but I don't like the idea of ringing [in] all those capitals, or the words themselves which the capitals emphasize. "The Enthusiast" is "all right," though I do not feel sure that a little retouching might not better it. That, however, is all with you.

I have not been to see Mr. Macy, and I suppose he has naturally given me up for a beast. I took a great fancy to the man, but owing to the fact that it takes all of my hypocritical "strength" to keep up my false note of cheerfulness with those who know me, I cannot, at present, pose before strangers who think, quite innocently and naturally, that I have one of those excellent situations which breed, or ought to breed Mr. Stephen Phillips' "eternal smiles."[2] Of course you will object to this; but the fact still remains that I cannot transform myself into an utterly different sort of human being from that which I am. The place itself is not the cause of the trouble:—to an active, practical and generally smart youth who could make the work his chief interest, there is a chance to be more or less indisposable, as the Irishman would say; but for me, who cannot dictate letters as fast as I can write them, who cannot by any stretch of my practical realization of things bring the concern really within sight, who cannot, on certain days, quite stand the grotesque and ridiculous side of it all or do anything to change it—the probability or possibility of making anything of it in the future is out of the question. There is something about it that I cannot name or describe and that something is what I have to look out for. Please assure Mr. Macy that I am very far from indifferent to him, and that I appreciated fully his coming out to Cambridge to see me—though of course you put him up to it.

I feared I had offended Chilton, but I have just received—five minutes ago—a copy of the *Sun* with a long drivel in it by Goldwin Smith on Tennyson and Browning.[3] From what I have seen, he thinks Tennyson is great because he can call "hydraulics, astronomy, steam railways, balloons etc" by poetical names. He gets after Browning; I have not read the thing, so cannot tell just how. Nothing in the world tickles me quite so much as this prophetic analysis of the poetry of the future. When it gets to be great it will be very much like certain very smooth and inevitable places in Sophocles and Shakespeare. It will be great for what it is, not in spite of what it is—which is partly true, I am afraid, even of *The Ring and The Book*. You see, I have softened towards it infinitely [since] I was in New York; but even now I cannot help looking on it as a sort of sublime "stunt." Its very individuality is enough to bar it from being really great—except in spots. Nine-tenths of it is not poetry; nor is all of one-tenth of great poetry.

You see I am having a nice time today and hate to leave off. Tell Miss Marjory that I am likely to write now almost any time.

Very sincerely,
E.A.R.

1. The two sonnets referred to here are "The Enthusiast, who said: 'I feel power and enthusiasm in me, burning like twenty devils!'" and "To Edward MacDowell (After playing his 'Sea Pieces')." The Enthusiast is Carroll Brent Chilton. Another sonnet which celebrates his views, "La Pianola," is also among a sheaf of typescripts now in Modesta Ximena's possession. Part of the note appended to the last reads: "Written particularly for a friend who was for years with the Aeolian Company and who is devoting his life to propagating the idea of *pure music* disassociated from the worship of mere virtuosity, in other words, of the Performer." Despite Robinson's preference, "The Enthusiast" seems never to have appeared in print, while "To Edward MacDowell" was published in the Boston *Evening Transcript* on October 2, 1899, page 9.

2. Stephen Phillips (1868–1915), English poetic dramatist. "Eternal smiles his emptiness betray" is line 315 of Alexander Pope's "Epistle to Dr. Arbuthnot."

3. "The Future of Poetry," New York *Sun* (May 14, 1899), p. 4.

56

HARVARD UNIVERSITY
CAMBRIDGE, MASS.
6 June 1899

Dear Friend:

I don't know whether you are still in the wilderness or not. If you are, this will be forwarded to you and you will learn that I am still in Cambridge earning money by the sweat of my brow. Just now it is more a matter of sweat than anything else. The world is drying up and I doubt not there would be chapel prayers for rain were there not so many Unitarians on the faculty. The Unitarians do not pray for rain, or, to my knowledge, for the President of the United States. I am not sure, however, on this last point.

I can look out through my window and see no end of green leaves but they have a tired and rather flabby appearance—somehow as if they had stood it about as long as they could. It may be that they are tired of hiding Sever Hall, which is the noblest work they do in this part of the Yard. Sever Hall was designed by the same Richardson,[1] I think, who designed Trinity Church, but that does not make the Hall any more endurable. It is probably the smallest building in America and gives one the impression of having been built for the sole purpose of finding out how many bricks could possibly be used—I can't say utilized—in so many cubic feet of architecture. The next time you come to Boston, you will do well to come out here and try to imagine how the thing looked before the ivy got a good start. Eventually it will be very beautiful, for it will be entirely covered up.

You say nothing about your literary achievements this winter. Am I to understand that you have written a novel or that you have just lived? I hope you have done both—more or less. I do not expect you have written a whole novel, but I have hopes that you may have done three or four chapters. Personally, I am not doing as much as I should like to do, but as long as I am doing something, I manage to keep above ground. The one thing I cannot do at all is to branch out and make new acquaintances. My position in the world is so particularly ridiculous that while I can make a joke of it for my own private use I cannot use the joke as a social crowbar. There is an element of injustice in this both to myself and to others, I suppose—but I cannot bring myself to believe that a fellow who has not brains enough to meet the practicalities of the world can be held in any very great esteem by those who are more generously endowed. It is true that I may make up for this in the course of time, but for the present I may keep with the inferiors even at the risk of giving occasional offense, as I may possibly have done, to a small extent, in the case of Mr. Macy. I do not forget that the man came out to Cambridge to see me, nor do I forget the man himself, for what he obviously is; but all this, as I told you before, does not alter the fact that I am, to use a very expressive bit of slang, "not in it." Very likely you are beginning to change some of your notions in regard to my strength, but perhaps you need not change all of them. I have really done some things, and I have done some of them under rather trying conditions. Because I cannot seem to make a living does not necessarily imply that I am a total failure, even though it does put me in a position where I cannot expect or always accept the recognition of independent men. If this carried with it a corresponding sense of self-discouragement I should in all probability go and shoot myself. As it is, I am not going to do anything of the kind. I am going to finish up my two books and then if things go at all decently I am going after bigger game. It may get away from me but I shall have at least the satisfaction of a few shots at it. So do not think that I am giving up the ghost because I do not see so many people as you would have me, for I am not. I merely lack, for the present, the not altogether usual faculty of living two lives with a very ordinary outfit for living one. I can see in the eyes of some of my old friends that they would be much better satisfied with me if I were to make a thousand a year, even if I lost the other thing, than they are today. Literature is very good as an extra, they think, but they can go no further. When it comes to being the main thing—well, a fellow will outgrow that and be starved into a little common sense. They are partly right, too. If they were not, I shouldn't bother my head about them. I suppose a man, in order to be a credit to his planet, should make money somehow: not for the sake of the money itself so much as for the sake of the social balance reflected in the accomplishment. It is all very well for us to say that we do not care, but we do care just the same.

Mr. Chilton seems to be "booming" the Pianola.[2] By the way, what do you think of [that] interesting machine?

Very sincerely,
E. A. Robinson

1. Henry Hobson Richardson (1838–1886), American exponent of romanesque architecture, designed Trinity Church and Sever Hall, as well as the state capitol in Albany and the Marshall Field Building in Chicago.

2. Recent issues of the *Aeolian Quarterly* carried a profusion of full-page advertisements and testimonials, in addition to the department, "Editorial Paragraphs," which averaged some ten pages of extravagant claims for the virtues of the mechanical piano manufactured by the Aeolian Company of New York City. Chilton edited this short-lived periodical, "a magazine devoted to analyses and descriptions of the operatic and classical music published for the Aeolian."

57

HARVARD UNIVERSITY
CAMBRIDGE, MASS.
13 June 1899

Dear Friend:

While the learned men in the Faculty Room are filling themselves with crackers and cold tea—a combination that ought to kill a hippopotamus—I must send a line or two to assure you that I took your letter with a most hopeless lack of indignation. I did not know that I asked you to plead my cause a second time with Mr. Macy. If I did it was without any consciousness of how it would sound or that it would be taken with any particular seriousness. As for your own feelings in the matter, why don't you let them go? If I choose to behave like a beast, why do you bother your head over me until I am a decent again? If it is too late then, so much the worse for me. In the meantime I have all of your own realization of the falseness of my existence, and I know as well as you that if I do not get out of this mental climate before long I shall go down the slippery path like a jellyfish down whatever you think the most appropriate. It is too muggy today for figures. It is not my purpose to make this very unhappy slide, but if I do make it, it will be because I have been harnessed to a heavier load than I can haul. I know enough about farming to know that some "critters" can draw more than others and that if you are obliged to make one lean beast do the work of two fat ones there is going to be an inevitable collapse unless the animal in question has a most convincing change of diet: or to shorten all this, it begins to look as if I had not the stamina to live two lives. It takes a tolerably good man to live one and make anything of it and it takes one of those peculiar things called geniuses to live two; and even they are likely to make a most miserable mess of it. So if it turns out that I, who have a certain talent—enough to be taken seriously here and there by some isolated "admirers"—but no genius—should happen to prove a disappointment, why should you not rest satisfied with the consciousness that you have thrown out a friendly hand on every possible occasion and left not the slightest possible chance for me to doubt your sincerity and earnestness? I do not expect you to think no more about the business, of course—in spite of what I said a few moments ago—but I hope that you will not feel in any way obliged to identify yourself with my shortcomings. If Mr. Macy thinks me a cad, do you suppose that is going to change his opinion of you? Because you put him on the trail of what you believed to be something worthwhile, do you [think he] will hold you responsible for the mistake? I do not say this to get back at you, but to put this ludicrous notion out of your head and at the same time to cultivate your sense of humor. Your sympathy is infinite but, if you will pardon my ungraciousness, you do not always see the joke. For, in spite of some rather unpleasant flatness there is [something] almost akin to Mr. Squeers' "richness"[1] in my present position. If it were in my power to set down the complete ridiculousness of it you would understand better why I hesitate [to] go about. I have four or five good friends—all I can really handle, with anything like intimacy—so you need not fear for my solitude. I shall go to see Mr. Macy before very long but the fact that I was so strangely attracted to the man is the very thing that will make me go unwillingly. Perhaps there is no need of your trying to understand just what I mean.

I have hardly been corresponding with Mr. March. I sent him a small note two or three months ago in reply to a letter he wrote last summer. That is not exactly correspondence.

Whenever you are hungry for a legitimate stirring up, read Coppée's *Pour la Couronne.*

E.A.R.

1. In chapter V of Dickens' *Nicholas Nickleby*, Wackford Squeers, the hard headmaster of Dotheboys Hall, tastes the diluted milk he ordered for the boys' breakfast, smacks his lips, and declares, "Ah, here's richness."

58

HARVARD UNIVERSITY
CAMBRIDGE, MASS.
16 July 1899[1]

Dear Friend:

I do not see why you should not find as much fault with me as you have found before. If ever there was a being on this earth who invited that sort of thing I was that being when I answered your long remonstrance as I did. Luckily you took it all in good part but I did a foolish thing in making so commonplace an affair of what is in reality, a serious matter—serious in that it affects, as a precedent, my whole future. I am conscious of all this, I assure you, but I cannot quite bring myself to feel that I am utterly culpable for my present deficiencies. Now and then something comes up in the way of unexpected proof that I am not losing ground and that I am at least partly justified in my notion that I must work this thing out in my own way in spite of all friendly objections on the part of those who do not and cannot understand the things that give me the greatest opportunity for "guessing." I know well enough that I guess too much and act too little; and I know equally well that there is, even in Carlyle, a distressing percentage of fool-talk mixed in with the world's time-honored precepts about thoughts and deeds. A man may work with his thoughts and achieve nothing, but another man may work with his arms and do pretty much the same thing. The mechanical fact of having earned a living counts for something more than it seems; but to the one-sided individual who is so built, the filling of his belly—for all the fact that it keeps him alive—is merely an incident and largely a nuisance. I fear that the loveliness of mere doing must always be ungloriously qualified with artistic selfishness. It may be that the great fellows could overcome this—given a quick pulse and an elephantine constitution the thing might be possible—but the second-rate neophyte like myself will hardly attain to this kind [of] superhuman Yankee which seems to be the natural expectation of any American who has any sort of interest in "a cuss that writes." The man with a literary worm in his head is expected to be a maker of three-dollar shoes, an alderman, and incidentally a bank president; this being brought about, he may spend his odd moments writing books. And even this is all right for the genius; he may do all this and a good deal more, but there is a fighting chance that he may not. Beethoven might have been a capitalist if he had not lost his ears; but he might not have written any greater music. Schubert would have made a particularly good bookkeeper had it not have been for a few limitations which he should have overcome. I have always had a notion that Shakespeare would have made a remarkable sea captain.

All this talk is of no consequence and of course it has a touch of remorse in it; but when I have to listen, as I do, to the well-meaning chatter of certain people I must confess that I get out of patience now and then. It never occurs to them that a man may be less than Beethoven, or Shakespeare, or Titian, or Thomas B. Reed,[2] and be of the least consequence whatever. They do not know that the measure of a man's enthusiasm is not made in accordance with his capacities or that the lesser victim goes through pretty much the same process as the greater. One achieves a great thing and one achieves a little thing, but both pay pretty much the same price. I will give in, however, to the extent of saying that I never dream of kicking against fate for messing up my days; all I have is a feeling of wonder that I let the thing go on with, as far as I can see, no power in myself to make a change. The idea of disappointing myself is rather sickening sometimes. My standards are too high to be realized but there may be something in having had them to work for. I say "may be" as if I were not sure, but that will not frighten you. You have met with this kind of thing before. You may not think it from what I have been writing, but I am wonderfully good-natured this morning. There was a good rain last night and this morning everything is green and growing, including

Your very sincere friend,
E. A. Robinson

1. Robinson wrote "16 July, 1899," but Miss Brower crossed out "July" and inserted "June" above it.
2. Thomas B. Reed (1839–1902), was a Maine Congressman, noted for his leadership as Speaker of the House of Representatives.

59

14 Oxford Street
6 August 1899

Dear Friend:

I did not curl up my toes because I had the privilege of lying in bed but because the incubus of that College Office was not hanging over me any more. I told them that I was in the wrong place and [they] agreed with me; they agreed with me so heartily, in fact, that I have not been there for over a month. There is no trouble or ill-feeling on either side, so you need not begin to conjure up shadows. I expect to go to New York this fall and stay through the winter. There is no other place where I can feel easy or half comfortable. I shall eat some queer things and very likely live in a queer place, but I must have the town. Probably I shall not see very much of the "Boy,"[1] as you call him, though I shall by no means let him go. He is a good fellow and we have an antipodean friendliness for each other which I hope will last. No, he said nothing about disposing of you. What is he going to do with you? And when are you going into exile?

I don't remember just what kind of stuff I wrote to Marjorie Hanson, but considering the character of the child you must give me a good deal of credit for writing anything at all. As long as she giggled and her mother was not offended, I suppose it was all right. I have a great interest in that "young one," and hope you will let me know what she makes of herself. Also, tell me about your own schemes, as far as you care to, and believe me

Always sincerely yours,
E. A. Robinson

This room is like an oven tonight—or I would not be so generous in the matter of margins.[2]

Do not misinterpret my statement about not seeing much of Chilton. All I meant was that I shall not like seeing a great deal of anyone who knows anything about me. This feeling is rapidly winning for me a reputation for conceit, incivility, indifference and the Lord knows what other things that are as far from the truth as Provincetown is from Paradise, but as the boy said, "I can't help it." The "Boy" would say the same thing if he were in my place and he were "me." As it is, he is beginning to show signs of pity—which is worse than prussic acid. I am not quite through with the game yet.

E.A.R.

1. Carroll Brent Chilton.
2. Apologetic for the width of his margins, Robinson wrote in the right margin of the first page: "This is a large paper edition."

60

1716 Cambridge Street
17 August 1899

Dear Friend:

I have just been reading Burns—for the first time, I think—in six or seven years—and he has given me several things to think about. He was a devil of a fellow and a genius; and the first two stanzas of "Holy Willie's Prayer" make me wonder what all of my poetical hydraulics are coming to. I am beginning to [think] that if I do not manage somehow to overcome my habit of squeezing things out of all reasonable proportion, my immortal poems will be shot back at me like wooden bullets. I never cared very much for the rather decadent Doctor John Donne, but I am asking myself this afternoon if he be not my poetical grandfather. Browning called him the "revered and magisterial"[1] but that does not make me feel any better. Speaking of Browning, I think I have proved to my final satisfaction that I cannot read *The Ring and the Book*, as a sustained poem, with any honest pleasure. I do not object to the "prosiness" of two-thirds of it but I do object to the self-conscious and self-satisfied grotesqueness of the carefully prearranged poetical scheme on which the whole thing is founded. If you tell me that the first book of it atones for all that sort of thing, I shall have to say that I do not agree with you. Of course I do not question for a moment the intellectual magnitude of the poem as a literary achievement (it is, in fact, this very impression of achievement that makes it hard for me not to consider it rather in the nature of a sublime "stunt") but I do question very seriously the possible artistic sincerity of any such performance. Time, however, will settle the whole matter. If the poem holds its present place in nineteen hundred and fifty—for a round number—I shall be all wrong in my judgment. You may remember that I said something like this two years ago and thereby roused your ire. I fear I have roused your ire a good many times—particularly, of late, in my apparently shabby treatment of Mr. Macy. I cannot say any more about him now except to repeat that I took a mighty fancy to him and that I hope sometime to know him.

My life in New York this winter [will] be of necessity one of more or fewer thistles, but I shall not make a hermit of myself on that account. I hope to see you often and to get your feminine criticism of some female things that I have done. They seemed to come quite naturally and I fancy there may be some truth in them. Still, you might detect a false touch where I might not know the difference. This sounds very elementary, but I think you will be generous enough not to read it the wrong way. At present I am still pegging away at the long thing—"The Captain," "The Pauper," or whatever it is, and I doubt if I bring the women[2] out much before March or April—bring them out of their hiding places, I mean. Their publication is [a] matter of the dim future, like the settlement of the Philippine business—and the problem of aerial navigation. I have sold *The Children* to a business man in Boston[3] who thinks he would like to do a little gambling on future possibilities and at the same time see my other work brought to some sort of finish. I do not think there is any danger of anyone doing me an "injustice." You forget that I may have had altogether too much "justice" in times past.

From all I can learn, there are four people in the world who think I am likely to do something. You are one of them and I hope you will hang on, say, for a year longer. I shall keep on working just the same, even if I have to work entirely alone; but it is a good deal better to have two or three human threads that you can feel pulling a little now and then. I am not at all sure you or Mrs. Richards or Pope will care much for either of the books now in process, but I have hopes that it may be on the ground of subject matter rather than on that of "size," if it turns out that you do not. This long thing that I have called "The Pauper," is, I am afraid, just a little queer. I have no desire to be queer. Observe the minimum of margin and believe me

Most sincerely yours,
E. A. Robinson

1. From stanza 114 of "The Two Poets of Croisic," in *La Saisiaz: The Two Poets of Croisic* (London, 1878), p. 161: "Better and truer verse none ever wrote / . . . / Than thou, revered and magisterial Donne!"

2. "Aunt Imogen," "The Growth of 'Lorraine,'" and "The Woman and the Wife" appeared for the first time in *Captain Craig* (1902).

3. It was suggested to Robinson that acceptance of *Captain Craig* by a publisher would be more likely if sales of *The Children of the Night* were more encouraging. William E. Butler induced his father to buy out the lot and place the books on sale in his Boston department store.

61

1716 Cambridge Street
4 September 1899

Dear Friend:

Did I say anything about "water Mediterraneous" in your Bach sonnet?[1] I don't think I did but I have thought a good deal about it—so much that I cannot help asking you to canvass a little for "expert" opinions on the subject. The rest of the sonnet is so tremendously good that I hate to feel in doubt about any of it. "Mediterraneous" takes one to the map immediately and the "ous" part somehow accentuates rather than conceals this (to me) unpleasant sense of localization. If I am finicky, as very likely I am, so much the better for the sonnet. Of course I am aware that you can come back at me with the same weapon—perhaps I refer now rather to "ponderosity" than to geography—but even that will not satisfy me. I want to know whether "Mediterraneous" is the word or not.

I said something about feminine criticism in my last letter which must have put you on the wrong track entirely. A friend of mine told me the other day that I was to be misinterpreted in every question more complicated than what time it is, and I think he was about right. About half of my object in publishing the book that I am working on now—it will be cruelly long, nearly two thousand lines—is to test the sense of humor of about a dozen people I know.

From your silence I gather that you are getting ready to emigrate.

Sincerely yours,
E. A. Robinson

This is not a letter, it is a Mediterraneous complaint. Tell me what you think about the matter, and if you think that such waters can well be characterized as "loud." I suppose you include all the oceans on earth, but one must think first of the "tideless dolorous midland sea etc."[2]

1. Miss Brower's "Bach" appeared in the *Aeolian Quarterly*, II (March 1899), 43:

"Ein Bach? Nein, 's ist ein Meer"—No Brook, a Sea!
Not inland Sea, imprisoned by rock-cliff shore;
Not Lake, soft-walled by grassy Mountain; nor
Loud Water Mediterraneous, rolling free
Amid the Continents. We liken thee
Rather to that great Ocean without roar
Whose azure Gulfs around the World do pour
And wash the Sides of Stars eternally.

Illimitable art thou—fathomless
Thy fugal Depths, undreamed thy Choral Heights;
We know, yet know thee not—like men who gaze
Wistful along the pathway of those Lights
That show them where the Suns and Planets blaze,
Nor their immeasurable Distance guess.

2. From Swinburne's "The Triumph of Time," stanza 41.

62

8 September 1899

Dear Friend:

I will answer your request for an interpretation of my strange remark by saying that the word you took for "quarter" is, or is intended to be "question." I, therefore, am to be misinterpreted in every question more complex than "what time is it?" And I think he was right.

As for the "Mediterraneous" matter, you have as much on your side as I have on mine—perhaps a little more. "Loud water" is good; but I don't believe the long adjective is altogether the best thing in the language to follow it. I'll admit that it has a great noise, but it still irritates me—which, of course, is too bad. If you are convinced that it is all right, the chances are that I am all wrong.

I started this letter with wide margins again, but I did it without thinking of your very recent complaint. You are the only one of my correspondents who clamors for a full page, and for that reason you ought surely to get it; but I'm afraid you don't very often. The next time I write I'll try to make you glad. Your last letter was as good as a three-volume novel and a good deal better than most of them. Something must have been amusing you of late, so perhaps there is no need of my telling you that I have been playing golf. I did wonderful work, but did not get full credit for it.

One of the best things about you is that you do not persist in looking on me as an absolute object of pity. If you do, you hide your feelings, and [that] answers the same purpose. I have friends—yes, I think some of them are friends—who make me feel like starting a dime museum with my own God-forgotten self as the chief attraction; and the worst of it is that I can say nothing in the way of remonstrance. I have made some literary capital out of these people, however, and you will have a chance to see how much I have done with it when "The Captain" gets between covers. Captain Craig, his name is, and he is rather a queer sort of devil in his way. There is undoubtedly a certain amount of self-caricature in him, but that will not hurt anybody if it doesn't hurt me. And I don't think it will hurt me very much.

I do not think I would make a very good eagle. Better call me a terrapin—magnanimous, if you like, but hardly "libre." But I am not magnanimous, either. Ask Mr. Macy what he thinks [of] that. He will tell you that I lack the first principles of mud-turtle respectability. If he doesn't, he is the one to be called magnanimous—not I. No, don't call me any of those fancy names, I can't carry them. They don't fit. The more you try to make a hero of me, the more will—I mean *shall*—I remain the other thing. I can't help showing my literary appreciation of your compliment in regard to packing things for long journeys. The journey will not be for so long as you think, but your phrase is just as good.

I don't think my criticism of your opera article[1] will be of any value but I shall be happy to let you have it. I am rather on your side in damning that form of art, but I do not claim that my damnation is very intelligent. I can't get over the [*phrase blotted out*][2] (you will never know what that was) bigness of it. I expect to go to New York about the twenty-fifth.

Sincerely yours,
E.A.R.

No, I did not refer to the erotic in Donne, but to the *style* of his mystical poems—say "The Ecstasy." If I am not erotic I have been accused of being very immoral in "John Evereldown." I thought all the time that he was merely unfortunate.

1. "The Passing of Opera," *Aeolian Quarterly*, III (September 1899), 5–12.
2. Robinson has obscured what appear to be two words here.

63

71 Irving Place
New York
29 October 1899

Dear Friend:

I have had all sorts of times finding a place to live in this village and have already cancelled two addresses. Now I am over east, close by Gramercy Park and in a house where everything is new even to the sheets. In the light of my experience during the past two weeks I feel that there is nothing in town that is too new for me. I had a great old room in Washington Square but it was not new enough. I think the natural historians have a fancy name for them that ends in "zoa," but I may be mistaken. I never paid much attention to natural history until now, and you must not frown on me if I make blunders.

I had a glimpse of Chilton on Broadway one windy morning about ten days ago but have not seen him since then. As soon as I feel that I am settled I shall hunt him up and get him to tread out some music for me. Tomorrow afternoon I am going to find the genial Doctor[1] and see what he has to say for himself. I had a note from him just before I left Cambridge in which he made reference to "corded bales." He takes me for a shy trafficker with no end of things to undo, but there he is wrong. I have positively nothing to talk about—except things in general—and

Wuthering Heights, which I am reading with a good deal of labor but yet with deep interest. The other day I came across a remarkable criticism of it in Maeterlinck's *Wisdom and Destiny*, a book which all should read—you and your "Boy" in particular.

My friend with the wooden leg[2] is in town again and I find it good to be with him. I am still wondering how it is that I have friends. I have them—lots of them—but why or how I cannot imagine. To me I am a stick without the stick's virtue of standing up straight. By the way, I saw Mr. Macy one evening in Boston and had a good four hours with him. He has a genius for suffering and is a man of the right sort. When are you coming this way?

Sincerely yours,
E. A. Robinson

1. Dr. Titus Munson Coan.
2. George Edwin Burnham, a law student Robinson met while at Harvard, had suffered freezing and amputation of both feet.

64

71 Irving Place
22 November 1899

Dear Friend:

I am very sure that I wrote you a long letter in which I said, among other things, that I could not easily go to Wilkes-Barre this winter, no matter how much I should like to do so. I hope there is no need of my laying particular emphasis on the fact that I should like to go, for you ought to know that without my telling you. Sometime when I am differently situated I'll be in a better mood and condition for that sort of thing—that is, if the time ever comes. I am not very sure of myself now in any way but I keep on working as if I were. There are some things ahead of me that I can see and some that I cannot see; and there are some of each kind which I am unphilosophical enough, at times, to think I might get along without. And yet I am in a decent frame of mind; and if you come to New York I hope I may not be quite so negative as I was when you were here two years ago.

I have not yet seen much of Chilton. Somehow I feel that we have not much to say to each other just now, and I know that his time is pretty well taken up. He is "growing," as you say, and I have given up fearing that he may grow too much. He seems to know what he is doing and I have not a doubt but that he will come out all right. This, from me, may amuse you, but it is good for people to be amused now and then and I am never sorry to know that I have made anyone happy. I have only this way to do it, and this way is perhaps not the worst. I am told that I am an amoozin' cuss when I speak of others as if I forget myself. "Lord God of Hosts be with us yet," they seem to say, but there is really no need of it. There are some things that I always remember. Let us hear from you whenever the machine is in order.

Sincerely yours,
E.A.R.

How is your cousin who went into the hen business?[1] He is a good fellow and he ought to raise good hens. Tell me something about him.

1. Archibald Parsons, brother of Effie and Catharine, left his law practice for reasons of health and raised chickens for a living.

65

71 Irving Place
4 December 1899

Dear Friend:

I have just paid a long green dollar to hear Mr. Ian Ignace Paderewski do things on the piano sometime in the near future. I don't know just when, but I suppose the date is on the ticket.[1] My engagements are so few that I do not have to worry much over these matters. Next Saturday evening I am going to hear Mendelssohn's "Scotch Symphony" and I am looking forward to it as I might look forward to an extra two feet in the height of my room. I suppose you have long outgrown all such flowery halfway stuff, but we fellows of limited appreciation still think Mendelssohn was a good deal of a man. He had the disadvantage of staying married but even then he wrote some good things. Petschnikoff[2] played his violin concerto the other evening and I had the bucolic [pleasure] of hearing that too for the first time. I tell you there is a good deal in being an unsatiated rustic when it comes to matters like these. The wonder is that I care so much for Brahms, and so little for Schumann. I am told that this arrangement will be inverted sometime but no symptoms of such an inversion have yet made their appearance.

You ask me what I think of your article on "The Passing of Opera," but I am sorry to say that I have not seen it. I'll get a copy of the "Boy's" review tomorrow and tell you frankly—no matter what other things I may say—that I think your title a little misleading. With the fearful exception of the oratorio, the opera is the form of music for which I care the least, though I know that the oratorio has much more to defend it. I am afraid I don't care much for the human voice anyhow, except as an accidental chorus in a college yard or under any other natural conditions. I could easily spare the singing from all of Wagner's operas and everything else from those of a great many others. I say this, and get promptly smacked for it. I am not supposed to know; I don't know—I only feel.

Sincerely yours,
E.A.R.

1. On December 12, after an absence of three years, Paderewski played a concert of Liszt, Chopin, Beethoven, and Schumann at Carnegie Hall.

2. Alexander Petschnikoff (1873–1949), a Russian concert violinist and teacher, winner of the gold medal at the Moscow Conservatory, toured extensively in Europe, the United States, and South America.

66

71 Irving Place
24 December 1899

Dear Friend:

I read your article on operas with a good deal of unexpected pleasure and surprise. Unexpected surprise may be a little queer, but unexpected pleasure is correct, for that is what I felt after finding out that you were not going to be too radical, as I feared you might be. It seems to me that you handled the subject in the proper way and as a writer who knew the ground that he, or she, was standing on; and this last thing is always the most important. I have not heard any of the operas yet, nor do I expect to hear more than two or three—*Don Giovanni* and the *Götterdämmerung*, with the *Barber*, possibly. You may be surprised at my choice, but I maintain that I have a strong argument in my favor. I want *Don Giovanni* to offset the *Götterdämmerung* and I want the *Barber* because I want it. As for *Siegfried*, I can do without him. The *Walküre* was enough of that sort of thing. I don't know just what I shall find in the Twilight of all these people, but I know there is something in it that I need.

I did not "weep" at Paderewski but I felt his power as I never felt the power of any public pianist before. I should not care to hear him again in public, though I should like to know him and have him play to me in his own den. That is what the piano is made for, but the vanity of humankind has dragged it out of its proper place and filled the world with false impressions. I would give more to hear Petschnikoff play his fiddle for fifteen minutes than I would to hear Paderewski play the piano for fifteen hours—that [is] if he, Petschnikoff, would play what I wanted him to. After this it is only fair for me to say that I was unfortunate in striking Paderewski's most impossible programme. What is there in Schumann's interminable "Carnaval" that any sane person cares to listen to?

Sincerely,
E.A.R.

67

26 December 1899

I wrote you a letter the other day and forgot, I think, to wish you a Merry Christmas, which was not at all kind. Please accept this belated message of good will and all the other things and this further certificate of my complete appreciation of your persistent friendliness. Kindly remember me to your Aunt, your cousin, and—if you can make him understand it—to your cat.

Most sincerely yours,
E.A.R.

68

[January 1900]

It was impossible for me to see you today, but I'll try to see you tomorrow morning about ten o'clock. I am afraid it will be out of the question for me to do Chinatown this week. Explanations tomorrow.

E.A.R.

Tuesday evening

69

[January 1900]

I shall be free, I think, both Friday and Saturday. Here are the programmes I spoke of.[1]

E.A.R.

1. Probably the Paderewski and Petschnikoff concerts alluded to in Letters 65, 66.

70

4 March 1900

I have read Mr. Wood's[1] verses with a great deal of interest and agree with you in thinking there is an unusual amount of meat in them. But like nearly all literary work of the spontaneous order, they are too crude to give pleasure as "objects of art." In the resurrection piece there is a real poem which can easily be brought out with a little chiselling. No poet ever lived who could write safely of his "Essence" as a thing to be sipped by droning bees out of flowering canopies. To be perfectly honest, I think it is the man himself, rather than his verses, that attracts me. I hope to meet him some day and have a talk with him about his machines. I am infinitely more interested in machines than [you] can possibly suspect, only I don't like the Kipling method of treating them. There is nothing truly "modern" in that; it is merely halfway groping—a cleaning-out process to make things easier for the real man when he comes. I think Mr. Wood would agree with me in this and I think it very likely that he may use some of his coming leisure in the cultivation of a new art and thinking, [and] produce songs which will be as good, in their way, as his printing-presses; but I have so little faith in art as an accident that I cannot believe that they will come from him or from any other man without sustained effort. I mean, of course, that previous grinding is the mother of inspiration, or whatever you call it, quite as much in literature as it is in mechanics. If I am wrong, so much the better; but whether I am wrong or right, I should like very much to meet this man whenever he happens to feel like meeting me. My passing reference to Kipling has nothing to do with these poems. They go beyond Kipling into Whitman—but they go too fast.

With my regards again to the cat, I am your obedient servant.

E.A.R.

1. Henry A. Wise Wood (1866–1939), engineer and inventor of the Autoplate and other mechanisms which accelerated the process of printing newspapers. He published half a dozen books and pamphlets on such subjects as naval policy, national security, newspaper manufacturing, morality, and one volume of verse, *Fancies* (New York, 1903).

71

[March–April 1900]

Mr. Wood is the real thing, and I am glad for a chance to tell you so. It is not likely that he will find much in a lopsided nature like mine to interest him, but that has nothing to do with him, nor will it be any cause for me to think less of him. I have given up trying to regulate human "affinities" and I find that things go much better.

I fancy he sees in me a rather complicated machine that has been running for thirty years "out of plumb." I don't know how much such a machine is likely to be good for, but we are trying to get some sort of product, as you know, and it is possible that the thing may hang together longer than we think. I was going to say longer than we desire, but that would not be quite true; at any rate, it would be misleading.

Mr. Wood's contrivance is a marvel but the man is the more important part of the combination. I thank you for letting me know him for he adds new proof to the things that I am feeling and always trying to say. We seem to do very well together and I trust there will be no bloodshed.

Yes, I am going up to see Miss Hanson and to take back the book that I borrowed. Probably she thinks I have stolen or forgotten it, but I have done neither.

Sincerely yours,
E.A.R.

72

[April 1900]

Your "Robinson Book" sounds ominously like another "Baby Book." What on earth is it anyhow? As for the sonnets,[1] I am quite willing to give you a copy of them, but I must ask you to wait until I have fixed them a little. In spite of all the good things you say I feel sure that there is something wrong in the way they "connect"—or rather in the way they don't connect. When I tinker them to something like my satisfaction I'll send them along. But I ask again: What in the name of all the gods at once, what is a Robinson Book?

Mr. Wood came in again the other afternoon and found me the victim of grippe (I prefer *grip*). I was rather a woeful object and I felt just as I looked; but he did most of the talking and did me more good than all the doctors in Manhattan could have done. I tried to make him hear *Tristan* but without success. The last performance is on next Saturday afternoon with Schuck[2] conducting. Try to make him go. He can't quite disbelieve the ambulance stories of his friends. You will see from this that I have changed my attitude a little. It was a second hearing of the thing that converted me to the first and second acts, which I had thought a little dull.

I am pretty nearly myself now, but still rather shaky. Next Saturday, by the way is a remarkable day. *Tristan* in the afternoon, the "Ninth Symphony" with choral, in the evening.

Sincerely,
E.A.R.

1. "The Woman and the Wife" consists of two sonnets: "I. The Explanation"; "II. The Anniversary."

2. Ernest von Schuck (1846–1914), a child prodigy on the piano and violin, became conductor of many eminent opera companies in Germany, Switzerland, and Italy and general music director of the Dresden Court Opera. In the spring of 1900 he conducted three performances at the Metropolitan Opera House in New York City.

73

[April 1900]

The Woman and the Wife

I—The Explanation

"You thought we knew," she said, "but we were wrong.
This we can say, the rest we do not say;
Nor do I let you throw yourself away
Because you love me. Let us both be strong,
And we shall find in sorrow, before long,
But the wise price Love ruled that we should pay;
The dark is at the end of every day.
And silence is the end of every song.

"You ask me for one proof that I speak right
But I can answer only that I know;
You look for just one lie to make black white,
But I can tell you only what is true—
God never made me for the wife of you.
This we can say;—believe me! . . . Tell me so!"

II—The Anniversary

"Give me the truth, whatever it may be.
You thought we knew, now tell me what you miss
You are the one to tell me what it is—
You are a man, and you have married me.
What is it worth to-night that you can see
More marriage in the dream of one dead kiss
Than in a thousand years of life like this?
Passion has turned the lock. Pride keeps the key.

"Whatever I have said or left unsaid,
Whatever I have done or left undone,—
Tell me. Tell me the truth. . . . Are you afraid?
Do you think that Love was ever fed with lies
But hunger glittered after in his eyes?
Do you ask me to take moonlight for the sun?"

You and other people seem to like this, but it is poison to magazine editors. Probably the "me" in the last verse kills them.[1] You would say "him," but I can't possibly see the question from your point of view. I send it only because you asked for it.

E.A.R.

1. The sonnets were first published in *Captain Craig* (1902) with two verbal changes: "Only the price . . ." in line 6 of "The Explanation"; "But hunger lived thereafter . . ." in line 13 of "The Anniversary." Robinson never altered the controversial "me."

74

8 May 1900

I think I must be a night-blooming idiot. At any rate I cannot, after trying seventeen different ways, bring myself to see that you and your doubtful adherents are right in supposing that any woman would not say "Do you ask me to take moonlight for the sun?," or something like it, after the "strong talk" that has gone before. The Doctor and Betts[1] condemned it because it contained the thought in the preceding question about Love's going hungry; and in doing so they made me very uncomfortable. I had tried so hard to do the thing they condemned me for doing that I felt no leg left to stand on. She asks that rather high-sounding couplet, and then, half to him and half to herself, she repeats the question for pretty much the same reason that she said "The dark is at the end of every day," or in the sunset above. Still, I suppose you are right. Four against one must mean something, even though I heard that last verse before I heard the rest.

What the deuce is Art, anyhow?

Sincerely yours,
E.A.R.

I can't make out your address, but I'll guess at it.

1. Craven Langstroth Betts, a bookdealer Robinson met in Dr. Coan's office, wrote verse prolifically and published at least five books. Like Miss Brower, he immediately discerned Robinson's genius.

75

16 May 1900

You are putting me down a little too far. I haven't got quite to the grovelling point yet—in fact, I haven't been thinking much about the sonnets of late. I have been too busy with the Big Thing[1] which is still a question. Betts refuses to endure it, the Doctor thinks he likes [it], and Mr. Stedman[2] is now struggling with it. Tomorrow it goes to the ancient house of Scribner, from which it will undoubtedly come back in due time.[3] It's a rather prodigious piece of business and a thing that must necessarily be pretty good or very bad. If it fails to go, the disappointment will be more to my friends than to me, for I have no end of other stuff in my head. Only you must give me time and remember that I am growing. At least, try to be good enough to think so.

As for the sonnets, I am almost beginning to think that I am obscure in my personification of Love. "His" refers, of course, to Love himself, as an abstraction; otherwise there should be no capital L, which is woeful nonsense when unnecessary. If you still think the last line strikes a false note I'm afraid I shall have to put the thing in pickle for a year; for I am positively unable to understand the difficulty at present, and equally unable to think of any line to take the place of the line where I say "Do you ask *him* etc." which would make—so it seems to me now—the whole thing rattle. If I keep on trying to write three-volume novels in twenty-eight lines, I suppose I ought to expect these obscurities and be willing [to] take unfavorable criticism as I would take ten thousand a year. I'll make another attack on the sonnets before long and let you know what I have left. You may look too for a sonnet on Emerson and one on Erasmus,[4] though you are not to think that the sonnet disease is on me again. I have mild relapses now and then, and I intend to have them the rest of my life—two or three a year—or more. I'm reading *Resurrection*, which is really great; not so good a novel perhaps as *Anna Karénina*,[5] but I think a more significant piece of writing.

I have not seen Wood for two weeks, but I think I shall look him up tomorrow. I am [not] doing very much "seeing" just now, as you know.

Sincerely yours,
E.A.R.

I have lost your street number. If it is necessary send it next time and I'll paste it to something.

1. "Captain Craig."
2. Edmund Clarence Stedman (1833–1908), Wall Street broker, poet, critic, and anthologist, admired and aided Robinson.
3. Scribner's rejected the volume as "at once too simple and too sophisticated" for its constituency.
4. "The Sage" first appeared in *Captain Craig* (1902); "Erasmus" in *Harvard Monthly*, XXXI (December 1900), 110, and reprinted with changes in *Captain Craig*.
5. Numerous British and American translations of Leo Tolstoy's novels *Anna Karenina* (1875–1877) and *Resurrection* (1899) were available at this time.

76

[May 1900]

Now you have mixed me all up again. I wrote "Do you ask him etc" merely to show you what I meant by "Do you ask me etc," never dreaming of making the change in sonnet itself. To me the "me" is absolutely necessary to give a kind of final turn or clinch to the whole thing; after the impassioned abstraction (wow!) of "Do you think that Love etc" I came back to the concrete because it seems to me that I must do so in order to be ARTISTIC. I don't know what you will say to all this, but I'm afraid I can't do any more for you. You and Miss Buttons[1] are [the] only people who have had difficulty with "him" and "me" and you have, between you, given me no end of trouble. Please let me know at once if you are disgusted with my contrariness and if you think, honestly, that "him" in the last line would not bother more readers than it would help.

Sincerely yours,
E.A.R.

1. Miss Brower's pet name for Harriet Jones (see Letter 94, note 1).

77

[May–June 1900]

Here is an irregular sonnet on Erasmus, which I ask you to straighten as well as you can. I sent it, as you see, to Pope, who tells me that it will go; but I don't want you to be influenced at all by his opinion. Please send it back when you write.

As for "me" and "him," it seems that you, Miss Buttons and Betts are for "him," while Mr. Stedman the Doctor and I are for "me." To be perfectly honest, we don't even see what you three are driving at.

I have lately been inspired by a golf-fiend, and I am making a very powerful poem on him.

Sincerely yours,
E.A.R.

78

[10 June 1900]

"Mean—that which is intermediate between two extremes."
—Webster[1]

Tell me at once, but without being offended, just what is the matter with all women. They are entirely willing to tell a man that he is a roaring idiot and at the same time they try to leave him with a feeling that they do not think it particularly strange that he should write contrary to logic, common sense, and all rhetorical decency. If you thought I mean what you found fault with why do you not call me "impossible ass" and so spare my feelings? I tell people sometimes that I have no feelings, but that is really a falsehood.

Sincerely yours,
E.A.R.

I return the sonnet for you to browse over at your leisure. You may find something else—something of a different nature. Believe that I am good-natured, even though I howl.

1. The fifth line of "The Sage" contains the phrase "the madness and the mean."

79

11 June 1900

When I had read your unexpected criticism of "the mean" yesterday morning I was so thoroughly bewildered that I sat down at once and wrote an Informal Note, which I suppose you have received and read by this time. I thought at the time that I was safe; but in the evening I tried the line on Betts, who found the same difficulty, only he was going to call it all right.

In the light of this I feel that the thing must be changed, though I am not yet reconciled to the idea. The possibility of taking "mean" as an adjective had never occurred to me; and I fear Pope's eulogy of this particular line may have had some effect. I can't say "the extreme and the mean" very well, so I shall have to rack my cerebral machine for something else.[1] Also, I suppose I shall have to thank you for calling my attention to the defection, even though it goes against the grain. When three intelligent readers fail even to dream of what I am driving at, I do not feel that my case is very strong. In the meantime I have done and am still doing a "symbolical" Twilight Song (sic) of seventy-two lines.[2] It will make you and Miss B——s wring your hands, and I fear it may drive Betts to drink.

I tried to find Wood the other day but did not succeed. I am as glad as you are to know that the big machine is exceeding expectations.

Sincerely yours,
E.A.R.

1. Despite this protestation Robinson never changed the phrase.

2. The original version contains six twelve-line stanzas (see Letter 80). On January 1, 1901, Robinson wrote to Josephine Preston Peabody: "I enclose a copy of my Song with the earnest request that you endeavor to tell me what is the matter with it. There is something that I have not cured even by throwing away twenty-four lines, which I did with joy at Moody's suggestion. If you can improve it by tearing out two more, do so by all means" (Torrence, *Selected Letters*, pp. 36–37). See also Hagedorn, *Robinson*, pp. 169, 178.

80

[June 1900]

I send[1] these two "symbolical" things, wondering what you will make of them. I know what I mean by them, but whether I can expect anyone else to know is another matter. Of course they are intended primarily to give a "feeling" to the reader, and that feeling will depend entirely on how much or how little intellectual (I suppose) sympathy I succeed in raising. The ballad[2] ought not to give much trouble as it is nothing more than a picturing of the grotesque way in which mystery, tragedy and joy mix themselves at times on this peculiar and amusing planet; but the song[3]—I call it a song and say *marcato* to keep you from jigging its anapests (the accent is more than half of it, I fancy)—may mean pretty much everything or pretty much nothing; and I do not expect you, in either case, to try to bring the thought down to a clear outline. "Feel" something of it, if you can, and be glad that it doesn't feel any worse. You may keep this if you care for it, but I must have the typewritten ballad back. I'm going to shoot it at an editor before long.

E.A.R.

1. In the right margin of the first page Miss Brower wrote: "Belongs to 1900 or 1901, I think." This letter and the enclosed manuscript of "Twilight Song" became separated and she did not connect the two in her later reconstruction. None of the original sheets are now in the collection but are present in photocopy. See Letter 91.

2. Miss Brower circled this word and wrote in the upper margin: "First called 'Intermezzo,' but printed under the caption 'The Return of Morgan and Fingal.'"

3. See *The Library of Bacon Collamore*, pp. *vi*, 10. The poem was first published in *Captain Craig* (1902), without dedication, in four stanzas of twelve lines each. Robinson made minor revisions of punctuation, and verbal changes in lines 17, 19, 25, 45.

Twilight Song

([redacted])

Through the shine, through the rain,
We have shared the day's load;
To the old march again
We have tramped the long road;
We have laughed, we have cried,
And we've tossed the king's crown;
We have fought, we have died
And we've tired the day down;
So it's lift the old song,
For the night flies again,
Where the road leads along
Through the shine, through the rain.

~~[illegible]~~
~~[illegible]~~,
~~[illegible]~~
~~[illegible]~~;
~~[illegible]~~,
~~[illegible]~~,
~~[illegible]~~
~~[illegible]~~;
~~[illegible]~~
~~[illegible]~~,
~~[illegible]~~,
~~[illegible]~~

~~[illegible]~~
~~[illegible]~~
~~[illegible]~~
~~[illegible]~~
~~[illegible]~~
~~[illegible]~~
~~[illegible]~~
~~[illegible]~~
~~[illegible]~~
~~[illegible]~~
~~[illegible]~~
~~[illegible]~~

Long ago, far away,
Came a sign from the skies;
And we feared then to ~~[illegible]~~ pray
For ~~Till~~ the new sun ~~[illegible]~~ to rise;
Side by side, hand in hand,
Not a child stepped or stirred—
So the light filled the land
And the light brought the Word;
For ~~But~~ we knew then the gleam
Though we feared then the day,
And the Dawn smote the dream
Long ago, far away.

So the road leads us all,
For the king now is dead;
And we know, stand or fall,
We have shared the day's bread;
We can laugh down the dream,
For the dream breaks and flies;
And we trust now the gleam,
For the gleam never dies;
So it's off now the load,
For we know the night's call, —
And we know now the road,
And the road leads us all.

—

Though the shine, though the rain,
We have wrought the day's quest;
To the ~~[illegible]~~ old march again
We have earned the day's rest;
We have laughed, we have cried,
And we've heard the king's groans;
We have fought, we have died,
And we've buried the king's bones;
And we lift now the song
Ere the night flies again,
When the road leads along
Through the shine, through the rain.

E. A. Robinson

June, 1900

81

[June–July 1900]

"The madness etc"[1] is even more than "me and him."[2] Now comes along another school of critics who "do not see," to quote one of them, how an intelligent person could have any difficulty with the line. This is the first time that I have ever passed my stuff around for individual criticism and I more than half think it will be the last. I discover too many things—and yet it paid in the sonnets on the woman.

Don't be afraid to stamp on the "symbolical" things[3] if you don't like them.

E.A.R.

1. "The Sage" (see Letters 78, 79).
2. "The Woman and the Wife" (see Letter 73 *et seq.*).
3. See Letter 80.

82

450 Manhattan Avenue
5 July 1900

Here are two comical sonnets[1]—the last of the lot. So you see the new book is to be made up wholly of different material from that in *The Children*—not over eight or nine sonnets in all.

"We have worn the sun's touch."[2] It says what I mean, but I'm not at all sure it means what it says. Tell me what you think of it. Your remarks on "Fingal and Morgan" fail somehow to reach me, though I appreciate your interest in setting them down.

I'm here for a little while with Betts and I am trying to persuade him for the love of God not to bake a pan of beans "the way his sister does." I don't know just where I shall be in a week from now, but anything addressed to me in Betts' care will reach me.

Sincerely yours,
E.A.R.

1. Ironic reference to "The Growth of 'Lorraine,'" a sonnet pair.
2. Line 5 of the original second stanza of "Twilight Song," eliminated before publication (see Letter 80).

83

[July–August 1900]

Of course I can improve my way of writing but I cannot take back anything in regard to the pan of beans. They have not yet been baked, by the way.

So you would like to punch my head because your remarks in regard to "M. and F." fail to reach you.[1] Well, I am very sorry, and I am sorry too that you have given up criticizing the things I send. Some day I shall agree with you and send you some sort of pretty present; so perhaps you had better change your mind and let me know what there is in "Lorraine" that displeases you. Also, I should like to know how many lines in the "Twilight Song" strike you as inadequate. After this, you may be glad to know that the things were not sent primarily for criticism, but wholly out of friendship and overwhelming esteem for your cerebral activity. And you would like to punch my head because I have never lived very much with Welshmen, and therefore cannot see the difficulty in the matter of Fingal. Go to, and let me know if I ought to read Trevelyan's book about Charles James Fox.[2] Betts is growing thin because I refuse to do so. The *Captain* has come back from the Scribners and is now ready for another journey. The thermometer is somewhere in the neighborhood of 100° and there are four bottles of beer in the ice chest. The Doctor fancies he is going to Europe very soon.

Sincerely yours,
E.A.R.

1. Robinson evidently intended to write *me* here.
2. George O. Trevelyan, *The Early History of Charles James Fox* (London, 1880).

84

450 Manhattan Avenue
5 August 1900

What right have you, after the lapse of time, to tell me that I have "no fine trousers?" How do you know that I did not go downtown even last Saturday and purchase the most resplendently subdued pair in

New York? And how do you know that I did not start out the following Sunday on a triumphal tour to Bronxville, that I might show them to Mr. Stedman and Mr. Tudor Jenks?[1] Mr. Stedman, by the way, is the most long-suffering of men and one to whom I am indebted in more ways than one—though none of these ways are of the material sort, as the trousers may have led you to suspect. I came home in the evening and found Betts—of whom it is my duty to sing. He is the fairest of ten thousand, and I don't think he really intends to bake any beans. I have had a chance to find out what he is like [as a] housemate and I hasten to say that no orthodox heaven could give him any more than he deserves. Almost the whole of his life has been given up to others and he is now well along on the road to fifty years old. When I think of what he has done and the spirit in which he has done it, I feel as if I had no real right to exist. The active and supposedly successful fellow who makes a lot of money and cuts his figure in Wall Street does not embarrass me in the least, but the fellow who knows in his heart that he is looked upon by his friends as one condemned to mediocrity and yet goes on as Betts goes, trying to make life a little pleasanter for all the hungry-looking victims who come his way—to say nothing of actual financial self-sacrifice in favor of those who would never think of doing as much for him—I feel that I have received not only, as you say, "what I deserve," but a great deal more. I have no illusions on the point whatever, only my standard of what counts is rather different from those of my friends and for that reason I am bound to be rated for much more or much less than I am.

I am glad that you have the letters all in one bundle, for now you can throw them into the fire. Of course I cannot command you to do it, but I can ask you to do so and assure you that I mean what I say. I never keep letters myself and I prefer to know that mine are torn up as soon as they are read—or, say, answered. There is so much in them that is none of the real "me," so much crass vulgarity and crazy "criticism" (written for the most part when I hardly knew what I was doing)—that I am sure you will not hesitate to put them where they belong—in the stove.[2]

Sincerely yours,
E.A.R.

1. Tudor Jenks (1857–1922), a practicing lawyer and student of art, writer of prose, verse, and juveniles, was an editor of *St. Nicholas Magazine*.

2. In the right margin of the first page Robinson wrote: "It is not yet 'the time for disappearing.' Be sure, too, that my feelings are not to be changed. I think I know you by this time."

In the right margin of the second page: "I have kept your first letter, however."

85

450 Manhattan Avenue
27 August 1900

I hope my last letter did not make you think that I wished never to hear from you again. I do not remember writing anything that could give you such a feeling, but yet I may have made use of my incomparable bulls and so set you into a fine frenzy. If I did that, please take my word for it now that I meant to do nothing of the sort. My remarks about "crazy criticism" did not apply to what I said about your stories and essays, but to what I said at odd times about works of art in general; but now I am going to tell you one thing that I hope you will choose to consider with some seriousness, for it is a thing that I have been getting ready to tell you for some time. Prepare, therefore, to know that you can write—within one year—or say two, just as you like—a book of essays in the vein of "The Musical Idea,"[1] though perhaps not always quite so long, that will give you something to live for and also to make whatever you do in the way of fiction much easier and probably much more satisfactory. Up to the present, you have shown a queer and *contrairy* reluctance to make fiction of a subject which is in itself really worthwhile. "Old Friends" is an exception, but even in that there is certain remoteness or something that will keep it just outside the line. You know about music, you know about musical people, and you can write this book of more or less humorous essays on whatever comes into your head, and you ought to begin by next Thursday morning. The job will not be half so difficult as you think; and when you have the thing between covers you will have fourteen times the confidence to go to work on the novel —provided it is musical—which I still believe you were born to write. Ipse Dixit, and all that, but no matter. Either I know what I am talking about, or I don't. If I don't know what I am talking about, then I don't know anything; and I'll be given to superfluous language if I quite believe that.

Betts has lately brought me a poem[2] (I don't remember whether I told you of it or not) which is big and real. It seems he did it some time ago, but never thought overmuch of it. I do not say that it is transcendant or splendiferous, but I do say that it is likely to live if ever it gets into print.

Please quiet my doubtful velleities and tell me that you ain't mad.

E.A.R.

Above all, do not take this for anything in the nature of an apology or a poultice. I should have written just the same if you had sent me a cinnamon bun on receipt of my letter.

1. Miss Brower's "Is the Musical Idea Masculine," *Atlantic Monthly*, LXXIII (March 1894), 332–339.
2. Possibly one of the poems in the second section of *Selected Poems* (New York, 1916), which contains odes to Spring, Autumn, Winter, and some lyrical narratives; or one of the two heroic ballads in *Two Captains, at Longwood, at Trafalgar* (New York, 1921).

86

71 Irving Place
3 September 1900

I shall not go so far as to question your sincerity in regard to writing that novel, but I will say that you have not yet made an inch of progress towards convincing me that you can't do [it] if you wish to. If you don't wish to—why, of course that's quite another thing. As for those essays I quite agree with Chilton, though I have not seen him for four or five months. Coincidences are after you with picks and sticks, and I think you may as well make up your mind to write. I am not so ready to let you go in the matter of the essays, for I know you can do them without much trouble, and I know they will be good reading when they are done. Even if you do not feel just like doing them, I think you ought to try three or four, if only for the sake of discipline—which I feel somehow that you need. She was too far away to shoot, so she merely went to the shore of the lake and cursed. She didn't get mad though, for she never does that.

You see I am back here again in my old quarters. Betts' sister and nephew pounced down on us from Nova Scotia and I got out. For some unexplained reason I got up early that morning and so made, I hope, an excellent impression on Miss Betts, who is a lady of many activities and much humor. If she knew that my early rising was a miracle she might not think so well of me as she seems to; and the consciousness of this fact has turned the matter into a sort of habit. For the past three mornings I have been up ridiculously early—that is, with the exception of this morning, when I lay rather late to make up for not sleeping any during the night.

To go back to the novel, let me assure you again that the whole thing is merely a question of interest and courage. If you care to write it, and dare to write it, you can; but if you "dassent," you can't. Possunt qui posse[1]—that's wrong, but the first part is all right. I remember how it looks in Virgil. I used to read Virgil by the hour, but I can't read him now at all. My Latin has gone with my ambition to play the clarinet. The influence of both stay with me, though, and it is to Virgil, I think, that I owe nearly all of my daylight. If it wasn't for my daylight, I'm afraid I should be pretty much in the dark; and as it is, things have a crepuscular appearance at times.

I'm reading Baden-Powell's book on Scouting,[2] but I don't think I shall be a scout. I have some of the requirements, but I am not "specially active" and I can't see very well. I can read and write, however, and that gives me courage to think that I may take to scouting when everything else has failed. B.-P. doesn't say whether a good scout should be able to write sonnets, but I have a notion that he should.

I don't know whether you are in the mountains now or not, so I'll send this to Wilkes-Barre as usual. I suppose you will get it sometime.

As for Betts' poem, I'm afraid I cannot give you any satisfactory idea of what it is like. You will have to read it sometime for yourself. I have been trying to get him to do something with it, but he refuses to mind my advice, which is always very valuable.

Sincerely yours,
E.A.R.

1. After "posse" Robinson wrote "videntur" but drew a line over it. He was trying to remember "possunt, quia posse videntur" from book V, line 231 of the *Aeneid*—"they can because they think they can."

2. Robert S. S. Baden-Powell (1857–1941), a lieutenant-general in the English army, founded the Boy Scouts and the Girl Guides, and wrote many books and brochures on the subject of scouting.

87

17 September 1900

No, I don't see the good of keeping letters; nor do I see just why Betts and the Doctor should take every chance word I happen to let out as the utterance of anything more than what it is most likely to be when I say it. I think I did tell them once that I thought it might be a good plan to send the *Captain* to you but I think the thing was in the hands of the Scribners (they had it for nearly two months) at that time. Anyhow, I have not yet had an opportunity to send it. Just now the manuscript is in Boston, where it is likely to stay for two or three weeks longer.[1] On the whole, I don't think that I shall let you see it until it is between covers; for I know that at least five hundred places in it that you will not like, and I know that some of them are places that I can't fix.

As for those letters, I will ask you—formally and explicitly—to destroy them. As I said before, I can't command you to do so, but I can ask you to and I can ask hard. If I destroy yours as fast as I read them, why should you be unwilling to do as much for me? Letters are good things to get, good things to read and to keep for a day or two maybe; but at the end of that time they are the best things in the world to tear up. So if you wish to prove your good feeling toward me, you have only to tell me that the things are gone. If you wish to keep the poems I have sent from time to time, I shall be rather glad; but for heaven's sake burn up the letters.

By the way, you are to make this change in the "Twilight Song"—"And we feared then to play" (which says just what I mean but still is clumsy) I have changed to

"And we feared then to pray
For the new dawn to rise etc"[2]

Any suggestion you may have to offer in the way of other changes will be considered, suffered over, and possibly acted on. I say "suffered," but I mean tortured. Did you ever try to pull a brick from the side of a house? But then, of course you have, for you too have done things in verse. Vide "Bach" etc. Et tu in Acadie[3]—and in New York again, I hope.

Sincerely yours,
E.A.R.

My handwriting is worse than ever today. I must be losing what little character I have ever possessed. Pray for me—don't get m—. I beg your pardon.

1. *Captain Craig* had been rejected by Scribner's and was now in the hands of Small, Maynard & Company, who held it until December before notifying Robinson that it would publish the book in 1901. However, after another period of silence (during part of which the manuscript was lost in a brothel), the company also rejected it. Houghton, Mifflin published *Captain Craig* "on commission" in October 1902, with John Hays Gardiner and Laura E. Richards as guarantors against loss.

2. The word "play" never appeared in print. Robinson effected the change to "pray" on the manuscript (see first and last paragraphs of Letter 91).

3. Miss Brower seems to have taken a trip to Nova Scotia (Acadia), and Robinson is punning on the celebrated pastoral landscape by Nicolas Poussin in which three young people are reading the words "Et in Arcadia, ego!" inscribed upon a tomb.

88

71 Irving Place
18 October 1900

After my elaborately humorous statement to the effect that I hope you ain't mad (I supposed the ain't would save it) it is particularly irritating to know that the good Betts has got me into more trouble. If I told him that you had gone back on me, I made no more than one [of] those famous remarks of mine which are said with no thought in particular on my part and are taken constantly in the most deadly earnest. Such remarks are the natural result of my being temporarily down to a certain extent and I assure you that they do not call for any such consideration as my friends seem inclined to give them. I may be in many ways a sort of ass, but I am not a two-year-old baby. Please remember this and so do me a great kindness.

Chilton made his semi-annual visit of inspection a while ago. Probably you have heard from him, and learned that I am very solemn and incapable of any useful effort. Now don't take this as venom, for it "ain't." It ain't anything in particular. Wood reminded me of his existence too by sending me a copy of Stedman's *Anthology*,[1] which I happened to want. Just why he did it, I don't know, for I have not given him any reason for thinking of me since last June. He is the real thing, as I told you some time ago; and I hope I may shake myself together some day and be able to talk with him without feeling that he has succeeded in everything where I appear to have failed—that is, in Doing Something.

Ex pede Herculem—which is to say that one can tell an impecunious Child of Letters by the looks of his hat. You will see it if you come to

New York; and if you come early enough you will see Mansfield in *Henry V*,[2] which is really a big show. Burnham has come back with his two wooden legs, and the Doctor is expected tomorrow.

Your obedient servant,

E.A.R.

Don't believe Betts again—no matter what he says. It would be indecent of me to criticize him in any way, but I must say in self-defense that he has a thoroughly well-meaning habit of saying too many things with the idea of being friendly. He doesn't quite see the line—sometimes. And I wonder if I do.

1. Edmund Clarence Stedman, editor, *An American Anthology, 1787–1899* (Boston, 1900). Robinson's copy of this book in Colby College is inscribed: "To E. A. Robinson, with the sincere regard of an appreciative, if eccentric, friend, H. A. Wise Wood, 1900."

2. Richard Mansfield (1857–1907), a leading American romantic actor, played such roles as Cyrano, Nero, Don Juan, and the schizophrenic Dr. Jekyll and Mr. Hyde. In the Shakespeare canon he re-created Richard III, Shylock, and Brutus, as well as Henry V. In the current play he made a spectacular appearance, riding a white horse in the interpolated procession after Agincourt.

89

91 Palisade Avenue
Yonkers
10 November 1900

You asked me sometime ago to tell you what things of mine Mr. Stedman selected for his *Anthology*, and I think I failed to reply. So I will say now that his somewhat lugubrious admiration turned to "Luke Havergal," "The Ballade of Dead Friends," "The Clerks," "The Pity of the Leaves," and "The H[ouse] on the H[ill]." I fancy that he has rather given me up for a hopeless lot, though I have really no right to say that, I suppose. You see he doesn't understand that the thing I need is about two years of manual labor—or "at hard labor"—instead of the newspaper work which I detest and cannot do. I have been wondering of late whether Wood might know of some sort of ten-hour treatment at a dollar and a half a day which would give me a chance to connect with what are known as the Realities—just a job, I mean, and a job of the worst sort. There are many things in this line that I could really do and do pretty well—much better than I can do editorials for the *Tribune*.

In the meantime I am trying to think up a way in which to get Betts calendered. Saint Craven of Harlem is nothing to what he deserves. The more I find out about his past and the farther I see into him, the more do I feel like tying a grindstone to my neck and jumping into North River. There is one little thing that I can do in a sort of way, but I can't seem to make myself, as such, worthwhile. Up to the present I have managed partly to keep down the vagabond in me, but I think now that I am sailing along for about what I am. I'm honest enough, and I have a few good points; but I shall find my level actually with the esoteric hodcarriers and the illuminated motormen. Only I can't be a motorman, for a dozen obvious reasons.

I saw Mrs. Hanson today and heard from her that your cousin[1] has been in town. I should have liked to see him, for he is altogether of the right sort, as I have said before. I'm glad that he got out of the law and into the hen business. Please remember me to him in all sincerity.

I have lately written a few things which will please you sometime—when I get them rubbed down. *Captain Craig* (who is the king of all tramps) is still in Boston, where I understand he is looked upon with favor, in spite of his clothes. He will please you exceedingly when you see him*; for he is highly interesting. And I think he is Art.

My friend Moody[2] has just published *The Masque of Judgment*, which I want you to read. I'll let you have my unbound copy as soon as Betts gets through with it.

Sincerely yours,
E.A.R.

* if I succeed in getting him published

1. Archie Parsons (see Letter 64, note 1).
2. William Vaughn Moody (1869–1910) was an established figure in undergraduate literary publications at Harvard at the same time Robinson was having little success breaking into that circle. They became closer friends later. See Maurice F. Brown, "Moody and Robinson," *Colby Library Quarterly*, V (December 1960), 185–194; and Richard Cary, "Robinson on Moody," *CLQ*, VI (December 1962), 176–183.

90

91 Palisade Avenue
Yonkers
28 November 1900

I have just time to send you a word of thanks for your invitation to Thanksgiving and to tell you that it will be impossible for me to accept it. Sometime in the course of the winter I shall be rejoiced to take a trip to New York to see you, however. You might not like Yonkers,[1] in spite of the fact that I am gradually getting attached to it. It is a beautiful place—in spots—though my particular spot is not so beautiful as some of the other spots are supposed to be.

I'll write to you in the course of a few days. Also to the Man of Hens. There are hens in "Captain Craig."[2]

Sincerely yours,
E.A.R.

1. To save expenses Robinson was sharing a room with Burnham in a boardinghouse here.

2. Robinson portrays the Fates as three fearful, crafty, foolish fowls (pages 42–43 in the 1902 edition).

91

91 Palisade Avenue
Yonkers
16 December 1900

Please be good enough to send me your copy of my "Twilight Song" as soon as you can do so. I have changed it in a way that will make you think better of me and still better of the song. You may be right about "Lorraine" but I hardly think I shall throw her away. As for the "Morgan and Fingal" thing, and "The Woman and the Wife," you may care to know that they have been refused by nearly all of the magazines; and you may be interested at the same time to know that I shall stick to books hereafter and let the magazines go, even though the "W and W" should stay with the *Cosmopolitan*, where it has been for the past five weeks.[1] I am glad to say that the book business is looking a little better with me and that *Captain C* will be brought out by Small, Maynard & Company sometime in 1901. So you will have a chance to make his acquaintance before long and to tell me whether or not he is disreputable. He has been both praised and damned by the five or six who have seen him, but I am told that Mr. Bliss Carman[2] took a great fancy to him and desired that he should be published. On the whole, I think he will go, though I doubt if the cherrystone critics will be able to make much of him. Even Mr. Stedman, who is given to look kindly on all sorts of so-called innovations, fought rather shy of him; and our good friend the Doctor appeared to take pretty much the same ground. Betts, making due allowance for his constitutional fear of Giving Pain, got hold of him at once, I think; and this thought goes as far as anything to make me believe that the old reprobate (I mean C.C., not Betts) will take care of himself if he is once fairly started on the road.

The other book[3] should be done by this time, but it isn't, and it won't be before fall. It was written two years ago, in the rough, but the greater part of the work is yet to be done. I am inclined to believe there is something in it, and I am also inclined to believe that if a few people will "stay quiet," as Wood puts it, I shall still be able to square up my accounts with the universe. I know very well that my notions of squaring up are not quite like those of some other people, but they are my notions and I have to abide by them. I have reasons to hope that I shall not have to speak to Wood on the subject of hodcarrying—a subject which would be unpleasant to me for the reason that I like the man and would not have him think that I was trying to make use of him—and to believe that the next few years are going to be a little different from the past few years of Our Devil 1896–1900. They have been good years for me in one way, but I think I could endure a change. I don't pretend to know just what sort of bewildered mechanism I have been in the eyes of those who have seen the outside of me, but I do know that the machine has been at times almost a total stranger to me—to say nothing of you and several others. But I shall always have an excellent opinion of you, for you are not one of those people who insist that a fellow shall live more than seven distinct lives at the same time. The ability not to do this is a rare quality and you should congratulate yourself on having it. And I suppose you do.

I have not yet written to Mr. Parsons, but I shall do so some day when the feeling comes over me. I know it will come, for it always does—sooner or later. In the meantime I like to think of him as a fellow worth a dozen of the smug sort who stand for ten times what they are. I don't know why he, or hens, should make me think of Howells, but he does—or they do—and I have to report that I have been reading him for the past month. I find him much better and bigger than I supposed he was, but he has not the largeness that he needs for doing his work as it should be done. I'm afraid his lighter things are the best, though *A Modern Instance* and *The Minister's Charge* just fall short of being permanent. If you haven't read them you will find them to your fancy—if I know anything about your fancy. W. V. Moody, the man of the *Masque*, has been in town (N.Y.) for some time past, and I have convinced myself that he is one of the fellows whom the future will have to deal with. Waldo[4] fiddles to us, by the way, and this makes me think that I met your friend Miss Lyford just before I left Irving Place. Waldo brought her in a cab and showed her to me, and he seemed to be very much pleased with her. I hardly think, however, that they have found their destinies in each other.

Please send the "T[wilight] S[ong]" at once, for I want you to see what I have done with it and what you think of the change. You'll have to take it, anyhow.

Sincerely yours,
E.A.R.

1. All four of these poems appeared for the first time in *Captain Craig* (1902).
2. The Canadian poet (1861–1929) who, with Richard Hovey, led a revolt against domesticated verse with *Songs of Vagabondia* in 1894. After publication of *Captain Craig*, however, Carman wrote that it was "worse than Browning . . . only saved from being the most dreary of failures by the very marked power of the author" (quoted in Emery Neff, *Edwin Arlington Robinson* [New York, 1948], p. 128).
3. Robinson planned a separate volume for the shorter poems which were later incorporated into *Captain Craig*.
4. Fullerton Waldo, a Harvard classmate, owned a Storioni viola which he played for Robinson on request.

92

91 Palisade Avenue
Yonkers
7 January 1901

This will come to you as a somewhat belated acknowledgement of your Christmas letter, but I think you have had experience enough with my methods by this time not to think strangely of it. I have intended two or three times to write during the past week, but the writing did not come to pass. It would not come to pass this time were it not for the fact that I do not wish you to think me indifferent to your good wishes, particularly when you take the trouble to put them down on paper; for my letters all come hard nowadays—maybe because I am spending nearly all of my time on that other book which is gradually—but surely, I think—getting itself together. It will be as unlike *C[aptain] C[raig]* as any two things of mine can possibly be—a difference which is in some ways perhaps not very great. This new book is not funny, or not so funny as *C.C.*, and I suppose you will be pleased to hear me say it.

Moody is beyond doubt the coming man. With his *Masque* just out and his book of miscellaneous poems soon to be published by Houghton Mifflin Co. he can hardly fail to take something like the place he deserves; and beyond all this he is a rattling good fellow, which I take to be the biggest thing of all. If he lives to manage his moods a little and tempers his defensive method somewhat towards his superfluous acquaintances, he will leave little to be desired in the way of the humanities. But I forget that you do not know him or anything about him. You will know, or hear, a good deal about him before long. He's a jaynius, and he will be a good deal more of a jaynius when he really finds himself —sometime in the course of five or ten years. He assures me very gently that my octaves are rubbish and that "Cliff Klingenhagen" is great— an observation that convinces me that he can make two mistakes at once. Not that the Octaves, as literature, necessarily amount to anything; but I always take it upon myself to feel that a fellow has not quite grown up when they mean nothing to him. Moody has not grown up in that way, but he has grown so much more than I have in other ways that he will indisputably be making a big noise in very short order. This in itself does not mean much to me, but in his case I think the noise will last. At any rate, I want you to keep your ears open for its music and to remember what I have told you. I like to pose once in a while as a prophet.

Now I have Moody off my mind, I'll go back to the beginning and wish you a happy new year and all the other things. I don't know just what you want, but whatever they are I hope you may get them. I hope you don't want any more "Twilight Songs," for I have come to the conclusion that I cannot produce the right sort. The four stanzas I have kept of the one I tried to do seem to me now to be pretty doubtful, though I fancy they have just enough of the quality I was after to make me keep them and publish them—to my regret sometime in the future. I am sorry now for about one half of *The Children*, and I hope to be still sorrier before I republish any of it.[1] If I have not asked you already, let me ask you now if you will be good enough to tell me what you would throw away. I do not ask this wholly out of curiosity, for I have a good deal of faith, sometimes, in your judgment. Which is a compliment, of course.

Sincerely yours,
E.A.R.

1. A second edition of *The Children of the Night* (1897) was brought out by Charles Scribner's Sons in 1905. Despite his expressed dissatisfaction, Robinson made only one change in the text—eliminating the sestet from "Boston" on page 51—even the typographical error in line 23 of page 78 ("When loves goes . . .) was retained.

93

22 February 1901

If I keep on neglecting all my friends as I have for the past month or two I shall soon be qualified to call myself the King of Peccaviators. My conscience has been pretty active on your account for some time, and I think I may as well take time this morning and put it to sleep—so let me say in the first place that I like to think of you addressing a lot of tearful mothers and telling them how to be happy. I think you can do that sort of thing; and when I say this I mean to say something that will tickle you and make you feel charitable and puffed up. Charity is always puffed up, but I have observed that it is not always as long-suffering as it should be. This, of course, does not apply to your kind, for you are a miracle in that way. So is Betts, and so am I—only you don't understand just how. Perhaps I can partly explain myself by saying that I do not damn Henry James for having written *The Portrait of a Lady* and *The Bostonians*. It would pay you to read three or four hundred pages of the latter just to see what a man is capable of when his logomania gets the better of him. I will not go so far as to ask you to read *What Maisie Knew*, for then you would lay violent hands on me and quite probably stop the progress of two or three new books which are of great importance to me. Whether they will be of any importance to other people or not is more than I can say, but I have some hope that they may find a few readers who will be able to stand them. One of these is pretty well along now. And this makes me think of your Index Expurgatorius in the last letter you sent me. I agree with you in regard to everything but "F.H."[1] and the "Charles Carville" thing and "The Tavern," and I don't say that these things are not bad. All I can say is that they mean something to me and that I cannot think of throwing them away. "F.H.," by the way, has been called by several more or less intelligent people the best thing I have done. So he[re] I am, thrown back as a poor devil always is, just where I started, and without any reason to suppose that any two of my critical friends will be considerate enough to weed out the same stuff.

I tried this as an interesting experiment, but I find that if I am [to] please everybody I shall have to throw away everything in the book but "The Clerks," "John Evereldown," and "Cliff Klingenhagen"; and even two of these have been questioned—one for its immorality and one for its prose. You will see that I have had some innocent amusement—which was really all I started out for, I fancy—and that I shall have to go back to my original idea of throwing out a dozen or fifteen things which are such utter rubbish that they make me sick when I think of them, and of letting the rest stand—partly for filling, I must confess, and partly because now and then a mortal finds something in them to like.

I have heard a good deal about *The Religion of Democracy*[2] but I have not yet got hold of it. The polite ladies in the library here did not know anything about it but they were good enough to let me carry away a copy of Phillips' *Herod*, which I have read with a good deal of interest. It is disappointing, like everything he writes, but it has the saving grace of being interesting, and that is enough, with me, to atone for a multitude of sins and limitations. It is better, as a play, than *Paolo and Francesca*,[3] but it contains nothing in the way of poetry that is so good as the bad things in the earlier book. On the other hand it contains nothing so bad as "usher me to oblivion"—though Herod's "O liquid language of eternity!" when Mariamne says something to him, is a dangerous second. The play is an oddity in one way. The tragedy is all settled in the first act, and the other two are drawn out from it. The conventional tragedy would be represented by > while Herod would have to be represented by < which is rather a good idea when it doesn't leave too bad a taste. The aftertaste of this play is rather nasty and it has a general flavor of belated decadence about it. Still I think you will like to read it sometime. I should not call it comparable with Moody's *Masque*.

I saw the Doctor last evening and learned from him that you are to be here the first of next week. On the strength of this information I enclose a "dead head" ticket to Bauer's[4] last recital with some hope that it may be the means of my seeing you on Tuesday afternoon. Mason[5] tells me that he is not a man to be omitted, and Mason ought to know,—but I can say no more about him than this. But you know what a potent attraction I am, and as I expect to be a part of the show—your show—I think perhaps you may be there if you have nothing else to do. I am going primarily to please Mason, but now I shall go primarily to see you if you tell me that you are to be there. All of which might be represented by diagrams. Moody is not Moody, by the way. Please send me a word or two between now and Tuesday.

Sincerely yours,
E.A.R.

1. "Fleming Helphenstine."
2. Charles Ferguson, *The Religion of Democracy* (New York, 1900).
3. *Herod* appeared in London, 1901; *Paolo and Francesca* in London, 1899.
4. Harold Bauer (1873–1951), English-born piano virtuoso, first appeared in the United States with the Boston Symphony Orchestra in 1900. He was particularly noted as an interpreter of Brahms, Schumann, and Franck.
5. Daniel Gregory Mason (1873–1953), author, critic, composer, and MacDowell Professor of Music at Columbia University, was for a time Barrett Wendell's assistant at Harvard, where Robinson met him.

94

91 Palisade Avenue
9 March 1901

I have just received two big volumes of Stevenson's Letters—which I have wanted for a long time—and I am wholly at a loss to know where they came from. If you can enlighten [me] on the subject you will relieve my feelings very much by doing so—for then I can make my proper—or more likely improper—acknowledgements to the large-hearted and sagacious friend who sent them. I fancy the friend is feminine, but I don't know. Also tell me how much longer you are to be in town, and when I may see you.[1]

E.A.R.

1. In the lower margin Miss Brower wrote: "I was stopping at the Union Sq. Hotel with Harriet Jones. It was there that we read the *MS* of 'Capt. Craig.'" Harriet L. Jones, a teacher of English at the Wilkes-Barre Institute for girls, was Miss Brower's neighbor and intimate friend, with whom she shared numerous intellectual and artistic pursuits. Miss Jones also wrote minor verse.

95

UNION SQUARE HOTEL
NEW YORK
[March] 1901

Will call again Thursday morning—at eleven.

E.A.R.

96

450 West 23rd Street
Wednesday evening
[March 1901]

Perhaps it is just as well that I did not find you this evening, as I am feeling a little queer nowadays. I am engaged for tomorrow, but I will call on Friday evening at eight unless you tell me not to. And it is possible, though hardly probable, that I may be able to drop in tomorrow morning a little after eleven.

Please let me know a little about your plans and at the same time pardon these ruins of stationery.

Sincerely yours,
E.A.R.

97

29 East 22nd Street
1 April 1901

It's all gone, whatever it was, and I am now feeling very frisky. I think *Die Götterdämmerung* must have cured me—at any rate, it did me a lot of good, no matter what it did to Betts. Wood brought his book[1] the other day, and I told him just what I thought of it. There is no doubt whatever that he has it in him to write poetry of a high order, but what he has done thus far is for the most part so crude and amateurish that one cannot be his friend and at the same time advise him to print anything just yet. I honestly believe that he will surprise people, including himself, in the course of two or three years; and when the time comes for him to do it I shall take much satisfaction in the thought that I may have been the means of opening a few doors for him. He takes my slating with equanimity for the most part, but I make him squirm once in a while.

I have just sent a new thing to the typewriter and I intend to make you read it sometime. It is 400 lines long and perhaps a bit experimental.[2] You will like it in spots, but whether you will be able to stand the whole of it or not is another question. I shall have a Parable[3] for you pretty soon; and when that is finished I think I may say to myself that I have finished the book that I have been pegging at for the past three years. It could have been done long before this, but it was interrupted by *C.C.*—and several other people. It won't be a big book, and it may not be one that you will care much for, but it will be a book, and one that I have enjoyed writing—even though I have worked like the devil over it. I fancy that "Aunt I."[4] will give you a general notion of its character as compared with *The Children*. I have not used the hydraulic press quite so much and I have a notion that I have acquired something that has a faint suggestion of color. I don't make much of this, though, for I know that I am by nature a black and white man. I am going to be musical one day but I don't think I shall ever be crimson or purple. Still, I have had symptoms even of that now and then.

Moody's *Masque* is striking hard wherever it hits at all. You will hear a good deal of the man in the course of the next year, I think. If you don't hear it so soon as that, you will hear it later and correspondingly louder. In the *Atlantic* for last May you will find his big "Ode,"[5] and you will find something by him in nearly every number since then. Houghton Mifflin & Co. are booming him.

Sincerely yours,
E.A.R.

1. Probably a manuscript of *Fancies*, a book of verse which Wood published in 1903.
2. "Isaac and Archibald."
3. "Sainte-Nitouche."
4. "Aunt Imogen."
5. "An Ode in Time of Hesitation," *Atlantic Monthly*, LXXXV (May 1900), 593–598.

98

450 West 23rd Street
28 April 1901

I am slowly going west. In another year I may be as far as Hoboken, though I don't quite think so. Nobody believes me when I say it, but I am a chronic optimist; and I am glad to say that a new headful of ideas goes only to aggravate the condition. When they have taken a definite form I shall have things to amuse you. During the past month I have

[been] trying various compounds on Wood. He continues to make all of them go down, but in one or two cases I have fancied that his eyes bulged a little in the effort. I may as well confess however, that I gave him some pretty strong doses—too strong for Betts and probably too strong—I mean rank, of course—for you. I'll try them on you some time and find out.

I was rather puzzled at your objection to "Aunt Imogen" as a title, for I had thought that for once at least I had struck one that no person could find fault with. If you thought it was too "homely" or provincial, or something of that sort, you must have forgotten that I am an incurable myself in that way, and that it will always be folly for me [to] be afraid to say what I mean on that account. The rural note has been pointed out so often in my stuff that I am almost beginning to consider it as something to do with the afflatus—perhaps the only thing I have that has to do with it. Speaking of this sort of thing, I will say again that "Luke Havergal" is the most rural of all the things I have done—not excluding "Isaac and Archibald," which will make you say more than one cuss-word when you read it. Wood prefers it to the others and therein shows his sagacity—so I like to think. I suppose, though, that his primary reason for liking it is that it takes him out of the city and out of doors. What makes me more encouraged in regard to Wood's intellect is his immediate respect for the sonnet. He takes hold of it as if it were some new sort of printing press and sweats over it accordingly. By and by he will "fix" one as he did the stereotyping machine and have a war dance. You will not be sorry to know that he has given up the notion of publishing his book right away: he has seen fit to lay it aside until he has breathed a bit more of the metrical atmosphere, and I am sure that he has done wisely. "The Building of the Rose,"[1] and a few other things, convince me that he has the real thing in him; sometimes, in fact, I am more than half ready to believe that that single poem will give him a place, though I don't say this to him. To me the thing has the very rarest quality and has it to such an extent that the suggestion of inexperience, or rather carelessness, that it gives tends rather to make it all the more attractive and satisfying. Anyhow, I wish I had one like it to put into my next book.

I feel a kind of musical disturbance somewhere in me nowadays, and I have forewarnings of things that will jingle. It's the "Wilderness" microbe acting up again. Whatever you do this summer, don't take the trouble to read *La Tragédie du Nouveau Christ* by Saint-Georges de Bonhelier. Miss Peabody[2] is here with a five-act drama called *Marlowe*.

Two acts of it gave me an impression that it may take a pretty high place. I haven't said anything to her about Phaethon.[3]

Sincerely yours,
E.A.R.

1. In *Fancies*, (New York, 1903), pp. 20–21.

2. Josephine Preston Peabody (1874–1922), poetess who turned to poetic drama under Moody's persuasion, used her professional influence unsuccessfully upon Small, Maynard & Company to publish *Captain Craig*.

3. In several instances Marlowe passionately declaims his desire to live briefly and brilliantly then plunge in flame into eternal darkness. In view of the numerous specific classical allusions in the play, either Miss Brower or Robinson may have felt that Miss Peabody should have made this analogy to the careers of Marlowe and Phaethon more explicit. Robinson had mentioned Phaethon twice in "Captain Craig," describing how he "did . . . Go gloriously up," then "Did famously come down."

99

450 West 23rd Street
14 June 1901

I am sending a couple of things which may possibly interest you. If they do not, you will not hesitate to say so and to say why.

I saw Chilton on the street the day before he left and I was sorry to see that he was so badly broken up. When he comes back I hope he will be all right again; and I am tempted to say, even at the risk of being misinterpreted, that he will make a more consistent use of his philosophy in the future. Philosophers ought not to go to pieces, even though they have the musical microbe to contend with.

This is merely a note to acknowledge your letter of a few days ago. I shall undoubtedly write a letter again sometime but I can't say just when. The Doctor is deliriously happy nowadays, and Betts has forsaken the arts for billiards. I don't know just why the Doctor is so happy unless it is because he anticipates lifting up his voice in Buffalo—where the Liederkranz Fellows are going to sing "Die Allmacht," "Old Black Joe," and "Yankee Doodle."

Always your obedient servant,
E. A. Robinson

Please return the pomes in a week or so.

E.A.R.

100

4 July 1901

Gracious Lady:

I have a horrible confession to make—to wit, that I did not wake up this morning until 11.30. I got up dutifully at 11.32, but I felt so much like not going to ferries that I did not try to go. You people who know how to sleep will not understand this, but maybe you will excuse it.

I was sorry not to have had more talk with Miss Jones, but I hope there may be another opportunity sometime. I have lately finished two things, one of which you will like as much as you will dislike the other.

Sincerely yours,
E.A.R.

101

UNION SQUARE HOTEL
NEW YORK
[July] 1901

I shall not be able to see you tomorrow, I regret to say. Will leave *C.C.* for you to treat as you like. I suppose he may tell you that he has been waiting for you since Saturday.

E.A.R.

102

450 Manhattan Avenue
12 July 1901

As I wish to try *C.C.* with the publisher again as soon as you are through with him, will you be good enough to send him back sometime in the course of a few days? I am sorry that the delay at the hotel made it necessary for you to do it up, but as there seems to be no way out of that, I will ask you to wrap the thing in some newspapers—or better still, to stiffen it with a piece of pasteboard if you have such a thing.

I am keeping Betts's house in order after my own ideas, doing some work of my own, and reading *Sentimental Tommy* for recreation. The title has kept me away from the book up to this time, but now I find it almost great. I had no suspicion that Barrie had it in him. I won't be so reckless as to ask you to read it, but still I should like to know what you would make of it.

Tell me if you find *C.C.* tedious in the opening. Stedman did; and if he did I suppose others will. I was cherishing a fond notion that it was rather frisky—for me.

Sincerely yours,
E.A.R.

103

[July 1901]

I thank you for reading *C.C.* three and one half times, and for finding something in it. Much that should be there is somewhere else, I fancy.

I enclose 25¢. I did not mean to make you pay the bills.

Sincerely yours,
E.A.R.

104

450 Manhattan Avenue
27 July [1901]

I have been occasionally conscious during the past few days that my last note to you was rather snappy and altogether inadequate as an expression of my feelings in regard to your appreciation of *C.C.*, however well it may have expressed my toothaches; so now I write this to assure you that I meant well. Of course I knew there would be qualifications; and I supposed there would be much more adverse criticism than I found.

Sincerely yours,
E.A.R.

105

450 West 23rd Street
14 October 1901

You may never have suspected such a thing, but I can assure you that your long letter of some time ago was received and duly appreciated. My ways of appreciating things—or rather of showing my appreciation—are as varied and peculiar as Samuel Weller's[1] knowledge of London, but I appreciate just the same. So I hope you will not be discouraged by my inaction, and that you will not wait as long as I have waited this time before writing again and telling me all about it—what you think of it, and how you think it is likely to turn out. I refer, of course, to this existence of ours and to the planets we see by reflected light. I don't care so much about the stars.

The nimble man Betts is much elated over his *Perfume-Holder*. It appears that he has made arrangements with a pair of fellows who are going to bring it out in the spring[2] with illustrations by Mr. Ibbetson Zeigler,[3] and there is a rumor that large numbers of copies have been engaged for (is that English? I don't know about such matters today. I don't much think it is, however), and that Betts is likely to do another of the same sort on the Troubador question. I hope this is all true, though I could wish that he might not be so cussedly objective. I may be all wrong, but it seems to me that this romantic story-poem writing is not just what the public is likely to encourage nowadays; and on the other hand I am well aware that my own poisonous dislike for all that sort of thing may make me one-sided in my judgment. But anyhow, the poem is to be published, and I am mighty glad of it. It will do the man no end of good.

I am inclined to believe with you that there is wisdom in Mrs. Hanson's suggestion in regard to an English publisher for *C.C.*[4] but for all that I shall continue to irritate the American houses for a while longer. Just now he is with McClure, Phillips & Company, at Wood's suggestion, but I don't know what they are doing with him. I must look Wood up, by the way, and find out how he feels—and what he thinks of it, also. The last time I saw him he was drinking a cocktail and trying to persuade me that I might do all sorts of things that I don't do. I told him that he was entirely wrong, but I didn't swear at him as I shall tomorrow. On the whole I think Wood is the most promising specimen that I have met in New York. I encourage him all I can, and I try to make myself believe that I am right when I damn him for dropping the -ugh from his *thoughs*. Of course I know that there will be no -ughs eventually, but somehow I hope I shall be dead before they are.[5] And yet I am modern enough in some ways—too modern for publishers, apparently. By the way, my new book[6] is with the Scribners. I think there is an apparition of a chance that it may be taken, but I can't say anything about it now.

The book contains a string of verses called "The Wife of Palissy"[7] which may trouble you a little—possibly.

Sincerely yours,
E.A.R.

1. Mr. Pickwick's witty and resourceful manservant in Dickens' *Pickwick Papers*.

2. *The Perfume-Holder; a Persian Love Poem*, originally published by Sealfield & Finch (New York, 1891), did not achieve a second edition (New York: Monarch Press) until 1910, which was dedicated "To Edwin Arlington Robinson."

3. In the lower margin Miss Brower wrote: "Lee Woodward Zeigler, whom I named Peter Ibbetson. The illustrations never came off."

4. Although not formally published in England, an English edition did technically precede the American by almost two months. See Hogan, *Bibliography*, pp. 7–8.

5. To the left of this Miss Brower wrote: "Me too!"

6. The selection of shorter poems which Robinson eventually included in *Captain Craig*.

7. Retitled "Partnership" beginning with *Collected Poems* (1921).

106

28 January 1902

If you still have a copy of that "Intermezzo,"[1] as I called it once on a time, please be thoughtful to tear it up.[2] It has been largely rewritten and some of the kinks have been taken out of it, I hope. If your friend Mr. Pershing[3] likes it in the old form he is a charitable man. Of course I shall be glad to see him if he finds time to take a journey to this part of the village.

This is not a learned letter, but just a word in the way of decency. I know nothing more concerning Small & Maynard, and I have no wish to investigate. I wish them well, on principle, but I don't understand how such rapscallions can succeed. Everything, however, seems to be possible with publishers. I have nothing yet to tell you in regard to the new book. H. & M. has not passed judgment on it.

Believe that I am your faithful servitor even though I don't write when I should.

Sincerely yours,
E.A.R.

1. Later titled "The Return of Morgan and Fingal" (see Letter 80, note 2).
2. To the right of this Miss Brower wrote: "I didn't."
3. Above this name Miss Brower wrote: "Theo Pershing."

107

[March–May 1902]

Dear Madam:

I fear that I have no better reason for not writing than the ancient one called laziness. Do not think me so silly as to pretend that I am not glad to get *C.C.* and the rest of them off my hands, for I am—devilish glad, in fact. The book will be out sometime this spring, probably in about a month. Then you will have a chance to consider the old fellow at your leisure and very likely to find him pretty bad in places. If you can drop him without breaking him I shall be satisfied, and I give you leave to drop him—though perhaps you had better not throw him. In that case his head might come off.

Betts is looking badly. He wants something that he will never get in this world—or perhaps I should say several things. I fancy his sister has taken several years from his life,—but on the other hand the man is so put together than he can't live alone, so perhaps I should [not] say this after all—even though I know it is true. The Doctor is writing poems about stars and goats. What are you doing?

Sincerely yours,
E.A.R.

108

15 Prescott Hall
Cambridge
8 July 1902

Dear Madam:

"There's this about the Hindu:
He does the best he kin do,
But when he wants
A pair of pants
He has to make his skin do."

This is what I learn in Cambridge. I learn also that this part of the world is nothing other than a long debauch of green. I see green, hear green, smell, taste and feel green. Probably I am green—I always was, in many ways. What I mean to say is that I am not a lost soul after all. Mason plays all sorts of Beethoven and things to me. I hope you got the *Marlowe*[1] this morning and that you are enjoying it.

Sincerely yours,
E.A.R.

1. Five-act tragedy published by Josephine Preston Peabody in Boston, 1901.

109

450 West 23rd Street
13 October 1902

I have been in no hurry to send you and Mrs. Hanson a copy of *C.C.* as I understood either from you or from her that you ordered the thing last June. Of course you would have got them eventually from me, but you know I'm awfully slow. I appreciate your last letter and it is good for me to know that your interest has not died out. "There was a pale artist named Ransom, whose hands were exceedingly handsome. To be sure they were seen he painted them green and held them all day through the transom." I hope to see you in New York this winter and I congratulate you on your coal. I will remember what you say of your study. Maybe I'll come along some cold day and snatch you out of it.

Sincerely yours,
E.A.R.

110

27 October 1902

It seems to me now that you may have been very much surprised after all at not receiving a copy of *C.C.* at the first. I had a few copies sent to me the afternoon before I left and I bundled them away as quickly as I could to such as I knew would not know what to make of it if they did not get one. Of course I thought of you first, but I understood that you had a copy on the way and so let you wait. Besides, I was so weary of the whole thing and so much in a hurry to get—forever, I hope—out of Boston, that I forget for the time all about such things as feelings and sentiments. I have lots of them but they aren't always on the surface, as you may have seen. I have not yet been up to see Mrs. Hanson but hope to some time this week. Meantime here I saw the Betts household, which has increased to the necessity of moving into larger quarters. I'm writing this in the dark, and you may find it easier to decipher under the same conditions. Didn't sleep until six this morning—ergo I'm nervous. At any rate my handwriting is.

Sincerely yours,
E.A.R.

III

450 West 23 Street
9 October 1903

I hardly know what [to say] to you, Edith Brower, now that Mrs. Hanson has told me of the death of your Aunt.[1] She must have suffered, and when one's sufferings are over I am not sure that it is always, or ever, kind to forget what one has gained in the light of what another has lost. I am vaguely aware that her death will make a complete change in your way of living; and I hope that the new life may somehow prove itself, as a development out of the old, something freer and larger (as regards your own choice) than anything that you have known before. I feel almost guilty for saying such commonplaces as this at such a time, but you know me too well to take anything amiss. At this moment I am only stupid. Forgive me for not replying to your letter from the mountains, and believe me when I tell you that I was strangely glad to get it.

Always sincerely yours,
E.A.R.

1. Miss Laura Gardiner Brower died on October 5, 1903, at seventy-eight years of age. She was cited by the local newspapers as "a member of one of Wilkes-Barre's pioneer families" who "possessed a noble character and lived a useful life"; and commended as "an earnest Christian woman" with a "charming personality" and deep sympathy "for those in distress." Shortly afterward, Miss Brower made her home with cousin Catharine Parsons, then moved to the Wyoming Valley Woman's Club.

112

OFFICE OF
SPECIAL AGENT TREASURY DEPARTMENT[1]
NEW YORK
23 August 1905

Thank you very much for your letter, for it does away with a fear of mine that you might think me your mortal enemy, or something of that sort. Still you must be sure that my silence has been more the result of a consciousness on my part that I had done what little (if anything) there was for me to do for you and that I should never fulfil your expectations. Perhaps I might have done that once, more or less, but now I seem to be pumped dry. Now and then I do a small thing, but it is always something that I had in mind some years ago. You will be satisfied if you take a few of my things that you like best and try to imagine that they represent Me. (I use a big M not out of vanity, but so that you can read it.) I shall keep on writing and sooner or later bring out my new book[2]—out of habit, apparently. No doubt I and a dozen others will like it as in the case of *C.C.*—and no doubt I shall believe in it in my blind way, but all this will have nothing to do with my feeling out of the game. This doesn't sound just like "enthusiasm," but yet I don't know what else to call it. It is something that keeps me going and knocks pessimism on the head. To be born without gas in one's make-up is not quite the same thing as it is to be born without illumination. It may be that I have electric lights—like the man who took Electric Bitters and wrote a testimonial. Anyhow; whether I have or have not, I have not forgotten you or the way in which you first called to me through my northern fog and made me realize that miles are nothing to speak of. I am sorry for much of the rather callow criticism that I made of your stories, but I don't see what I can do about that now. Sometime when you are at Mrs. Hanson's again I shall want to see you. I suppose you have heard about Betts and his romantics.[3] This makes me feel old.

Always sincerely yours,
E.A.R.

1. In June 1905 President Theodore Roosevelt appointed Robinson to a sinecure in the New York Custom House.

2. *The Town Down the River* (1910).

3. Possibly a reference to Betts's "Defence of the Long Sant," a versification of Parkman's account of the defense of Montreal by seventeen Frenchmen and five Algonquins against the whole armed power of the Iroquois Nation. Robinson may have seen an earlier version of this poem of thirty-three quatrains in iambic heptameter which appears in *Short Stories and Poems by American Authors* (New York, 1909), pp. 5–14.

113

NO. 1766. TREASURY DEPARTMENT
2 October [1905]

You are undoubtedly right in calling me a swine for not replying to your letter. If I had any reason for doing as I did, I suppose it was because I thought the matter was not of sufficient importance. Of course this is no reason, but still it is true that when I found that "U.A."[1] was to be tucked away in small type I felt that I was placed in a false suspicion.[2] After that I felt rather silly for taking a small matter so seriously. But it is still a question in my mind just why R.W.G.[3] should pay twenty dollars for a few lines to go along with J. K. Bangs & Co. No, dear child, I am not puffed up, but puzzled, and peradventure a bit punctured, as to my amazing dignity. *The Children* is coming out in a new dress in a week or so—a green dress, by the way. The Sons of Charles Scribner are doing it.[4]

Let me know when you come to town and I'll be as solemn, no doubt, as in times past. You make me solemn by taking me too seriously. I'm the jolliest cuss that ever was, but I have to be encouraged.

Adieu,
J. Brahms

1. "Uncle Ananias."
2. Above this word Miss Brower wrote: "position(?)"
3. Richard Watson Gilder (1844–1909), editor of *Century Magazine*, published the poem in August 1905 in the department "In Lighter Vein," which was devoted to trifles of comic prose and verse.
4. This second edition appeared on October 14, in green cloth with gold-stamped front cover and spine.

114

Gardiner
7 October 1909

Dear Madam:

Your letter has just come to me, having been forwarded from the Judson[1] after many days, which is unusual. As a rule letters are not forwarded from the Judson at all. You need not worry[2] about my becoming good to you. I hardly ever change unless people put toads in my pockets; and I have never suspected you of such proceedings. What you say of your wards is mostly new to me though I believe Mrs. Hanson talked of them last time I saw her—which was *rayther* long ago. I must change my ways, I fear, and not assume everlasting fidelity on the part of others without even giving a sign.

I expect to be in New York this winter and to finish a book. The good Gawd knows that I have been long enough at it.

Yours sincerely,
E.A.R.

1. In the autumn of 1906 Robinson went to live at the Hotel Judson in New York's Washington Square, where he consolidated his friendships with Percy MacKaye, William Vaughn Moody, Ridgely Torrence, Louis Ledoux, Daniel Gregory Mason, and May Sinclair, and became acquainted with others in the world of the arts.
2. In the lower margin Miss Brower wrote: "I didn't 'worry.'"

115

Chocorua, N.H.
1 November 1910

Dear E.B.:

I should have answered your first letter before this if I had not been a brute beast, as ever. I was very glad to get it, as I was duly humiliated today by the receipt of the second. There is no need of my telling you how much I appreciate everything you say about the book[1]—and you may be sure that I do not want you going back and digging out the blue-covered beginnings.[2] If my poetry is really good for anything, the same quality should be found in both books. I like to believe that the last one is a little better done and, as a whole, rather more worth doing—but my opinion may not be of much value.

I appreciated what you had to say about Moody. The last time I saw him I could not help knowing what was coming, sooner or later; and I am sure that it is only kindness and good sense on my part to be glad that it did not wait to come later.[3] He did enough as it was to give him his high place in English poetry—probably much higher than most of us realize today.

I have been down here in the mountains since the last of July and have written two-thirds of what I call a novel[4]—for the sake of a better name. Perhaps you will be able to classify it properly when it comes out. I am feeling pretty well considering and hope to be in New York before New Year's. Just what good I shall do there seems to be rather a problem. Please write whenever you feel that I ought to be stirred up and be sure that whatever you say will be gratefully "eyed over." Who was it said that? Oh yes, Simon Tappertit in *Barnaby Rudge*. I suppose you wouldn't read it for a thousand dollars.

Always sincerely yours,
E.A.R.[5]

1. *The Town Down the River* was published by Scribner's on October 8.
2. *The Torrent and the Night Before* (1896).
3. William Vaughn Moody died on October 17, 1910, from the effects of a brain tumor and typhoid fever.
4. Robinson spent the latter part of 1910 in Chocorua, New Hampshire, as the guest of Truman H. Bartlett, an old sculptor and rustic philosopher who had known Walt Whitman and who had a wide acquaintance among contemporary artists and writers. Robinson was attempting to turn his yet unpublished play *Van Zorn* into a novel. *Van Zorn* was brought out by Macmillan in September 1914, but Robinson never succeeded in converting any of his early short stories or later plays into publishable novels.
5. Following this letter, Miss Brower inserted one written by Dr. Coan to her, interesting for his opinion of Robinson's quality. The first and last paragraphs, irrelevant to this volume, are omitted.

New York
11 January 1911

Dear Ebee:

Yes. I have received and read the new Poems of Robinson. The best of them I think are his very best; "The Town Down the River," "Leonora," "For a Dead Lady," "The Gardener"—these have given me more pleasure than I would like to confess. There is a sacred beauty in them. What exquisite art in metre and rime—and what melody, what *ease*, what emotion! His admirers are not likely to be many, for a full half of the poems are obscure: and the greatest poets are not obscure. But his gift is intensely individual—that is the charm of it; his poems are full of distinction; they efface other poets as long as I am reading, which for me is the best proof of their quality; and so I pass by the failures. There are so few to forgive—"Saint Helena"* perhaps especially: this I do not like to read a second time.

T.M.C.

*In the left margin Miss Brower wrote: "Does he mean 'Saint Nitouche'?" She is referring to "Sainte-Nitouche," which appeared in *Captain Craig* (1902), but Coan means "An Island," subtitled "(Saint Helena, 1821)," in *The Town Down the River* (1910). The poem is a soliloquy by the exiled Napoleon, dying in a squalid atmosphere of omnipresent rats.

116

New York
2, 3, or 4 October 1912

Dear Lady:

Your letter found me only the other day, and it reminded me of all the letters that I have [not] written to you during the past year and a half. I'm glad that you have such a forgiving nature. I don't know that I have anything very new to tell you except that I am still worshipping strange gods.[1] Sooner or later I'll get back to my proper business I suppose, but I can't say for certain. I shall not be really settled anywhere until the first of November. I made a mighty and impressive huntsman, being so thoroughly disguised that nobody recognized me. I didn't know that Kilmer cared for my books until I saw him in the *Times*.[2] Ledoux's commentary[3] seemed to me to be rather necessary, and it came all the better being unexpected. I hope to see you when you come to town.

Yours always,
E.A.R.

1. Robinson spent much of the time between this letter and the last in converting his second play, *The Porcupine* (1915), into a novel and trying to ease his financial stress by turning out a popular drama. He published no poem in 1911 or 1912, and only one in 1913 (December).

2. In "A Classic Poet," *New York Times Review of Books* (September 8, 1912), p. 487, Joyce Kilmer reviewed *The Children of the Night*, *Captain Craig*, and *The Town Down the River*, calling Robinson "a student of mankind" whose poems are "compounded of sympathy and wonder."

3. Louis V. Ledoux, a generous friend of Robinson, responded to Kilmer's critique in the *Review* (September 29, 1912), p. 533. His letter, titled "A Discussion of the Exact Value of Robinson's Poetry," emphasizes its realism of characterization and the cryptic quality which does not yield itself lightly to casual readers or critics.

117

129 West 83 Street
21 December 1913

Dear E.B.:

I'm glad you liked Levi,[1] and that you did not think that he was one of the Twelve Tribes, or an East Side Jew, as several of the doubtful-owlish have seemed to think. It *was* rather nasty of his old mother to look him up and down as she did, but even then I suppose he couldn't run away. And he wouldn't have done much if he had.

I made him merely to let the Race-Optimist explain his optimism, and to justify it, if he can, from a materialistic point of view. Perhaps I've been hearing too much about the "race." Anyhow I'm sick of it.

Yours always sincerely,
E.A.R.

1. In "The Field of Glory."

118

129 West 83 Street
15 March 1914

Honored Lady:

I'm glad you liked my "Clinging Vine." Some do, some don't; and some (this time I'm really at sea) don't understand it. I thought it was, if anything, a little too clear. As for the obscure line in the "Dead Lady," I never thought of meaning or indicating anything more than her way of presuming on her attractions and "guying" those who admired her. Perhaps you looked for something deeper. Others have had similar trouble with "Vickery," trying to read into it all manner of stuff, when I merely meant that the gold was waiting for him, but that the Fates and devils wouldn't allow him to accumulate sufficient sense and energy to go and get it. Maybe there is so much Vickery in all of us that we don't recognize him when he is set before us.

I'm sending a copy of *Poetry* with this containing one of my more recent offenses entitled "Eros Turannos."[1] You aren't obliged to like it, though I rather hope you will.

Yours sincerely,
E.A.R.

1. *Poetry*, III (March 1914), 206–207.

119

129 West 83 Street
1 April 1914

Dear E.B.:

I'm glad you liked "Eros" and I thank you for all you say about it. A few have called it cynical, but I haven't the smallest notion as to what they mean. You will find another ensample of my wurruk in the current *Scribner's*.[1]

You are good to think of writing another article, but I don't like to give you much encouragement. I'm afraid you will have the devil and all of a time in disposing of me. And when you do, please don't quote that incriminating first "Octave,"[2] which is a little the worst thing that I have done—and that is saying much.

Yours sincerely,
E.A.R.

1. "The Gift of God," *Scribner's*, LV (April 1914), 485.
2. Robinson is referring to the first of the series of octaves in *The Children of the Night* (1897), p. 91—"To get at the eternal strength of things." He retained it in the 1905 edition but omitted it from his collected poems thereafter. Miss Brower had quoted the octave in full in her 1897 article (see Appendix II).

120

Wednesday [15 April 1914][1]

Dear E.B.:

Thank you for your good nature and for your second invitation. I am booked for Saturday evening with the man who wrote the *Forum* article.[2] I had never heard of him at the time of its publication and have met him but once or twice since. He seems to be a very good sort. So you may look for me next Monday at five-thirty.

Yours sincerely,
E.A.R.

1. This date penciled in here by Miss Brower.
2. Otto Frederick Theis, "Edwin Arlington Robinson," *Forum*, LI (February 1914), 305–312.

121

129 West 83 Street
23 April 1914

Dear E.B.:

I was glad for your letter and especially for the P.S. which contained a great deal of truth, although it did not explain all my foolish talk about your friend[1] the other evening. That was almost wholly a matter of nerves. I have those "attacks" now and then, and am always sorry for them afterwards. The kindest thing you can do will be to forget it. Of course I know that he did not realize how unpleasant he made himself on certain occasions or how utterly impossible it was for him to understand my condition at the time. Sometime or other I may be communicative enough to tell you something about myself.

Yours always sincerely,
E.A.R.

1. Carroll Brent Chilton.

122

Care L. V. Ledoux, Esq.
CORNWALL-ON-HUDSON
25 October 1914

Dear E.B.:

It was surely good of you to read my drammer[1] aloud to your friends and it was surely good of them to stand it—the drammer I mean, not your reading, which I'm sure was effective. What you say gives me great pleasure, for I've never pretended not to be human. Some people think I'm not, but that's because I don't know how to talk. By the way, I wish you would tell me how long, or about how long, it took you to do the reading. I fancy the thing will have to be cut if it gets near to the stage—within egg-distance of it, so to speak.

Yours sincerely,
E.A.R.

1. *Van Zorn,* a comedy in three acts, was published by Macmillan on September 23, 1914.

123

51 West 84 Street
30 November 1914

Dear E.B.:

It begins to look as if *Van Zorn* has missed fire and all for reasons that might have been rectified in ten minutes if it had ever occurred to me that there were any difficulties. I am beginning to realize, considerably to my chagrin, that the very people who read it in MS. praised it, and seemed to understand it, could not have known what it was really about. I am going to be mean enough to ask you to give me the briefest possible sketch of the plot, or rather the situation, as you understand it. If you "fall down" you needn't be at all worried, for you will be one of a rather large company.

The disgusting thing about the whole matter is, as I have said, that I could have made everything clear by the insertion of fewer than a dozen short speeches before the play went to press.[1]

Yours sincerely,
E.A.R.

1. There was general agreement among the reviewers of the book that the plot of *Van Zorn* was fairly easy to follow but the characterization was puzzling, indistinct, and ineffective. The anonymous critic in the *Dial*, LVIII (January 16, 1915), put it most succinctly: "As the reader begins to turn the pages of Mr. Edwin Arlington Robinson's *Van Zorn*, various questions rise in his mind. Who is Van Zorn? Who is Villa Vannevar, the heroine? What have been their past relations with each other? with George Lucas? with Farnham? There is no exposition to satisfy his curiosity; but he consoles himself with the thought that as he goes on these matters will become clear. On the contrary, he becomes more and more bewildered. . . . Mr. Robinson keeps his secrets, or reveals them only in riddles. . . . The play will be a good subject for some future doctor's thesis" (p. 48).

124

[7 December 1914][1]

Dear E.B.:

A woman told me the other evening that she understood *VZ* and I told her that I would give her one minute to tell me the plot. "Why of course I can do that." she said. "Van Zorn believed it his destiny to marry the girl, and probably would have got her if Lucas hadn't been in the way." Now put that book away and forget it—but please don't forget *me*.

Yours sincerely,
E.A.R.

This is in reply to your card.

1. This date penciled in over the salutation by Miss Brower.

125

51 West 84 Street
18 December 1914

Dear E.B.:

I am sending with this a Boston interpretation of *VZ*[1] which is in the main correct, though I doubt if he would have gone quite so far as to "declare his love" just then, even if Lucas hadn't been in his way. In the same small magazine you will find your old friend "The Burning Book."[2]

I am glad to get your letters, and you needn't be so sorry over a small matter.

Yours sincerely,
E.A.R.

1. The *Cornhill Booklet*, IV (December 1914), 90–91, carried a four-paragraph review by W.S.B. (William Stanley Braithwaite). The first two paragraphs praise Robinson in general as "America's foremost poet." The last two consider *Van Zorn* a play "of the very tightest texture" which "demands very careful reading and intelligent sympathy." The statement Robinson questions is "To save the happiness of Farnham and Villa, and himself, [Van Zorn] compels his friend to arrange an interview with the girl in which he intends to declare his own love."
2. "The Burning Book" appears on page 69 of this issue.

126

[1914][1]

It's all over, as I thought. What you say is well enough, so far as it goes, but like most readers, say eight out of ten, you seem to have missed the plot itself, which envelops everything that you have talked about. Apparently you have been so much interested in Lucas's drinking that you have not stopped to consider why VZ should take up so much room or so much time. I don't know whether the trouble is with me or with you and all the others or with the English language; and I don't know that it makes much difference. Not to mention twenty or thirty other places, you (and the others) seemed to have skipped from page 58 to the end of Act I, to have read the second half of Act II, and the long scene at the end of the play between VZ and Farnham, with no regard whatever for what it is all about. Don't think I'm "mad at you" for I'm not. I'm only a little mad at myself for working eight years over a thing and only to find it a puzzle for the public. I can only suppose that the plot is so simple and so obvious that you didn't notice it, and yet a sufficient number do get it to convince me that I'm not altogether an idiot.

So much for Buckingham. I wrote the "Dark Lady" in twenty minutes and got twenty dollars for it. If I could keep this up I could have a King Ludwig[2] performance of *Van Zorn.*

May all health and happiness attend you—and please put the play out of sight and forget it.

Yours always sincerely,
E.A.R.

1. This date penciled in at the end of the letter by Miss Brower.
2. King Ludwig of Bavaria invited Richard Wagner to stage his operas in Munich and provided him large grants to realize his large ambitions.

127

Tuesday [January 1915][1]

Dear E.B.:

The enclosed[2] will make you a little mad[3] and it may at the same time amuse you.

Happy New Year.

Yours,
E.A.R.

1. This date penciled in at the bottom of the letter by Miss Brower.

2. In the upper margin Miss Brower wrote: "Cassandra." The poem appeared in the Boston *Evening Transcript* (December 21, 1914), p. 17.

3. In the lower margin Miss Brower wrote: "Evidently he thinks me a 'pacifist.' But Cassandra is here addressing the pocketbook pacifists."

128

51 West 84 Street
Thursday [January 1915][1]

Dear E.B.:

I'm glad you aren't "mad." I may write a sonnet to you sometime. As for "The Stalwart Oak," of course, I should like to see it. I'm a little puzzled at what you say of my "Old Lady."[2] I don't remember sending you the MS. and I didn't know that Hapgood had published it in his toy *Weekly*.[3] If he has done so, can you tell me when, or about when? In the current *Outlook*[4] you will find a thing of mine that several people insist upon liking. I'm not sure that I don't like it myself.

Yours,
E.A.R.

1. This date penciled in the upper margin by Miss Brower.

2. "The Voice of Age." See Letter 130, note 4.

3. Norman Hapgood (1868–1937) was editor of *Harper's Weekly* from 1913 to 1916.

4. "Flammonde," *Outlook*, CIX (January 6, 1915), 37–38.

129

51 West 84 Street
Monday [January 1915][1]

Dear E.B.:

I wished for certain reasons to get a copy of *Harper's Weekly* containing the "Old Lady"[2] but I have heard nothing from the editors since writing to them. Now it seems to me that you may possibly have seen the thing in MS. though I cannot understand where or how. Will you kindly send me a word by return mail? My relations with the *Weekly* people are a bit strained on account of their methods and I should like to be sure that the poem has been printed before stirring them up again.

Yours,
E.A.R.

1. This date penciled in the upper margin by Miss Brower.
2. In the lower margin Miss Brower wrote: "Does he mean 'The Voice of Age' in *The Man Against the Sky*?"

130

[27 January 1915][1]

Dear E.B.:

I like the poem[2] and the way in which the man gets after her. Incidentally I feel highly complimented. The sonnet[3] is a good tribute to you, although it isn't a very good sonnet. At the same time it has internal evidence to indicate that the author could write a good one if she cared enough to try. If you want the long poem back let me know.

I suppose you noticed the proofreader knocked my "Old Lady" dead in the first stanza—twice, in fact.[4] I knew something would be wrong in that sheet.

Yours,
E.A.R.

1. This date penciled in the right margin by Miss Brower.
2. In the upper margin Miss Brower wrote: "K.M.'s 'Stalwart Oak.'"
3. To the right of this Miss Brower wrote: "to E.B."
4. "The Voice of Age" in *Harper's Weekly*, LIX (September 12, 1914), 250, contained these errors: in line 2, *Rhadamanths* for *Rhadamanthus*; in line 3, *ane* for *one*.

131

Peterborough, N.H.
29 July 1915

Dear E.B.:

I was on the point of saying How are You when your card came. I see that you are alive and I trust that you are moderately happy and that you may find your way to this place[1] again this year. There is to be no regular festival, but there will be some more or less irregular choral singing in the Town Hall sometime about the 29th of August. Your name comes up rather often, from which I gather that you left a not altogether unpleasant impression.[2]

I've just sent away the last proofs of another play, and I shall have another book of poems for you some time in February.[3] After that, the good Lord only knows.

Yours always sincerely,
E.A.R.

1. The MacDowell Colony for encouragement and support of creative work by composers, writers, and artists was founded in Peterborough, New Hampshire, in 1908 by Marian Nevins MacDowell as a memorial to her husband Edward, the American composer. Consisting of a large central house and numbers of secluded, individual cabin-studios set amid mountains and woodlands, the 400-acre retreat was maintained largely through the proceeds of Mrs. MacDowell's lecture-recitals. Robinson was persuaded by Hermann Hagedorn to spend the summer of 1911 here, found the privacy and pastoral quiet so conducive to the writing of poetry that he returned every summer until his death. Besides himself, some fifteen others produced Pulitzer Prize winners here (e.g., Thornton Wilder, Aaron Copland, Willa Cather, Stephen Vincent Benèt).

2. Miss Brower never went to the MacDowell Colony as an artist, nor specifically to visit Robinson. She accompanied Modesta Ximena there to study with Mrs. MacDowell on two occasions and stayed briefly.

3. *The Porcupine*, a drama in three acts, was published on September 15, 1915; *The Man Against the Sky* on February 16, 1916—both by Macmillan.

132

Peterborough, N.H.
31 August 1915

Dear E.B.:

I don't think I acknowledged your good words about "Pauvrette."[1] Whether I did or not, I appreciated them. I fancy somehow that it will make a more general effect than most of my things, for nearly everyone must know somebody to whom it will apply to some degree. I wish it were not so, but unfortunately—from one point of view—it is so. I remember your cousin and have thought of her many times when I have been inclined to whine over little difficulties. It takes a woman always to make a man feel really foolish in the face of trouble.[2]

There seems to be nothing new about myself. You will be getting another play in the course of two or three weeks, and sometime before very long a book of pomes. I wish for the sake of appearances that I were a more voluminous producer, but someone else appears to have control of that part of my inferior destiny. I can only hope that it won't seem altogether too inferior when I have said the last of my say.

Yours sincerely,
E.A.R.

1. In the upper margin Miss Brower wrote: "Printed under title 'The Poor Relation' (in *The Man Against the Sky*)."

2. Catharine Parsons suffered from chronic disease in the last years of her life. She had conducted a private nursery school for girls and later taught at the Wilkes-Barre Institute.

133

66 West 83 Street
16 November 1915

Dear E.B.:

Thank you for your last message, such as it was,* and for your praise and admiration in regard to "Bokardo." If by any chance you saw my "Unforgiven" in *Scribner's* for November you saw that I have really a better opinion of men than "The C.V."[1] may have led you to fancy. The whole immortal mush is now with the printer and the book will be out sometime.

Yours to command,
E. A. Robinson

* Referring of course to its length. Why don't you write long letters —like me?

1. "The Clinging Vine," appeared originally in *Atlantic Monthly*, CXIII (February 1914), 218–220, and was reprinted in *The Man Against the Sky* (1916).

134

THE COVENTRY STUDIOS
121 WASHINGTON PLACE
Tuesday [1915][1]

Your note just received. Will see you as soon as I can get around—perhaps tomorrow.

Yours,
E.A.R.

1. 121 Washington Place was the site of Mrs. Clara Davidge's home, in the back yard of which she had a cottage-studio built for Robinson, to his own specifications. This letter and the following three, also undated, were placed in this order by Miss Brower.

135

[1915]

Dear E.B.:

Did I ask you to change Rachel's name to Brewster[1] and did I thank you for your good words about "Bokardo"? I'm afraid it's too late to do anything about the former, and if the play isn't big enough (it is supposed to be passably big) to live down one mistake, it doesn't matter much anyhow. Your interest in the poem gives me joy, for I doubt if many will care for it. It isn't pretty enough. When you write again, try care George Burnham, 99 St. Botolph St., Boston.

Yours sincerely,
E.A.R.

This is the last of my paper, and it isn't even mine.

1. In the upper margin Miss Brower wrote: "in *The Porcupine*."

136

Monday [1915]

Dear E.B.:

Here is the poem,[1] but [I] know your friend will not be able to read it. The only way to read my poems is get my books and then read 'em. I didn't even know that autograph poems were supposed to be read.

Well, I wish you good luck in your new attempt with *C.C.*[2] There are no changes to speak of. I don't expect you to spot them.

Yours sincerely,
E.A.R.

1. In the right margin Miss Brower wrote: "'For a Dead Lady,' copied on my request, for Mrs. F. W. Hart's (4 Marlboro St., Boston) Autograph Book."
2. The first revised edition of *Captain Craig* was published by Macmillan on February 10, 1915.

137

129 West 83 Street
Tuesday [1915]

Dear E.B.:

I seem to be really working just now, and as long as you are to be in town for some time, I'm going to be contrary enough to ask if you can let me see you some day—almost any day—at five-thirty. I do all my work between one and five—when I do any—and as my work is the only thing that gives me an excuse for staying alive, sometimes I have to seem perhaps a little selfish. I'm not that really, as you know.

Yours sincerely,
E.A.R.

138

66 West 83 Street
17 January 1916

Dear E.B.:

Thank you for "them kind words." Both plays have fallen utterly flat, and the few people who have read them—with one or two exceptions—don't even know what they are about. I may as well confess that all this leaves me a bit bewildered, for they seem to me at least to be interesting. I still nourish a more or less idiotic faith in their coming to life some day. The enclosed from the *Transcript* may explain correctly the chief difficulty.[1]

By the way, let me apologize once more for my careless and foolish talk about your friend C.C.[2] I was in a miserable state of mind and nerves that evening, and I suppose I simply had to let off steam. I wish him well, and have no feeling for or against him that is worse than the indifference that he has, in all probability, for me. We can't control these things.

The new book is due to appear about the first of February.[3] When it comes out you will receive a copy with my benediction.

Yours sincerely,
E.A.R.

1. William Stanley Braithwaite, "A Poet as a Dramatist," Boston *Evening Transcript* (December 24, 1915), III, 6. Braithwaite's most incisive comment is: "In *The Porcupine* as in *Van Zorn*, the action is deep, so deep that the mind has got to dive underneath the surface to feel it." Robinson's murky psychologizing and dearth of dramatic vigor put the stamp of closet drama on both his plays.

2. Carroll Brent Chilton.

3. *The Man Against the Sky* was published by Macmillan on February 16, 1916.

139

66 West 83 Street
1 March 1916

Dear E.B.:

It is good of you to like as much of the book as you have read and I hope you may succeed in reading the rest of it without too much labor. I am particularly glad that you like my "Man." I suppose, as you say, that superficial readers will call it "pessimistic,"[1] that being one of the easiest words to toss about. For instance, it has the great advantage of not meaning anything.

Yours always sincerely,
E.A.R.

1. Robinson's reference is to his poem "The Man Against the Sky." In the lower margin Miss Brower wrote: "*Amy Lowell* does! Ha! Ha!"

140

[1916][1]

Dear E.B.:

If I had written "No fate has made the man a beggar," you would have had no trouble with the construction, which is the same as that of the passage that puzzled you. "No irritant has made a waste a foretaste." You may put "of" after "made" if you like, but I don't see the need of it.[2] I glanced over the article in the *Poetry Review*[3] but didn't have a chance to read it. I'll send and get a copy if you think it so illuminating. I haven't seen *Poetry* but will look it up.[4] I understand that Amy Lowell is to get after me in the *New Republic*,[5] also that she thinks my "Man" a message of despair, which isn't at all what I meant it to be. The end is, as you say, a *reductio ad absurdum*. I thought that sufficiently obvious.

I met C.C. some time ago, unexpectedly, and while I was trying to think of something to say to him he disappeared. I suppose he thought I cut him, but I had no intention of doing so. He gave Betts a finger to shake the other evening, and Betts in his turn disappeared. I haven't the slightest ill will towards the man, but someone should tell him not to patronize his inferiors quite as he does.[6]

Yours,
E.A.R.

1. This date penciled in the upper margin by Miss Brower. In the upper margin she also wrote: "In reply to my expressed difficulties with passage on p. 144 in 'The Man Against the Sky.'"

2. On the reverse of this letter Miss Brower wrote: "This puzzling passage would appear to mean that none of the practical issues of life involving material necessities, no dream of social reform, no hypotheses of science can explain our *raison d'être*. And the argument that follows is based upon the simple, obvious absurdity of living at all and reproducing ourselves unless there is Something Else, Somewhere Else worth going on for. Same thought as in letter of June 1, 1919—there expressed with perfect clarity."

3. Edmund R. Brown, "A Master of Thought and Speech," *Poetry Journal*, V (March 1916), 82–89.

4. Harriet Monroe, "A Pioneer," *Poetry*, VIII (April 1916), 46–48.

5. Amy Lowell, "E. A. Robinson's Verse," *New Republic*, VII (May 27, 1916), 96–97. In the left margin Miss Brower wrote: "She did finely—see clipping." Miss Lowell did praise Robinson more than she "got after" him. She found his poems "dynamic with experience and knowledge of life," conceived with "original thought, original expression." Regarding "The Man Against the Sky," she observed that "Mr. Robinson is constantly affirming his optimism, and each affirmation only seems to bring out more clearly the innate pessimism from which he is forcing himself to flee." In closing, she remarked: "This poetry is 'cribbed, cabin'd and confined' to an unusual degree, but it is undeniably, magnificently noble."

6. Miss Brower, still smarting over Robinson's outburst against her friend Carroll Chilton, scrawled lines across the entire passage.

141

66 West 83 Street
5 February 1917

Dear E.B.:[1]

I don't know what B's book[2] will be like when it comes out, or whether it is ever coming out. On the whole, I rather hope it won't for the present. The new poem[3] is due some time this month, and there is worse to come. Therefore, cheer up and pray. *Van Zorn* is to be enacted in Brooklyn on the 26th, and if it survives will be taken to Philadelphia and New York.[4] If it should prove a total failure,[5] perhaps nothing could be better for me. I hope seriously that all my friends will stay away from the first night, for there may be no second—although the thing is billed for a week, with matinees Wednesday and Saturday. It will be funny, anyhow, and will give you another chance to laugh.

Happy New Year.

E.A.R.

1. On the reverse of this letter Miss Brower wrote: "The numbering of letters from No. 129 [138] to 131a [141] seem curiously mixed. The dates, too, for R. in 129 [138] writes of the failure of both plays, tho only one—*Van Z.* was then out and it hadn't been played." The confusion is Miss Brower's. *The Porcupine* was published on September 15, 1915, and Letter 129 [138] was written on January 17, 1916. Her numbering of the letters shows inconsistencies throughout the collection.

2. Craven Langstroth Betts's *The Two Captains, at Longwood, at Trafalgar*, a volume of poems, appeared in 1921.

3. *Merlin* was published by Macmillan on March 14, 1917.

4. The Brooklyn Community Theatre Company performed *Van Zorn* in the Central Auditorium of the Brooklyn Y.M.C.A. for a week beginning Monday, February 26, 1917. It did not survive to travel.

5. On the reverse of this letter Miss Brower wrote: "Mrs. MacDowell, writing me after its presentation in Brooklyn, said it was admirable and *most notable* and that all who saw it—a picked audience—thought so. Yet it did 'fail' —then."

142

Peterborough, N.H.
24 June 1917

Dear E.B.:

I'm glad to know that you like *Merlin*—if you do—although I am sorry that you are having such a hard time with him. For once in my life I thought I had written something that would read straight along, and even now I don't quite see how it can be read in any other way. But as I have long given up pretending to know anything about myself or my work, you needn't mind what I say, only, I wish you wouldn't call the poem "sad" for I'm——if it is anything of the kind. There is nothing especially sad about the end of kings and the redemption of the world, and that is what Merlin seems to be driving at. He is also a suffragist, as you must have noticed.

You may or may not be pleased to learn that I am halfway along with "Lancelot and Guinevere,"[1] which is another breed of cats. I expect to leave Camelot sometime about the first of September.

Yours sincerely,
E.A.R.

1. Robinson's working title for *Lancelot* (1920).

143

Peterborough, N.H.
9 August 1917

Dear E.B.:

As I haven't seen the *Bookman* for July or heard anything about the parody,[1] I'm afraid that I cannot enlighten [you] to any satisfying extent as to the purpose, import, or comport of the mysterious contribution. I'll send and get a copy and then I may be able to tell you something. I don't quite see the relation between "B.J." and R.B.[2]—but I suppose I shall have to be "like Browning" to the end of my days. The one man with whom I have a sort of internal affinity seems to me to be Heine, but no one else seems to have thought of it.

Was there any signature to the review of *Merlin* in the *Evening Post* of July 21[3]—or maybe you didn't see it. Patronizing, but otherwise rather good.

Yours sincerely,
E.A.R.

"G & A."[4] was written a year ago, as an ante-*Merlin* exercise, at two sittings. A few seem to like it.

1. On page 524 of the *Bookman*, XLV (July 1917), William Rose Benét caricatured Browning and Robinson wrapped in long, conspiratorial cloaks, huddled closely together under a lightless moon on a black night. The caption reads: "Edwin Arlington Robinson meets the man from Asolo at midnight." The satire is based on lines 1, 2, and 12 of Browning's poem, "Meeting at Night," which speak of "the long black land," "the yellow half-moon large and low," (Benét depicts a full moon), and "two hearts beating each to each!" Deny it as he might, in these letters and elsewhere, Robinson never escaped the implication of Browning influence.

2. Robinson's poem "Ben Jonson Entertains a Man from Stratford" and Robert Browning.

3. "Idylls of the Queen, Arthur and his court celebrated in a poem which does homage to woman," on page 4 of the New York *Evening Post* Saturday magazine section (July 21, 1917) was unsigned.

4. "Genevieve and Alexandra" first appeared in *Bookman*, XLV (May 1917), 252–259.

144

66 West 83 Street
12 December 1917

Dear E.B.:

Of course I am much pleased with all you have to say, but I don't yet understand that I am so darned (that's darned, not damned) successful. The specialists know me, but I don't believe there are fifteen people in say Oshkosh that ever read a line of me. Possibly it's better for me that I don't know. Miss L.[1] did pretty well in some ways, but she didn't see at all what I was trying to do in *Merlin*—which seems to have, as I understand it, both a beginning and an end; and tapestry is about the last thing that it would ever bring to my mind. But on the whole I'm grateful to her for what she says, and I think she meant to be sincere. Anyhow, she hasn't done me any harm. Be sure to let me know when you come to town.

Yours sincerely,
E.A.R.

1. In "Edwin Arlington Robinson," *Tendencies in Modern American Poetry* (New York, 1917), pp. 3–75, Amy Lowell said of *Merlin*: "Can the poem be said really to end? So little rounded it is, that it almost seems as though it might have stopped before or after the last line without affecting the result. . . . The poem is a piece snipped off a heavily brocaded tapestry, but the scissors might have cut either to the right or to the left of the line they did take without injuring the whole" (p. 69).

145

810 Washington Avenue
Brooklyn[1]
15 April 1918

Dear E.B.:

I was sorry to learn the other day through Betts, that you have been having a long illness; and I hope, in spite of my failure to write before, that you will tell me that you are much better. I appreciated all the good words in your last letter—of a long time ago, I regret to say—but of course I was careful not to let you know it. I have been rewriting my *Lancelot* this winter, and I'm now at work on what should some time or other take the form of a Book of Short Things[2]—although that isn't to be the name of it. More than this, I haven't much to say of myself. I go to town once in a while to see a good friend or a poor show, but for the most part I'm here in semi-exile, and doing very well considering.

Yours sincerely,
E.A.R.

1. For the next four years (excepting summers, which were spent at the MacDowell Colony) Robinson lived in a small apartment with his boyhood friend Seth Ellis Pope, who had left teaching to become a librarian.
2. *The Three Taverns* (1920).

146

Peterborough, N.H.
2 June 1918

Dear E.B.:

Your left-handed letter of some time ago was greatly appreciated although I fear you must have wondered whether the recipient was worthy of such an effort on your part. At any rate, he should have acknowledged it long before this. Please forgive his defection and send him a line to let him know that you are much better. I don't know neuritis, but I do know "shingles"—having had 'em good in my turbulent twenties. I'm sorrier for you than I can say.

I hope to do something this summer, but I shall feel [all] the time that I ought to be driving a mule in France,[1] and yet, if the world is worth having, I suppose it is best for one who is almost a rickety quinquagenarian (almost) to do what he can do rather than use himself up in trying to do what he can't do. There is no danger of my having too joyous a time, in any event. I can only hope that I may leave a little something that will add a little something to the lives of a few others. This sounds rather silly, and yet I suppose I mean it.

Anyhow, I am

Yours always sincerely,
E.A.R.

1. The United States had declared war against Germany on April 6, 1917, and American soldiers were fighting in France in the closing battles of World War I.

147

Peterborough, N.H.
20 August 1918

Dear E.B.:

I'm going to say Hello again in the hope of getting some sort of chirp in reply, and to the general effect that your damnable neuritis is better—or, better yet, gone. Why should a praiseworthy and altogether admirable person like yourself have to suffer, while others one wouldn't name go through this world dancing and waving jugs all their days! You don't know.

Nothing new as to myself except that I have "done" the better part of another harmless unnecessary book—"L & G"[1] in the mean (sic) time gathering dust.

Your obedient servant,
E.A.R.

1. "Lancelot and Guinevere," working title for *Lancelot*.

148

810 Washington Avenue
Brooklyn
26 December 1918

Dear E.B.:

It is good to see your proper handwriting once and to know that you are at least on your way to daylight again. I have been intending to write you for some time past and should have sent you some sort of Christmas card if I hadn't been so completely out of sorts. I thought I was going to have influenza and then decided to have something else—just what, I don't know, but I'm pretty well out of it now. I'm glad to know that you approve of "The Valley."[1] Some don't—calling it "pessimistic." I have about come to the conclusion that timidity is the besetting sin of the American mind. We can face germs and Germans, but we get behind the nearest tree at the approach of anything that really is. Besides which, the thing is full of the most engaging humor. May the New Year take away the last of your pain.

Yours always sincerely,
E.A.R.

1. "The Valley of the Shadow" first appeared in *Atlantic Monthly*, CXXII (December 1918), 783–785.

149

810 Washington Avenue
20 March 1919

Dear E.B.:

I am so tangled up this week with engagements that I cannot see an evening until Sunday. Will you let me know if that will be convenient for you? If you would like it better I can come late in the afternoon—or Monday between four and six, Anyhow, I hope very much to see you.

Yours sincerely,
E.A.R.

150

Peterborough, N.H.
1 June 1919

Dear E.B.:

You will see from this that I have come back to the woods; and I may add that it is infinitely good to be here. How are you? I was glad for that glimpse of you in New York, for your apparent patience under difficulties always has a good effect on me. The world, meanwhile, is undoubtedly a hell of a place; and I cannot see that there would be any logical reason for its existence if it were otherwise. For if we aren't continuous, what the deuce are we anyhow, and why? Which accounts, if anything, for the High Cost of Living. I'm sending you my St. Paul,[1] who touches lightly on the subject.

Yours always sincerely,
E.A.R.

1. "The Three Taverns," which appeared first in *Lyric*, III (May–June 1919), 6–14.

151

810 Washington Avenue
Brooklyn
17 November 1919

Dear E.B.:

It was good of you to assume that I am still alive. No man thinks of his friends oftener than I, or writes to them less frequently to let them know it. Consequently, I suppose they don't believe it. Well, it's true, and it's true that I'm back in Brooklyn, apparently for another winter. As for the books, *Lancelot* is likely to appear sometime before long as a prize poem[1]—God help us. It's too bad, but somehow it had to be so. The other book may be out before spring, or it may not. All that depends. As a whole, I think you will succeed in liking it, though you don't haveter. You might tell me about your visit from Myers, and what he had to say for himself. And you might if you can, tell me that you are all right again after your infernal neuritis.

Yours to command,
E.A.R.

1. *Lancelot* won a prize of $500 in the Lyric Society competition and was brought out for the Society in a special limited edition of 450 copies by Thomas Seltzer on the same day the first trade edition was issued.

152

Peterboro, N.H.
25 June 1920

Dear E.B.:

Whatever there may be in store for this place it is going on for this season,[1] and apparently I am going on with it. But I thank you and Miss Reynolds[2] all the same for your suggestion—or rather, invitation—and sometime or other, if it is still good, I may put in my superannuated appearance. Now that I am fifty years old, I find it fifty times harder than before to go anywhere, and I've lost all my social curiosity. But there are still a few people left whose word I am willing to take, and this willingness may take me to your mountains for a day or two sometime or other.

I am not at all sure that the new book[3] is better than *Merlin*, though I fancy it will be, for most of my fifty-seven readers, a little easier going. So far as my opinion is good for anything, my nearest to doing something is to be found somewhere in these two poems and in "Ben Jonson"—and I rather like some of the shorter things. Your persistent approval from the beginning has been of greater value to me than I have even so much as tried to tell you in language. But I have said it all in silence, much of which you have heard. The new book[4] will be ready in September.[5]

1. Established twelve years earlier, the MacDowell Colony was almost entirely dependent upon Mrs. MacDowell's fundraising tours. She used to say that she had put "about a penny down and the rest was mortgage." The Colony remained in precarious financial condition until 1927, when a group of New Hampshire clubs paid off the heavy mortgage.

2. Edith Reynolds, a younger and close friend of Miss Brower, studied painting under Robert Henri and wrote poems, biographical sketches, and plays. When the MacDowell Colony seemed in danger of closing, she offered Robinson the use of her studio, "Highfield," in Dallas, Pennsylvania, for the summer. See also Letter 166.

3. *Lancelot* was published by Thomas Seltzer on April 12, 1920.

4. *The Three Taverns* was published by Macmillan on September 7, 1920.

5. About one-third of this sheet is cut off below this line, presumably for Robinson's signature.

153

810 Washington Avenue
Brooklyn
2 November 1920

Dear E.B.:

I must be growing old. Anyhow, I cannot be sure whether I have or haven't acknowledged your letter in which you say so many pleasant things about my *Taverns*. You say so many of them, in fact, that I am altogether in a state of embarrassment when it comes to saying anything in return—even though I may have already tried to say it. On the whole, I am not displeased with your final preference for *Merlin*, for I am inclined to believe that my best work is there, though the subject matter of *Lancelot* is infinitely more appealing. If you think it is easy to make anything beautiful out of an amorous Merlin in his dotage, just try it for a hundred lines or so. Beauty wasn't just what I was after; and whatever it was, I'm lucky if I got it. I like still to think that Vivian isn't altogether a failure, though I grant that she may in reality have got rid of the old fellow a little sooner than she did in the poem. The new book seems to be starting well, and generally, so far as I can see, in accord with your highly valuable approval. I am rather surprised at the number who wax glad over "Tasker Norcross."

Always your obedient servant,
E.A.R.

154

810 Washington Avenue
6 January 1921

Dear E.B.:

This is just a word to thank you for your letters and for the article on Japanese stained glass.[1] I didn't know before that any Jap had gone in for that sort of thing—but good Lord, there are so many things that I don't know. Your approval of my *Taverns* gives me great satisfaction, and I'm glad to say that it seems to be taking hold. My dime novel[2] is now with the printer and my collected wurruks are due in the fall. You might run over the contents of *The Children* again, and tell me which of the poems you dislike most. I am tempted to make a pretty thorough job of it, and yet, if I do so, I'm afraid there won't be much left.

Yours, very much as usual,
E. A. Robinson

If I asked you to do this before, please forgive me. You are great at that.

1. Edith Brower, "Stained Glass in Japan," *International Studio*, LXXII (December 1920), supplement, pp. 45–54.

2. The title poem of *Avon's Harvest* (March 1921) contains elements of mystery and melodrama.

155

810 Washington Avenue
22 January 1921

Dear E.B.:

While I agree with you to a considerable extent it appears to be impossible for me to accept all your pleas for life. So I fear that you will not be altogether satisfied when told that in the book that is now ready for the printer the following are sentenced to death:

The World

Ballade of a Ship

Two Octaves

x Poems by Matthew Arnold — I can't agree with you here at all—at all.

Kosmos

Thomas Hardy

x The Miracle

The Night Before

Walt Whitman

Romance

Octaves I and III

and probably Ballade of Dead Friends.

There are several more that ought to go, but I have decided to let them die a natural death. I am very much obliged to you for going over these again and hope that the poems didn't bore you too much. Now I'm cleaning some of the rubbish out of *C.C.*—much, I fancy, to its advantage. Any attempt to change the general key and flavor of so ingrained a thing would be useless, and I am not attempting it.

Yours always sincerely,
E.A.R.

156

Peterborough, N.H.
23 August 1921

Dear E.B.:

I have been a little worse than ever this time, but don't think that my not writing signifies any indifference to all your good words in your last letters. *Avon*[1] appears to be well liked in most quarters; and as for mere verse it is probably as good as anything I have done. My last royalty report from the MacMillans indicates a quadrupled sale of my various books—from which I like to believe that my peculiar stock is picking up a bit. They have good courage in bringing out a collected edition, but it begins to look as if they would get out alive. Rather to my surprise the *Taverns* has had the largest first half-year sale of any of the books. Just now I'm working on another long thing that bids to finish me before it is done.[2] Having got halfway through it, I'm looking around for a detective story. All this is highly personal, but the best I can do without any epistolary motor. Mine ran down[3] long ago.

Yours always sincerely,
E.A.R.

1. *Avon's Harvest* (1921).
2. *Roman Bartholow* (1923).
3. Miss Brower circled *Mine ran* and wrote in the lower margin: "Beyond me!" Above the word *down* she penciled "was?" in complete mystification over Robinson's handwriting.

157

810 Washington Avenue
10 November 1921

Dear E.B.:

I'm glad you like the book,[1] but I'm a little disturbed over your failure to find "The Revealer." The poem is included, and unless you have by chance a badly mutilated copy you will find it at the end of "The Town etc." I left out "Au Revoir"[2] simply because no one liked it, or seemed to "get" it—insisting upon taking it in dead earnest, when it was supposed, save in the last two lines, to be mildly humorous. Sometimes I'm tempted never again to write anything but dirges and epitaphs.

Will you kindly look again and let me know if you find the poem?

I am sure that Gorman would be pleased if you were to send him a few lines.[3]

Yours always sincerely,
E.A.R.

1. *Collected Poems* was published by Macmillan on October 18, 1921.
2. In the lower margin Miss Brower wrote: "Au Revoir" (found in R.'s 2nd Vol of poems. (*Town Down the River*)—Scribner's." It was in fact Robinson's fourth volume.
3. Following this Miss Brower wrote: "I did, but got no reply." Herbert S. Gorman had written enthusiastically of *Collected Poems* in the *New York Times Book Review* (October 30, 1921), p. 6.

158

810 Washington Avenue
11 December 1921

Dear E.B.:

I believe that you asked me a question some time ago, and I believe too that it was never answered. As for the omission of the first poem in *The Children*[1] about all I can say is that it was left out because it seemed to be rather young and futile, and because the same thing was said again in the latter part of "The Man Against the Sky." I don't know whether this will be satisfactory or not, but it's the best I can do for you—and, I'm sorry to say—for a few others. But when the pote himself doesn't like a thing, I suppose he can only act accordingly. Doubtless some one or other will cuss me for almost anything that was left out—and there you are, or there one is.

Your obedient servant, always,
E. A. Robinson

1. In the upper margin Miss Brower wrote: "*Children of the Night*—naming his 1st *published* book (Richard Badger)." She did not consider a book printed by the author—like Robinson's *The Torrent and the Night Before*—as published. "The Children of the Night" was not reprinted in *Collected Poems* (1921).

159

Peterborough, N.H.
2 July 1922

Dear E.B.:

Thanks for your letter, which shows again that you have a good heart and an admirable patience—to say nothing of all your other good qualities. Your persistent confidence in what I have been trying to do has meant more to me than you will ever know, and for the simple reason that I haven't brains enough to tell you how much. For about a fifth of a century things were pretty gray and rather tough, but I've managed to come out of it somehow, on to this point. "It's all right so far," said the Optimist, when he had fallen halfway down from the top of a twenty-story building; and I suppose that's a good way to look at life. Anyhow, I'm not growling.

Yours always sincerely,
E.A.R.

160

Peterborough, N.H.
1 October 1922

Dear E.B.:

Apparently no one is going to understand "Avenel Gray," originally called "Mortmain," but for the lines altered in deference to Miss Harriet Monroe's sensibilities. She wants something for her anniversary number and thought the title too suggestive of the end for a possibly dying magazine;[1] and being the gentle critter that I am, I succumbed to her whim. You are too normal to care for such morbid psychology, and Seneca himself was rather a long time in finding out just what was the matter—at any rate, in letting himself know that he knew.

I haven't the book at hand, but will look at "Tact"[2] with sad eyes. I hope it [is] not one of those diabolical errors that make a sort of sense. Thank you many times for your missionary work.

Yours always sincerely,
E.A.R.

1. *Poetry: A Magazine of Verse*, founded by Harriet Monroe in 1912, was observing its tenth birthday.

2. The first word of line 3 in stanza 3 is rendered "That" instead of "The," on page 474 of *Collected Poems* (1921). Robinson was continually plagued by careless typesetters and editors (see Letter 130, note 4). Besides the lapses cited here, at least four other poems were marred in their first periodical appearance, and eight of his books contain up to three misprints in the first issue. Of the variety he describes as "diabolical," the two most prominent are the rendition of the final line of "Reuben Bright" as ". . . and tore down to the slaughter house" (in *Collected Poems*, 1921), and the misquotation by a reviewer of the first phrase in the last quatrain of "Veteran Sirens" as "Poor fish."

161

CORNWALL-ON-HUDSON
31 October 1922

Dear E.B.:

I haven't seen the *New Republic*[1] this week but will look at it when I get to town. As for your question, I can only say that in some instances the use of rhyme is to my mind a gain, provided it is used unobtrusively —that is, if the rhyme appears to be inevitable and not sought for. My chief objection to free verse is not that it doesn't mean anything but that it impresses me in most cases as being merely the subject matter for poetry. I don't care what form poetry takes so long as it fills the mould —or, to use a better figure, the instrument. In most cases free verse seems neither as one or the other.

My address this winter will be 28 West 8th Street, where I lodge again with the good Frasers.[2] F's Hamilton by the way, is soon going up in front of the Treasury Building in Washington.

Yours always sincerely,
E.A.R.

1. Reviewing John Erskine's *The Kinds of Poetry* in *New Republic*, XXXII (October 25, 1922), 18–19, Joseph Warren Beach mentions the use of free verse by Amy Lowell, Carl Sandburg, H.D., and John Gould Fletcher.

2. James Earle Fraser and his wife Laura, sculptors, provided Robinson with a congenial home in the upper floor of their Greenwich Village studio until 1926, and after that in their remodeled house at 328 East 42nd Street.

162

28 West 8th Street
21 November 1922

Dear E.B.:

Thank you for the Bridges article,[1] which covers the ground rather well, though he might have gone much further without giving the slightest offence so far as I am concerned. If your reading was the means of selling three copies of my poems, you are an amazing reader. My gratitude is boundless, as my regard is eternal. You were about the first that ever burst—I've forgotten Coleridge's adjective, but don't believe it fits.[2]

Yours as heretofore,
E.A.R.

1. Robert Bridges, "A Paper on Free Verse," *North American Review*, CCXVI (November 1922), 647–658.

2. ". . . the first that ever burst / Into that silent sea," from "The Rime of the Ancient Mariner," part II, lines 105–106.

163

[17 April 1923][1]

Dear E.B.:

I am very sorry not to have given you my date of sailing but surely thought I did so. I'm leaving Wednesday next on the *Tyrrhenia*, and don't see any possible way to get to your place between now and then. But I'll be back sometime before very long. Please forgive my queer oversight and write me a letter to that effect.

c/o Hambros Bank, Ltd.
21 Cockspur St.
London, S.W.1

Yours always sincerely,
E.A.R.

Tuesday evening

I'll be more explicit on the boat—if the billows permit.

1. This date, penciled in the upper margin by Miss Brower, is obviously erroneous. Robinson sailed for England on Wednesday, April 18, the next day. Except for short jaunts to Oxford and Cambridge, he stayed in London, not once going to the continent. He gave no readings, lectures, or interviews to the press, spending most of his time driving or walking about the city and its environs with an American friend (John Gould Fletcher) or English acquaintances (Lawrence Binyon, Alfred Noyes). He sought out Edmund Gosse, May Sinclair, and J. C. Squire, met Arnold Bennett, and went to gatherings at the homes of John Drinkwater and John Galsworthy. He attended one meeting of the P.E.N. and came away without enthusiasm. Although initially repelled by the city's "feverish" and "rather desperate" atmosphere, Robinson gradually became attracted to its beauty and traditions, and thought of England on the whole as "paradise." But the lure of MacDowell Colony was stronger. He embarked for the United States on July 26. If he wrote to Miss Brower during this interval, she did not see fit to file the letters in this collection.

164

ON BOARD THE
CUNARD R.M.S. "TYRRHENIA"
25 April 1923

Dear E.B.:

I was almost sure that you had my date of sailing, though I'm old enough to know myself well enough never to be sure of anything. Anyhow I like to gather from your telegram, which I found on the boat, that you are not yet my enemy. Please don't be that, for I think a whole lot of you, even though I never say or do anything to make you suspect it. I expect to be dropped at Plymouth next Friday, early in the morning, and so rather suspect that I shall have to get up. I think you have my address, but won't take any chances.

c/o Hambros Bank Ltd.
21 Cockspur St.
London S.W.1

Your obedient servant,
E.A.R.

165

Peterborough, N.H.
2 September 1923

Dear E.B.:

My epistolary faculty would be now about the same as ever if it wasn't just a little worse. Your letter came to me while I was in London and gave me the same pleasure that your letters always give, and received, I'm sorry to say, the same sort of prompt acknowledgment. But you are good enough to know me and my reprehensible ways, and since you have been for so long on such good terms with Saint Peter, perhaps you can afford to honor an erring worm once more with your forgiveness. If you don't, I don't know what the devil there will be left for me to do about it. London is a mighty town, and in many ways I was sorry to leave it. But here I am again, trying to believe that I am writing sonnets.

Yours to command,
E.A.R.

166

28 West 8th Street
24 April 1924

Dear E.B.:

I have realized today, with a jump, that a kind invitation from you and Miss Reynolds has not yet been acknowledged. I'm sorry not to be able to accept it, but I thank you both, and most sincerely. I'll be getting away very soon, in the hope of finding my other self down in the woods —that self that does my work for me, or at any rate acts as an agent.

I am glad to know that you like the new book.[1] Many others are good enough to do the same, or to say *so*.

Yours sincerely,
E.A.R.

1. *The Man Who Died Twice* was published by Macmillan on February 19, 1924, in a limited edition; the trade edition on March 4.

167

28 West 8th Street
10 May 1924

Dear E.B.:

I have mislaid your letter and so am not quite sure of the day and hour that you set. Will you kindly send me a word or telephone (Spring 2354) sometime tomorrow or Monday—not before one o'clock. I am all tied up for Tuesday, but can come around either [Monday?][1] or Wednesday afternoon.

Yours sincerely,
E.A.R.

1. Miss Bower penciled in this word here.

168

Peterborough, N.H.
9 September 1924

Dear E.B.:

Here I am again, as dilatory as ever, and trusting as much to your good nature as heretofore. Your letter of a month ago did not make me "vain," but it gave me a lot of pleasure as your letters always do. I'm glad that you like my later vintage of sonnets. Some people have trouble with them, but they seem to me rather good and I like to believe that some of them will stay for a while. Also I wonder sometimes if it makes much difference whether they do or not. What is New York going to look like in a thousand years, and what are people going to do with themselves? Maybe they are going to read sonnets, but there is just a possibility that the sonnets won't be mine. Perhaps by that time people won't read at all, but will just "listen in" and fly around the moon and chase after one another's wives—as they do now. Only by that time there won't be any wives, from present indications—which may simplify matters. Speaking of progress, some one with a far-seeing eye for trouble has prophesied that some generations of bobbed hair will result in whiskers on the faces of all the fairest women. It doesn't sound good, but the barbers may like it. Only there won't be any barbers, perhaps, by that time. God only knows what there will be, but one thing is certain, all sorts of people will be trying to do things that the Lord—if there is any Lord left—never meant them to do, and will make just as bad a mess of it as they are making now. It's a pity that the Almighty and Destiny (which I suspect very much to be the same person) couldn't get together and talk things over. In the meantime there is a fat young woodchuck just outside my window who doesn't worry in the least about such trivial matters. All he wants is something to eat—and I'm beginning to feel a little like him, having had a very light luncheon. It's raining, and it's getting dark, and I'm going home.

Your obedient servant,
E.A.R.

169

99 St. Botolph Street
Boston
24 April 1925

Dear E.B.:

I should like to see you while you are in New York, but unfortunately I shall not be able to get there again this spring. It is good to know that you liked the book, or parts of it at any rate. I didn't much expect that you would approve Dionysus his doubts,[1] and don't yet quite know whether you do or not. But it was good of you to write me such a good letter. Your play sounds interesting, and as if you might have had a good time writing it. I hope it will be produced before long—but it's a tough and woeful road to travel unless one is young and has the hide of a rhinoceros. If it was written for local performance, of course that's another matter, and the hide of a horse will do.[2] The way of the playwright is hard—except in the few cases when it isn't. I'm getting over a long grippy cold, which may account for my cheerful view of most things just now. But you know what my barking is worth.

Yours always sincerely,
E.A.R.

1. *Dionysus in Doubt* was published by Macmillan on March 24, 1925, in a limited edition; trade edition on April 7.

2. Miss Brower tried to get "The Gabtown Revolution" produced in Wilkes-Barre but failed to achieve a professional showing. Two of her contemporaries believe it may have been put on by amateurs at a local school or church. Robinson's wry observations stem from his own distressful experiences with *Van Zorn* (1914) and *The Porcupine* (1915). See Letter 116, note 1; 122, n. 1; 123; 124; 125, n. 1; 126; 135, n. 1; 138; 141, n. 1, n. 4.

170

Room 411
30 Ipswich Street
Boston
24 September 1925

Dear E.B.:

Your letter of June fifth looked at me all summer from my window in the woods, but like many others it didn't get answered. I won't apologize, or make excuses, but just say that it was not answered—a fact of which you are probably aware. And now that the summer is over, and I'm here in Boston[1] for a short time trying to recuperate and get some sleep, I don't seem to have much to report beyond saying that I'm pretty well tired out after "doing" twenty-eight hundred lines of a new sort of *Tristram*,[2] which will probably arouse more sorts of ire than *Merlin* or *Lancelot* did. Fortunately, many who hated these poems at first came later to like them, and I'm hoping that the same may be true of this one. I am trying (there are still a thousand lines or so to be written) to tell the story of what might have happened if Tristram and Isolde had been left human beings instead of impossible primates after swallowing an impossible drink that was supposed to be a symbol of fate. Even the naive writers of the early stories got over that part of it as soon and as briefly as they could. And this, may be, will be the last of my long things, and perhaps it had better be so. A long poem nowadays is at best a getting down on one's knees to invite disaster, and with everything going so fast in no apparent direction, it is quite possible that even short poems in the future will have about all they can do to survive. On the other hand, it is contrary to my nature to consider these contingencies, and you will have observed that no great amount of my time heretofore has been spent in considering them. Whatever I have done has been done by my insisting on doing as I have [been] told innardly to do, regardless of immediate consequences. As a result, and for God knows just what particular and sufficient reason, I am still alive and—as you found out in *Dionysus*—kicking. The timidity of our public men, who might really do something if they had the courage and vision of as many cockroaches, fills me with dismay and disgust. And their unanimity in forgetting the Fifteenth Amendment while they bury their heads in the sand before the Eighteenth, doesn't make them [any] the more impressive. I shall have [to] write something about changing our national bird—which is obviously the Ostrich, not the Eagle—who, while a pretty bad lot, at least doesn't fool himself.

Yours to command,
E.A.R.

1. In the left margin Robinson wrote: "Address / 99 St. Botolph St. / Boston."
2. *Tristram* was published by Macmillan on March 8, 1927, in a limited edition; trade edition on May 5.

171

328 East 42 Street
20 February 1926

Dear E.B.:

You have surely been nice enough to me—nicer than I deserve, but I haven't been decent to anybody during the past month, having been considerably out of sorts after a cold that went all over me and finally into my sinuses. Recently a medicine man has done things to me that have apparently solved my physical problems for the present and I'm beginning to feel something like right again. But I see now that the Long Poem[1] will [not] be finished this winter. All that I have done will be revised and put behind me and the rest of it, the Good God willing so, will be done next summer. We contrive to get along here with coke and soft coal but the cold weather today makes me shiver to think of those who haven't either.

There is a Worm of Imbecility eating his way to the heart of this country, and sometimes I almost hope that when he gets there he will make a square meal of it. I don't really hope anything of the sort, though it seems as if I did when I consider the sort of scared-cat intellectual that lives in high places nowadays—only I'm afraid it's something worse. I'm afraid the scared cats haven't any intellect worth mentioning.

Please continue to be nice and write me a letter when you feel so disposed. But I remember that you can't read Dickens—which you should.

Yours sincerely,
E.A.R.

1. *Tristram* (1927).

172

Peterborough, N.H.
22 August 1926

Dear E.B.:

Your old friend Mr. March looked in on me here today and told me of the recent death of your cousin,[1] which must mean a great change for you. There is not much for me to say, for of course you know that you have my sincere sympathy, which will not do you much good. Mr. M. is a most pleasant and satisfactory person, and his coming gave me a real pleasure—which is more than I am able to say of all comings. Your last unanswered letter was written long ago, and has not been forgotten—no matter what my bad manners may tell you to the contrary. I have simply been scratching away—or scratching away simply, perhaps—at my Tristram thing, which I hope isn't going to be entirely bad. It sounds hopeless enough—but you know what they say about hope and life—and I hope there is some life in this thing. There is some death, anyway. There isn't much left of either gentleman or lady after my treatment of them—which is pretty rough.

Yours always,
E.A.R.

1. Catharine Parsons, after an extended illness.

173

Studio 411
30 Ipswich Street
Boston
30 September 1926

Dear E.B.:

I am glad to know that you are so pleasantly placed after what must have been a great change for you, and that you appear to be in good spirits. You always appear to be in good spirits, and so that doesn't mean much, but I hope you really are. I'm well enough myself, but rather tired after *Tristram.* Perhaps the faithful who try to read it will be still more tired, but it's too late now to think of that. The thing has been after me for ten years and finally had to be done—without the potion. Much as I despise the Eighteenth Amendment, I'm a strict prohibitionist when it comes to potions. Even without one, there isn't much left of T. or I. when I'm done with 'em; and Isolt doesn't die of opera disease, as someone has called it. This is all that I have to say at present in favor of my poem, which is dreadfully long. Otherwise, I am very much the same and always

Your obedient servant,
E.A.R.

The enclosed letter was sent to me by mistake—as you may suspect.[1]

1. The only note by Miss Brower to Robinson in the collection explains this allusion. Her picture postcard, upon which someone has penciled "[Found in 1 of E.A.R.'s books.]," is addressed to him at 30 Ipswich Street, and is postmarked Wilkes-Barre, October 7, 1926. She wrote: "Oct. 7: Whatever became of that letter to you, in whose envelope I enclosed one to my cousin at Chestnut Hill? Heaven knows, I don't. She writes me *she* never got it. 'Twas a nice one, I'm sure. So poor Tr. and Is. are done for. And at some length? Thus far I've managed to live thru your long-windedness; like enough I can do it again . . . Yes, I really am 'in good spirits.' I'd be a Pig if I were not when everybody is so good to me. Besides, my life is too full of interest for me to be otherwise. Yours Allee Samee. E.B."

On the other side of the card is pictured the Giant Icicle at Niagara Falls, Canada. She circled the word "Giant" and wrote along the four margins: "No! really now—you don't mean it. Should have supposed it a dwarf icicle. Huh? To cool you off after getting so het up over those silly young ancient Britons."

174

30 Ipswich Street
Boston
[31 October 1926][1]

SENGEN[2]
CORNWALL-ON-HUDSON
NEW YORK

Dear E.B.:

I have neglected to tell you that your letter to me came in the same mail with the one that you sent by mistake, so nothing was lost. I'm here in the mountains for a few days, but shall go back to Boston this week for another fortnight or so, to the same address. New work is getting to be rather monotonous now. I'm not so eager to get back to [it] as I was once when things, and myself, were not so dry. This is not my world that we are in now, and I'm glad that I wasn't born any later. My two silly young people are killed off and out of the way, and I hope they have perished to some purpose. The few who have seen them seem to think so. Please let me hear from you whenever you are so disposed.

Yours always sincerely,
E.A.R.

I haven't your new address with me, but trust that this will find you.

1. This date written in the lower margin by Miss Brower.
2. *Sengen,* to which Robinson had an open invitation, was the country home of Jean and Louis Ledoux.

175

[11 February 1927][1]

My two silly young people will soon be before the public,[2] for better or worse. I have simply made their grand passion their career, so to speak, and that's about all there is to the story. There is no philosophy, no intellect, and no moral, except the obvious one that extravagant luxuries have sometimes to be paid for. There is absolutely nothing left of either of them when I'm done with 'em. In other words, I've treated 'em rough.

Please write before long and believe me

Yours most respectful,
E.A.R.[3]

1. This date written in the lower margin of page 3 by Miss Brower, corroborated by the envelope postmark, Wilkes-Barre, Feb. 12, 1927.
2. In the lower margin Miss Brower wrote: "Tristram and Isolt. They didn't come out till May."
3. In this letter of one sheet folded into four pages, only four lines at the bottom of each of the first two pages remain; the rest have been cut off. The fragment on the first page is heavily scored over in blue crayon, but Robinson's words are legible: ". . . one trifling matter that bothers me just a little, and for this reason I'm going to ask you to be good enough to destroy any . . ."

176

Room 411
30 Ipswich Street
Boston
20 May 1927

Dear E.B.:

It was a great pleasure and a greater surprise (I have the order wrong, but no matter) to see you at the show. If you came all the way to New York to hear that reading,[1] you are a most excellent lady and a faithful friend; and it was good of you to be there anyhow. I'm glad to know that a better acquaintance with the poem makes you like it better, for otherwise it had better never have been written. Apparently there are others who agree with you. Me, I don't know much about it.

Yours always sincerely,
E.A.R.

1. In conjunction with the Literary Guild's edition of *Tristram*, Carl Van Doren arranged a reading of selections from the poem by Mrs. August Belmont at the Little Theatre in New York on Sunday, May 8, 1927.

177

Peterborough, N.H.
3 July 1927

Dear E.B.:

Your letter of some time ago, June 23, to be exact, gave me a great deal of pleasure, even though I fear your superlatives may kick their heels a little too high,—a habit to which all superlatives are more or less addicted. But the knowledge that you and your two eminently discriminating friends think so well of the poem[1] makes me believe that others will do the same. Some have said so already, though I don't really know much of what those who have bought the book think of it, or how many of them wish they had their money back. There have been a few brickbats, which have gone, so far as I can see, rather wide of the mark—by which I don't mean to imply that the mark for them isn't there; and the Lord knows I don't mean to make a sick pun. Mark[2] is consistent enough as I saw him—*elementary* rather than *evil*, and requiring a bad jolt to bring him to the contemplative mood. I've known many of him.

I'm sorry to say that Mrs. MacDowell[3] has not been at all well for the past month, but she seems to be improving a little now. It's all very much too bad.

Yours sincerely,
E.A.R.

1. To the right of the dateline Miss Brower wrote: "Tristram and Isolde."
2. King Mark of Cornwall is the husband of Isolt and the uncle of Tristram in Robinson's *Tristram* (1927).
3. Mrs. Marian Nevins MacDowell (1857–1956), usually described as "frail-looking" and frequently in delicate health, was nevertheless an indomitable spirit who lived another three decades, just short of ninety-nine years.

178

Peterborough, N.H.
23 August 1927

Dear E.B.:

If I didn't answer your last letter, you have, I hope, forgiven me. You have had practice enough, and it ought to be easy by this time. I'm glad to be able to tell you, for the first time since May, that Mrs. MacDowell appears really to be better. For a long time there was nothing satisfactory to report, but during the past week she has been gaining in strength and spirits and yesterday was able to sit up for a little while. Nothing has seemed at all right here this summer with the knowledge that she has been suffering all the time, with everybody powerless to do anything. I hope before long to tell you that she is up and about. In the meantime you had better write me a letter and tell me how you are yourself. I am pretty much the same and am always,

Your obedient servant,
E.A.R.

179

328 East 42 Street
5 February 1928

Dear E.B.:

I have your note dated December 28, and I'm woefully afraid that it has not yet been acknowledged—which means only that my manners haven't improved. Mrs. MacDowell told me that your hospital experience was a short one, and I hope sincerely that there will be no repetition of it. Please tell me that you are all right. I have nothing now to report except that New York [is] getting to be too much for me and I'm wondering whether it will be possible for me to stand another winter of it. I'm sick of people, and yet can't quite get along without 'em. What to do? You can't tell me.

Yours sincerely,
E.A.R.

180

Peterborough
7 August 1928

Dear E.B.:

I remember your cousin[1] very well, and hope you will tell him. He seemed to me a real person—one who would always be found at the time and the place. I'm very sorry to learn that he is not well. Please give him my best wishes. Some friends of yours were here the other day and told me about your bad accident, and I was awfully sorry to hear of that. I knew that you had been in a hospital, but not for what cause. I hope your being able to travel is at least proof that you are much better now —and you might tell me so. Neuritis must be the devil and I'm woefully sorry that you have it again. May it leave you soon, and not come back.

I don't read modern novels, though I did read Wilder's *Bridge*.[2] I thought it beautifully written, but weak at the end. Perhaps there was no other sort of ending. You will laugh, I suppose, when I tell you that I still read Dickens. Each reading compels me to set the clock back a little further, but the genius and the miracle are still there, and there was never anything like him. Other writers write, but he makes a world; and you never know what he is going to say, while he works, to astonish you. But, good Lord, lady, you will never read him again. Well, you don't have to.

Mrs. MacDowell was greatly pleased to be remembered. She is really better.

Your obedient servant,
E.A.R.

1. Above these words Miss Brower wrote: "Archie Parsons."
2. Thornton Wilder, *The Bridge of San Luis Rey* (New York, 1927), a Pulitzer Prize winner.

181

26 August 1928

Dear E.B.:

It is a great relief to me to know that the report of your broken bones was a false one, but I'm still mortally sorry about your neuritis and your eyes. But I'm getting to the age when it is good for me to consider the relative good fortune of anyone past sixty who can still walk and eat. There isn't much comfort in this for you, but still there is some, though I suspect that you don't get dangerously excited over what you eat.[1]

My reading over of Dickens this summer has been attended by a mild sort of melancholy—for I have had to realize that it has been, in all probability, the last time. Only old affection and sentiment (oh yes, I can be sentimental, though I try not to let my readers know it)[2] has enabled me to get through parts of *Dombey and Son*. Some of them (the books) I have not even attempted. Perhaps *Our Mutual Friend* survives as well as any. *Bleak House* creaked badly and lived unhappily up to its name, and was all the time a work of genius. Dickens fell down worst of all in his photographic—or rather phonographic—realism. His women, who seem so silly sometimes on paper, talk just about as they would in really respectable emotional circumstances, without causing any especial comment or surprise, but in art it just won't do. It "did" for the Victorians, but it will never do again—though the valuable creatures will continue to talk in just about the same way. Well, we don't want men and women to use the same idiom, even if they do wear the same coats and trousers.

My collected sonnets are slow in coming out, but they are in type and will undoubtedly come out sometime before Easter. They are supposed to appear in September, but possibly they won't.[3] Some of them were written a long time ago, when the world was in some ways more attractive than it is now. The socialistic dark ages are coming, and the individual is going to "wither" as Tennyson foresaw,[4] but he'll swell up again after a few hundred years, and knock down the whole damned business—which is description, not profanity.

I wrote in care of Mr. Pershing only because you gave me explicit directions to do so. How the divvle else?

Yours to command,
E.A.R.

1. In the lower margin Miss Brower wrote: "I don't!"
2. In the lower right corner Miss Brower wrote: "He surely does!"
3. *Sonnets 1889–1927* was published by Crosby Gaige on November 1, 1928, in a limited edition; by Macmillan on November 13 in a trade edition.
4. Alfred Tennyson's "Locksley Hall," line 142: "And the individual withers, and the world is more and more."

182

30 Ipswich Street
Boston
4 November 1928

Dear E.B.:

If I ever said anything so ferocious about "people" as your quotation goes to show, it was just my way of saying that I am not a very good mixer.[1] Oh no, I don't hate 'em. I don't hate anybody. It is too expensive, and it doesn't do any good unless you intend to kill him or her. And I'm altogether too lazy to kill anyone—even a critic who calls me the American Browning, meaning apparently to give pleasure.

As for Josephine Peabody, I agree with you in preferring her poems of childhood, though there are many beautiful things in her other books. She insisted on giving bread to people who wanted cake—as I told her once, and was nearly slain for my good intentions. Her place is safe enough in American literature, but I'm not sure that the brainless neglect of her work while she lived didn't kill her. She felt it horribly, but never said much. Mankind is an ornery lot, in spite of its good qualities.

Yours sincerely,
E.A.R.

1. On the reverse of this sheet Miss Brower wrote: "He did say to me once, 'I love humanity, but I hate *people*'—which I took to mean the individuals he must constantly meet. He *isn't* a good mixer. Yet he *can* mix, beautifully. I've seen him do it."

183

328 East 42 Street
10 December 1928

Dear E.B.:

Mrs. Richards has sent me two copies of her new book on Laura Bridgman[1] by mistake, and I'm sending one of 'em along to you—not as a gift, naturally, but for you to read and pass on to somebody who will be interested. I found it most exciting—better than a detective story.

Many thanks for your letter, which was duly appreciated. You are much better off in Wilkes-Barre than you would be in New York, which gets worse and worse, but I hope to see you here sometime all the same. My new book is coming out in March instead of October.[2]

Yours to command,
E.A.R.

1. Laura E. Richards, *Laura Bridgman* (New York, 1928), a biography of the first blind deaf-mute to be successfully educated, at the Perkins Institution, then in South Boston, established by Mrs. Richards' father, Dr. Samuel Gridley Howe.

2. *Cavender's House* was published by Macmillan on March 26, 1929, in a limited edition; trade edition on April 23.

184

328 East 42 Street
24 February 1929

Dear E.B.:

You should have had yourself photographed as Mrs. Skewton.[1] By the way, I read *Dombey* again last summer and am still trying to find out what infernal force there is in Dickens that makes every page of him, even those that are only description, so different from anything else. He may be old-fashioned, and silly at times, but there's nothing like him, before or since. On the whole, I still have to call him the greatest thing since Shakespeare—he was such an all-fired (literally) engine. Please tell me how you are.

Yours always,
E.A.R.

1. The Honorable Mrs. Skewton, in Dickens' *Dombey and Son*, kept a bath chair when old in order to maintain her reputed resemblance to the Egyptian queen in her galley.

185

Colony Hall
Peterborough, N.H.
24 June 1929

Dear E.B.:

It is a great satisfaction to know that *Cavender* improves on further acquaintance and to be told so by you and by several others. Laramie isn't a "spook," but a projection of C's uncomfortable fancy. She is a part of him, so to speak; he brought her with him, and she can tell him nothing that he doesn't know—though she does tell him things about himself that he didn't quite know that he knew. A few ultra-radicals don't like it because it makes too much of love and marriage. But romance, judging from all the murders and suicides in the newspapers, isn't quite dead yet, and I shouldn't wonder if it outlived some of the ultra-radicals.

Mrs. MacDowell is pretty well, everything considered, but she has been overwhelmed with visiting women during the past week, and should, by all the so-called laws of nature, be dead. But she is very much alive, I am glad to say. I have long given up trying to account for her and her vitality. I suppose it is living for an idea, or ideal.

Yours always sincerely,
E.A.R.

186

Peterborough, N.H.
16 September 1929

Dear E.B.:

You are at home again by this time, I suppose, and from your letter it is pleasant to assume that you are feeling pretty well and that your summer has been satisfactory if not exciting. I'm glad to know that you are still able to read my poems, for if ever you should become unable to read them I should have to believe that they were no good. So perhaps it would be better that you should not tell me "if and when" that time comes. Mrs. M. is remarkably well, for her, and is all over the place. I leave Thursday for Boston (Room 411, 30 Ipswich St.).

Yours sincerely,
E.A.R.

187

Room 411
30 Ipswich Street
10 November 1929

Dear E.B.:

Strange as it may sound, I think I wrote, or had written, to you last before your letter came the other day. I agree with you about modern manners and the modern world in general, and about time and space, but I have to bristle and spit at any League of Nations that would include this mishandled republic of ours. We would get into all sorts of a mess if anything really happened. So I believe in a League of Europe and let it go at that—though I don't see how such a thing can be with Russia and Mussolini in the way. Sooner or later the yellow men will come over and get us, and in about five thousand years there may not be any white folks left. It looks sometimes as if our part in the business will have been to make the world ready for the tinted and colored races to use. They can't do much worse with it than we have done. Meanwhile time means nothing to them—no more than life or death—and they are in no hurry—except just now in India. But that is more or less a local issue, though of course it might develop into something else. England will have to fight or get out before long—and either way will be bad for all concerned. None the less, it's a fine day.

Yours always sincerely,
E.A.R.

Mrs. MacDowell continues to be wonderfully well, for her, and swears that she suffers comparatively little pain for the most part. And I'm happy to say that her face looks as if she might be telling something like the truth.

There will be a new book next fall.[1]

1. *The Glory of the Nightingales* was published by Macmillan on September 9, 1930, in a limited edition; trade edition on September 16.

188

328 East 42 Street
18 February 1930

Dear E.B.:

You will begin to suspect that there may be such things as time and space if you consider too much how far it is to New York and how long I have been in acknowledging your letter of December 30. I have a notion that time and space have about the same sort of existence that we have, and that there is a mighty lot of illusion in it somewhere. If I were to throw a brick and hit you on the head with it, you might say it was no illusion, but then again it might be. In fact, I'd rather not say too much about illusion to a lady who has her right hand cramped with neuritis. It might not be helpful, and it might not be altogether tactful. I hope the infernal thing is better by this time, and that you will tell me so. Thank you for Mr. Pershing's good words. There is something strange in the neglect of Josephine Peabody's poetry, but she has written several things [that] cannot easily die, and I don't believe that she is worrying about them now.[1] If your hand is willing and able, please send me a few lines to let me know How You Are.

Yours always sincerely,
E.A.R.

1. Josephine Preston Peabody died in 1922.

189

1 June 1930

Dear E.B.:

This paper is all that I can find—so I hope you will excuse it, as you have always been the best excusess that I could name. For that reason you should not be abused.

I'm starting off tomorrow for Peterborough, which will be my address until further notice. I hope you are pretty well and that your arm and hand aren't giving you too much trouble—by which I mean none at all, though I fear that is asking a great deal. I'm not a very good liar, but I improve with practice. How else is one to live in New York? And why should one live there at all?

I like Swan's[1] verses and don't miss the rhymes. Sometimes I wonder if rhymes are much good anyhow—only of course they help the poor poet along. But just whether they are stairs or crutches, I don't know. On the whole, I fancy they are both.

I haven't an idea in my head, and I'm wondering whether there will be any when I try to work. Perhaps there will be one or two.

Yours always sincerely,
E.A.R.

1. Miss Caroline Davenport Swan (1841–1938), author of *The Unfading Light* (Boston, 1911), lived in Gardiner during Robinson's youth. She maintained an élite literary salon at her house to which Robinson was admitted and where he first learned about the intricacies of prosody.

Appendixes · Index

Appendix I
MEMORIES OF EDWIN ARLINGTON ROBINSON
By Edith Brower

Begun 8 March 1920
Wilkes-Barre, Penna.

In thinking over the character of Edwin Arlington Robinson as I have known him through more than 23 years of personal acquaintance, by correspondence and by direct intercourse, as well as by a deep study of his work, it seems to me that of all men he is the most utterly honest. By *honest* I mean true to himself at all times and at whatever risk of misinterpretation, at whatever cost of advantages, social, financial, or otherwise. If I add here that he has never had a great amount of what he calls "social curiosity," and has no use for money outside the necessities and reasonable decencies (he once said to me: "If I had money I shouldn't know what to do with it"), his indifference to such advantages may appear to lessen the nobility of his character in sacrificing them to his high ideal. In one sense, certainly there is no question of sacrifice: he chooses not to regard what are generally prized as advantages—that is all. But that all is much, and means, to my way of thinking, a character formed from the start and built upon Right Valuations. In his early days in Boston, scratching along at poverty's sharp point, only beginning to be recognized,* Robinson was offered a position on a paper by a friend in St. Louis[1] at a salary of $2000. This he turned down at once and, I believe, without a serious qualm, for the sole reason that he would have had to bind himself to write not what he would, but what he must, not when inwardly led to do so, but when bidden to do so. He could starve and go raggedy, but he could not sign himself a slave to any man on

Starred footnotes are observations made by Miss Brower. The numbered notes at the end of this appendix were written by the editor.

* *Note.* Hardly recognition could it be called—not public recognition, even tho' Richard Badger, worthily famous for his daring in helping out worthy young poets whom all other publishers rejected, had at this time published *Children of the Night.*

earth. Several years later, in New York, after Houghton & Mifflin had brought out *Captain Craig*, and he was getting a wee bit famous, a beautiful lady of high degree did her cleverest to lionize him. She might as well have tried to lionize a lion: the King of Beasts himself would have been as amenable to society coddling. Again, some years later, another lady of high degree took him into her home collection of lions,[2] but that didn't work either with E.A.R. I never heard how the other King Beasts stood domestication of this sort.

My introduction to Robinson was by letter and it came off thus: In January, 1897, being in New York, I called at the office of Dr. Titus Munson Coan, chief of the "N.Y. Bureau of Criticism and Revision." For several years I had assisted Dr. Coan in his work and naturally saw him whenever I went to the city. Nearly always he had something especially interesting or amusing laid aside to show me—it was usually the latter: an impossible *ms*, perhaps, that could only be returned untouched, with a letter containing the minimum of justice—as expressed in strictural criticism—and the maximum of mercy compatible with entire honesty; for the motto of the Bureau was: "The truth, and nothing but the truth, but not all the truth"—unless definitely asked for! This time Dr. Coan handed me a small, thin book—in fact, a tiny pamphlet with blue paper cover. At top of this cover I read: *The Torrent and The Night Before*. At top of title page, the title again, and:
by Edwin Arlington Robinson
Gardiner, Maine.

At foot: Printed for the Author
by
Houghton, Mifflin & Co.
1896.

Not published, I commented, thinking how some folks were so bound to get into print as to be willing to pay for it. Midway of the page, a line from François Coppée—"*Qui pourrais-je imiter pour être original?*"—made me think a little more and differently, but the dedication on the following page really startled me: "I dedicate this book to any man, woman or critic who will cut the edges. I have done the top."[3] The not unpleasing New England flavor of dry irony was surely a curious preparation for a Book of Poems, and by this time I ought to have known enough to shake off my obsession and see that here before me was no matter for amusement. I began reading "The Torrent," a sonnet with which the book opens. The first quatrain made me exclaim in the tone of one cheated: "But this is poetry!" "Read on," replied the Doctor dryly. On another page another sonnet stopped me: "Dear Friends." Again I complained: "But this is Poetry (I'm sure my tone capitalized it)!" "Read on," was all the answer I got. A few more dips into the thirty little pages. Then I asked for a corner of Dr. Coan's crowded desk, and for paper, pen, and ink. And thus I wrote: "Please send me at once a copy of your book, if you have to beg, borrow, or steal one. Should it be necessary, kill somebody to get it."

How such an abrupt, almost fierce demand from an unknown person impressed the poet may be read in Letter 1, received by me at my home within a week. His curious disclaimer of any reason in his work to account for my apparent enthusiasm over it, galled me a bit, since never was I more sincere. Something of this was expressed in my acknowledgment of the book, and it is to this that he refers at the opening of Letter 2. At that time I could not understand his tone; it seemed to me like an insincere turning aside of praise, and made me feel as if accused of flattery. How *could* I then have guessed what bitterness of life experience, of deferred literary hopes, of persistent non-recognition, yes, of positive disapproval among his own, lay behind his rather sour response? It wasn't sourness, as I now know,—it was soreness. He had—before getting his little bunch of poems printed (Heaven knows what he left out of the bunch that we'd now like to see; his self-criticism has always been flinty-hearted)—he had reached the end of endurance. Get himself before the world he must, and the blue book served as a flag to arrest attention. A few copies, printed at his own expense and sent out to professional critics and literary folk of various sorts about the land, might do for him what, so far, every editor or publisher he had appealed to, refused to do. Moreover, it was—this book—as he later wrote me (Letter 3): "a protest against the materialism of a Down East community" where the sole ideals were "to get a job and vote the straight Republican ticket."[4] His own job had come straight to his hand; he knew it for his own, though it wasn't recognized in Gardiner, Maine, as a job worth working at. When, within a twelvemonth, he came to visit me at my home in Wilkes-Barre, he gave me a tiny sketch (Robinson's talk is always sketchy) of domestic obstructions almost prohibitive of any intellectual development, especially along poetic lines. His father, a lumberman, read Shakespeare, it is true—his only reading outside local newspapers—but not for the poetry of it, for poetry did not exist for him: he read for the action portrayed. As for his mother, while apparently pleased to hear of his first published book, she showed no desire even to look at it. The pathos—almost tragedy—of this made me bleed at the heart, but Robinson told it very simply and I gave no sign of thinking it extraordinary. We can here perceive the same home atmosphere indicated by Mr. Herbert Gorman of the *Sun* (January 4, 1920)[5] in his interview with Robinson, where the latter humorously describes himself, aged seven, declaiming from the floor to puzzled parents Poe's "Raven." They probably thought their little son a defective of some sort. His father, I fear, would have said degenerate; it is certain he thought him something quite reprehensible. The tragic autobiographical Letter 12 tells much more than it tells. The thing it tells me most strikingly is the *why* and the *how* of his poetical work—the sorrows of that dismal, blank, misinterpreted life of his,* and his noble surmounting of them all. A few years after he wrote me thus, I met a young man from Gardiner who knew R. well and who told me of the respect he had from everyone there for his dignified attitude towards the most trying conditions.

It's not to be wondered at that Father Robinson judged as he did. His ideals were those of Gardiner, and he had brought forth a Man from Mars! What should he "do" with such? Whether or not R. ever even tried to "get a job" in his native village, I know not,† but he at least showed no squeamishness elsewhere. In Boston, for example, he strongly contemplated taking a position as night watchman in a large warehouse, where his labors would be neither irksome nor engrossing, and, since his literary work was done largely in the dark, quiet hours, he would have plenty of leisure for it too. For some reason I have forgotten, this plan fell through, but later, in New York, he held for a year or so the position of "boss" (no one who knows Robinson can picture him as bossing anything or anybody) in the first subway, then building. What this would—theoretically—mean to a temperament like his, is hard to imagine,—he, the slug-abed, having to be on hand at 6 A.M.!—yet he told me afterwards that he had learned more underground than ever he learned on the surface. His soft voice—a dreamy voice with few inflexions—and his gentle, yet firm and direct manner must have been effective with the "Wops."

* Not to mention an untold domestic tragedy.

† His feeling towards jobs on general principles may be gathered from Letter 49.

About this time it was that a youngster hight Kermit Roosevelt, in school at Groton, spied in a classmate's room, a volume of poems entitled *Children of the Night*. The classmate was a son of Laura E. Richards (I have the tale from her), who had fondly hoped that he would value the book, at least as being the work of one of his townsmen, but the youth cared not at all for it, merely letting it tumble about on his table. But Kermit was his father's own child, and had an eye as well as a palate for literature. Moreover, as he had also an inherited love for the wilderness, he soon lighted upon the poem of that name.

> Come away! come away! there's a frost along the marshes,
> And a frozen wind that skims the shoal where it shakes
> the dead black water.

At once he fell for it, and at once sent a letter to the White House, where his daddy at that time was putting up, and told him of the book and the poem. At once Mr. President ordered a copy of the book,[6] and before many days he wrote to Mr. Robinson, inviting him to visit the White House. And—wonder of wonders!—Robinson went. Perhaps he construed a Presidential invitation as a command, yet I think such *perhapsing* is unjust to him. Rather, I imagine, he accepted on the wise principle of *Carpe Diem*. So long had the poor Down East chap waited for a day like this! How could he refuse such a frankly outstretched hand, such a friendly offer of sympathetic appreciation?

But there lay in wait an affliction that he couldn't have foreseen. "Teddy" gave a dinner for him, at which were some members of the Cabinet and other distinguished persons, and—*horrible dictu*!—after dinner, the President brought out *The Children of the Night* and read from it aloud, prancing up and down the room after his restless and enthusiastic fashion. It is next to certain that Robinson fell (metaphorically) through the floor into the White House cellar during the ordeal. He loves appreciation—when he can feel, not hear it—but he hates praise and publicity.

Mr. Roosevelt did not content himself with thus dining an unknown and deserving poet. He discovered that Robinson needed some material boosting, so he boosted him into a job at the New York Custom House. When Robinson discovered that his new position was a sinecure, he grew uneasy under it and within a year gave it up.[7] Mr. Roosevelt also wrote a pretty piece about him for the *Outlook*.[8]

The little visit of two days and two nights that Robinson made me in Wilkes-Barre showed me a lot of things that might never have come out otherwise. They were little things, *per se*, yet they all accorded with the impression of mental and moral sincerity given by his poems: a winning blend of profound philosophical understanding and provincial simplicity truly charming. (To show how well he understood himself—once, in these early days of our acquaintance, speaking together about his work, I said, "The most utterly poetic thing you have done is 'Luke Havergal.'" "It has a lot that spoils it," he replied, and pointed to his use of the word *some*—"The wind will whisper some"—for *somewhat*, or *a little*.[9] "It's provincial," he said, and added: "I shall always be provincial." He might have said *American*, for this use of *some* is given in our dictionaries under "provincial" but appeareth not at all in the English lexicons.)

I liked him for this very quality and I don't think he really lamented it himself; the point I make here is that he recognized it. The objectionable word gave, I thought, a quaintness quite accordant with the strange atmosphere of "Luke Havergal," but I couldn't get Robinson to agree with me. While content to be what he inalterably was, he wouldn't call one of his poems perfect when he knew it was not. Today I believe he would reject this poem entirely unless he could by re-writing it eliminate that single word.* His wastebasket receives about 9/10 of his output.†

In a letter to me written a few years ago (it is now 1920), just after one of his diminutive books had come from the press, he notes regretfully, almost as if ashamed, of his small output.[10] Yet I know for a certainty that he's better satisfied that it should be so. Doubtless his readers have lost much that they would like to have seen, but at least Robinson's uncompromising self-criticism and merciless sifting of his work will save posterity from volumes of unreadable stuff such as we find in nearly all of the great poets. He gives us only what he knows is his best.

Domestically and socially Robinson is full of what the English call "homely" ways. As destitute of *manner* as a bird, beast, fish, or savage, he yet has good *manners* of the quiet, unconscious sort. The most utterly unaffected person I have ever known. I'm sure this helps to account for the conduct of my cat Rory O'More towards him. All his

* I was wrong. See his *Collected Poems*.

† When Mr. Edmund Brown in his *Poetry Journal* (March 1916) speaks of R.'s *mss* as giving "little evidence of labored decision or *even excision*" it makes one who knows the truth laugh.

long life of fifteen years Rory had fled before anything wearing boots and trousers, and having heavy steps and deep voices, yet the moment he laid eyes on Robinson, he went straight to him, jumped upon his knees and made believe he had found a lap—which he hadn't, for R. is very long and was at that time very thin. I always like to recall this story, for I take it to mean that Robinson is all right. Rory was exceedingly discriminating in regard to the women folk who came to the house, tho' never scared by them.

One thing I liked about R. when he visited my home was the sweet tooth he displayed. According to Charles Lamb, he had not yet, tho' 27 years old,[11] lost his primal innocence. My aunt made a wonderful gooseberry conserve, and Robinson ate of it as one would eat applesauce. She gave him some to take back to Gardiner with him—enough, she thought, to last him a good while,—but he finished it in two days. It would have made some folks ill! Yet he was not a glutton at table: he just had that boyish sweet tooth, and one can fancy it had been underfed.*

There is in him a curious mixture of New England reserve and blunt outspokenness. Sensitive, of course, with a strong sense of personal dignity, he feels hurts keenly and deeply. When he does, he is likely to express it in some way. Once, sitting with me at a restaurant table, he burst forth, tho' nothing had led up to the subject, against a very dear friend of mine, whom he knew to be my friend, who had, he felt, taken an inexcusable liberty in advising him regarding his course of life. Later, Robinson made me a perfectly frank, manly apology, acknowledging that he had no right to hurt another while relieving his own personal feelings.[12]

I'm not sure that he ever does polite things for the mere sake of being polite, on the other hand, I'm equally sure that he never intends to be impolite. Simply, he ignores conventions unless it suits his disposition to observe them. For example: Mrs. Laura E. Richards was in New York while I was there. Robinson mentioned the fact to me and I said: "Of course you'll go to see her." No, he wasn't going to see her. Now Mrs. Richards was an old Gardiner acquaintance, and one of the earliest to recognize his gift. Indeed, I know she counted herself among his friends. But when I expressed surprise at his reply, I could learn from him only that calling on Mrs. Richards did not at that time appeal to

* I find I've done him a terrible injustice which I hurry up to confess. It was Blair—so it reads in Letter 49—that gobbled the conserve.

him as in the least obligatory. When he told me that she was visiting on Riverside Drive—was it, or West End Avenue?—it seems not unlikely that R. may have shrunk from paying a ceremonious call at a presumably "swell" house.

At that period, and for long after, he never had more clothes than he could wear at one time—and always a sack-coat suit. Me he could visit without compunction, for I was then stopping at nothing better than a very decent boarding house where he felt quite free to come by daytime. It mustn't be thought that these things ever trouble him on his own account; his self respect is too upstanding for that. His one suit was always exquisitely neat,—I've never seen him in the least soiled, or tattered and torn. There's nothing of the Bohemian in this sense about him. He likes clothes for covering purposes, and they must fit him and be immaculate. Further than that they are negligible. (Shortly before this writing—summer of 1920—Mrs. Lionel Marks[13] took away a part of my breath by telling me she had seen Robinson last winter in evening clothes! She said they became him charmingly—a dinner jacket, of course; no claw-hammer for E.A.R.—and that he seemed not displeased with them himself. It's good to know that he got those clothes and that they pleased him; it shows he's not purely superhuman on that side of his nature,—sometimes I've thought he was!)

Nobody can read him in the most cursory manner and not perceive how interest in the individual "human warious" (to borrow a term from Mr. Venus and misapply it)[14] predominates. Comparing him with the greatest in this respect—Chaucer, Shakespeare, Browning—he does not take a second place. Yet he has lived mostly by himself and to himself. "Society" in almost any phase bores—worse—repels him. He once said to me: "I love humanity, but I hate people."[15] This is strong language, for he has a faithful heart for real friends. One can't help wishing he could have found himself at an early age in an *understanding* circle and been spared the excruciating loneliness of soul indicated in Letter 12. Such totally uncongenial surroundings must have gone far to make a man of his peculiarly composed nature "hate people." On the other hand—there's always another hand—that peculiarly composed nature and the idiosyncratic genius springing from it, may have required what it got. Perhaps it would have failed of development had it had what it did not get that seems to us so desirable. Who knows? What we do know is that the up-state boy was "too mutch fer his condishun"; he played his poor hand well. This is the testimony of those who knew him in his early days, and it accords with all I have learned from a somewhat intimate acquaintance with him.

In Letter 24 (1897) he paints his social difficulties in characteristic fashion. He wouldn't find that camp with the unpronounceable—at least illegible—name so much of a purgatory now. In nearly all of these early letters is a strong note of morbidity, an egotism too often self-depreciatory, which is, however, readily understood and excused by anyone who reflects upon the singularly gifted nature of the young man swamped—almost—in such antipathetic surroundings.

I don't believe that Robinson hates people nowadays—not as extensively as he did, anyway. Never *very* adaptable to humanity, whether *en masse* or individually, he has gained much broader, more flexible liking powers. It is Peterborough that has done this. Seven seasons of close yet free intercourse with those of his own "degree"[16] (see *Our Invisible Guest*—not to be confounded with Maeterlinck's THE *Invisible Guest*)[17]—his very first opportunity of mingling with large groups of his peers—have brought out whatever he has of gregariousness. An absurd word used of him! He can't "flock" to save his soul. Notwithstanding this, one must insist that some enforced flocking—such as the wonderful Peterborough affords—has not disagreed with his soul, otherwise Mrs. MacDowell could not write of him as she has done in a recent letter to me (July 15, 1920), where she tells how "Everyone loves him here."

Harvard, where he spent two years (I don't know how he managed to get there, for his father looked upon extra education as decidedly "an extra") and where he "found two or three good friends"—see Letter 12—did much for him doubtless, in several ways. But there he would meet only men. At Peterborough the sexes are pretty evenly represented, thus it serves as a miniature world for him.

Barrett Wendell was one of the "good friends" he made at Cambridge, and Daniel Gregory Mason. Then there was Fullerton Waldo, the violinist, whom Robinson immortalizes as Morgan in his poem, "The Return of Morgan and Fingal," first entitled "Intermezzo." Probably R. would deny the identity of Morgan and Waldo—he denied to me that the prototype of Captain Craig was Alfred Louis, the remarkable English Jew who became a Roman Catholic, and was the most utterly perfect specimen of the raggedy Bohemian variety of high intellectual I've ever known. Yet every line of the Captain might be laid alongside of Louis and match without variance. Robinson said he didn't know he was painting Louis, and I believe him; I also believe that the pungently impressive personality of that strangely charming man was so embedded in his consciousness that, having selected the Captain's type, he worked it out subconsciously as we have seen, so that everyone who knew Louis is bound to find him in Captain Craig. And everybody except Robinson does! Similarly we recognize in Killigrew, the beloved, queer fish, Craven Langstroth Betts, perhaps a bit exaggerated, but not much. And I seriously doubt whether R. is aware of this. I fear he *is* aware of the original of Miniver Cheevy, but the name must not go down the ages, if *I* can help it.[18]

I consider R.'s critical powers to be of the highest sort. The severity of his self-criticism has already been mentioned here. He is slow to characterize others—one can hardly get an opinion out of him about any contemporary poet, and even for those who have "passed on" he has but a brief word. Yet what a word! It cuts in to the bare truth—good or bad—two-edged, dividing asunder the soul and marrow. Letter 5, and several following—especially Letter 7—show what he was capable of in this line even in those early days up in his little Gardiner, his "Tilbury Town" that he knew so well and that didn't know him at all. What is noteworthy in these critical passages is not the mere docketing of this or that thing (in my work!) as worthy or unworthy, but the bigness of his general view of what literature should be, the clear pronounced statements of universal principles. His wisdom is almost uncanny.

Everywhere in his letters he will be seen to be *very* hard on himself; I should say, perhaps, very doubtful and very requiring of himself. Somewhere at this date he speaks of his work as faulty, as if he had been almost ashamed to put it forth for the world to see. Yet it is astonishing to find how flawless is his technique, even in the poor little blue book, and (while he has grown enormously since this first desperate venture) how well-grown and well-formed his philosophy at that time. That philosophy he has never had to go back on. His "Torrent" and his "Two Sonnets" are re-echoed, perhaps in grander style, in his "Man Against the Sky," as they were in the earlier "Captain Craig."*

He may not be the greatest Monist that ever lived, but to my mind he is the purest Monist of the Idealistic sort that ever expressed himself in poetry. I never heard him discuss philosophical thought, or even mention a philosopher's name, yet it wouldn't be risky to say that Bergson

* In Letter 5 the blue-penciled passage gives it no compact clarity. (He would have "particular fits" over this phrase. It *is* pretty bad, but let it go: it's both *compact* and *clear*!)[19]

is *son homme*. And his philosophy is everywhere and at all times to be perceived, by one sense if not another, first as the armor of the knight could be felt through envelopings of cramoisie or of homespun.

It's astonishing as well as cheering to note the entire change of tone in his letters as one reads them straight through. In the earliest ones his delightful humor only occasionally oozes out; it is mostly overlaid with what I have, perhaps wrongly, called his morbidity, and by his clearly expressed philosophy which is never morbid. Also his fine critical dicta, apparently aimed at me, but, as I afterwards learned, expelled by way of relief from a mind in danger of festering for lack of opportunity of free social expression. Gradually, as he grows happier, more at home in the world, his humor gets full sway; he no longer preaches—whether at himself or anybody else, and his philosophy has become so real a part of himself as to need no restatement. Once in a while it comes out in some golden (and *always* humorous) passage, as in Letter 139a.[20] Here it may be seen that he is more than ever willing to accept "The High Cost of Living" because—so I know—he has never ceased to regard life as "a compensatory struggle towards the realization of the Infinite"—his definition of it in one of the 1897 letters.

Even at that time, however, brutally black as his horizon looked, he could laugh. *He* would never have "died because he couldn't laugh," as did Clavering in the poem "At Calverly's." Of course he has been helped to a full realization of his philosophy by his improved conditions, being no longer either ignored or misinterpreted.

But I love to remember that he didn't have to wait for recognition in order to put his faith into practice.

Many a question have I asked myself regarding the preservation of *all* these letters; many a qualm have I had when reading and rereading them, for some are very personal and intimate. But at last I've decided to omit none. Everything R. writes here throws some useful light on his mind and character. Those passages in the early letters which concern me so nearly, of no value to outsiders on my account, are important as proceeding from him. Once, in referring to our correspondence, he told a friend of mine that the writing of these letters saved his life, so to speak, at a time when he was bursting with the need of such personal expression. This I've referred to already in my "Memories."

I hope his ghost will forgive me for my decision not to expurgate anything he has written to me. And I also hope that his future editors or biographers will not think it necessary to print every word of the letters. *Almost* everything in them ought to be printed, for they are a choice and delightful revelation of his personality, better worth reading by the world at large, I think, than many, many collections that are made public.

The use of a magnifying glass will greatly diminish the difficulties of reading his minute and compressed hand. After many years I seldom have trouble with it, yet even now a telescoped word will baffle me. For my own convenience in re-reading I have frequently written out on the margin a term or phrase that has cost me agonies to make out.

1. He was offered the position of literary editor on the Kansas City *Star* (see Letter 51).

2. Miss Brower is evidently referring to Mrs. Clara Davidge and Mrs. James Earle Fraser.

3. Miss Brower was working from memory or transcribing carelessly. Following *Maine* is *1889–1896*. On the line below PRINTED FOR THE AUTHOR is simply MDCCCXCVI; "Printed by H. O. Houghton and Company" appears on the verso of title page. The dedication reads: "This book is dedicated to any man, woman, or critic who will cut the edges of it. — I have done the top." Her later statement about "the thirty little pages" is also misleading; the actual pagination for the text of the poems is [5]–44.

4. Miss Brower misquotes this passage, which appears at the end of Letter 2; January 26, 1897.

5. Herbert S. Gorman's "Edwin Arlington Robinson, and a Talk With Him," appears on page 7 of section 6 in the Sunday edition.

6. Miss Brower's account differs in several respects from that provided by Kermit Roosevelt in a letter to Lucius Beebe (*Scribner's*, LXXXIX [January 1931], 95): "I first became acquainted with Mr. Robinson's poetry through seeing a copy of his first book in the library of Mr. H. H. Richards who was my Dormitory Master in Groton School. Mr. Richards is a son of Laura E. Richards, and a grandson of Julia Ward Howe, and he and Mr. Robinson were friends as boys in Gardiner, Maine." Kermit obtained from Richard G. Badger & Company a copy of the 1897 limited, vellum edition of *The Children of the Night*—which he believed to be Robinson's first book—and sent it to his father on January 19, 1904.

7. Robinson worked in the New York Custom House from January 1905 until shortly after Roosevelt's departure from the White House in March 1909.

8. Theodore Roosevelt, "The Children of the Night," *Outlook*, LXXX (August 12, 1905), 913–914.

9. In *The Torrent and the Night Before* (1896), line 4 of the poem reads: "The wind will moan, the leaves will whisper some—." It remained unchanged in *The Children of the Night* (1897), and in the second edition (1905). In *Collected*

Poems (1921), Robinson revised it to read: "The leaves will whisper there of her, and some, / Like flying words . . ."

10. See Letter 132; August 31, 1915.

11. Robinson visited Miss Brower at Wilkes-Barre on January 8 and 9, 1898. He was then twenty-eight.

12. See Letter 121; April 23, 1914.

13. Josephine Preston Peabody married Lionel S. Marks, a professor of engineering.

14. Mr. Venus is a taxidermist in Dickens' *Our Mutual Friend*, an articulator of bones "human and various."

15. See Letter 182, note 1.

16. Robinson spent his first summer at the MacDowell Colony in 1911 and returned every year until 1934. At the time of Miss Brower's statement, he was in his tenth summer of attendance.

17. Miss Brower's allusions here are uncertain. No inkling as to the first title has been turned up; as to the second, she may have had in mind *The Unknown Guest*, published in London and New York in 1914.

18. It is the opinion of Mrs. William Nivison, Robinson's niece, that Captain Craig is an aggregate portrait of the poet's brother Horace Dean, of Alfred H. Louis, and others; that Killigrew was more probably Seth Ellis Pope; and that Miniver Cheevy is the poet himself, exaggerated.

19. In Letter 5 Miss Brower underlined in blue: "life is a compensatory struggle toward the realization of the universal mind."

20. In the revised numbering of the letters in this volume, this is Letter 150; June 1, 1919. Miss Brower misquotes Robinson in the next sentence. The passage is rendered correctly in note 19.

Appendix II
EDWARD ARLINGTON ROBINSON
By Edith Brower

People say a great deal about the world's not wanting poetry any more. "This scientific age"; "age of materialism"; "cycle of invention and discovery"; "the almighty dollar, etc., etc."—such phrases are eternally in our ears. And because they all point to a truth which is on every side evident—namely, that the present period really is astonishingly and unprecedentedly practical and materialistic—they have come to be accepted as expressing the entire truth.

This they are far from doing. Discouraging as the spiritual outlook often appears, yet if a man will only use his own eyes and not those of others; if he will forget for a few moments the phrases just quoted, and listen to certain quieter but just as insistent world-voices, he shall be cured of any transient pessimism to which he may have yielded; he shall see and hear enough to prove to him the full truth of Keats's saying, that "the poetry of earth is never dead,"—poetry here standing for all that excites or expresses the aesthetic in man's nature, not to mention any ethical or spiritual import it may have. It surely is not dead in our own land. That we have at the present moment in painting a Lafarge and a Sargent, in sculpture a St. Gaudens, in music a MacDowell, sufficiently proves it. These men, though working in different art materials, represent, each in his own person, the highest type of artist; that is, one whose faultless technical skill serves as the expression of a profound spirituality.

If one says, "but men such as these are scarce," I reply: Most certainly they are, and have been in every age and country. When nature executes her superfine in human shape, she does it after the artistic, not

This is Miss Brower's critical appreciation of *The Children of the Night*, to which Robinson refers in Letter 30. It appeared in the Wilkes-Barre *Times*, December 20, 1897, page 15. The error in Robinson's first name was made by the headline typesetter. Miss Brower renders it correctly in the text of the essay.

the mechanic, fashion;—in other words, she does not turn out her chefs-d'œuvres by the gross, but makes only one of a kind. The multitude does not require individual teachers; a single pre-eminent soul, gifted with whatever mode of speech, will speak to thousands. From the very nature of printed matter, the poet can reach a larger number of his fellowmen than any other kind of artist. This is fortunate, since his direct ethical force and influence are far greater than those of the painter or composer. I say, fortunate, always supposing him to be of the first order—ranking poets first by the importance of the message they have to deliver, and second by the power and beauty of their utterance.

That the poet whose name heads this article voices with a quite overcoming boldness and in an entirely individual manner some of the loftiest and most comprehensive thoughts that are stirring a few brave, unconventional spirits today, is not to be questioned. That certain large, plain, wholesome truths have uncovered to him depths and breadths of meaning not understood by "the general" without aid, is a claim verifiable upon almost every page of his little book, *The Children of the Night*. Yet, whether he has succeeded in uttering what he knows or divines of the World beyond the world, in a way that shall be acceptable and useful for all time, those who come after us must be the judges, not we. We can tell only if he has proved acceptable to us, if he has helped us; and if he has, and so filled the part assigned for him to fill, what more could an eternity of fame do for him? Edwin Arlington Robinson is not the man to ask for more.

Let him tell us in his own words what he thinks he is here for. This is the first of twenty-five consecutive short poems written in that highly condensed and severely artistic form known as the octave.

> To get at the eternal strength of things,
> And fearlessly to make strong songs of it,
> Is, to my mind, the mission of that man
> The world would call a poet. He may sing
> But roughly, and withal ungraciously;
> But if he touch to life the one right chord
> Wherein God's music slumbers, and awake
> To truth one drowsed ambition, he sings well.

These eight lines show us we need not expect to find much verse of the light, soft, sensuous sort in Mr. Robinson's book. Those who desire to remain in their sins and be soothed must go elsewhere. Poetry with him is not mere music, though he scorns not the music of it; it is more than a pleasant entertainment for thoughtless, idle hours. It comes, rather, as the voice of one crying in the wilderness, calling upon men almost sternly, at times, to look at Truth as she has been shown to him. The gist of that revelation seems to be that there is no commonplaceness in life, unless we view life through commonplace eyes; that man was not made to mourn but to rejoice;—to rejoice even in the darkness, since darkness presupposes "the coming glory of the light"; that there is no evil in the universe to those who have once glimpsed the true Real, in other words, the Divine Ideal, which must embrace all things.

And if God be God, He is Love;
  And though the Dawn be still so dim,
It shows us we have played enough
  With creeds that make a fiend of Him.

There is one creed, and only one,
  That glorifies God's excellence;
So cherish, that His will be done,
  The common creed of common sense.

It is the crimson, not the gray,
  That charms the twilight of all time;
It is the promise of the day
  That makes the starry sky sublime;

It is the faith within the fear
  That holds us to the life we curse;—
So let us in ourselves revere
  The Self which is the Universe!

Perhaps this is not a new communication. If it is not, so much the better for its success. Humanity rarely listens to what is wholly new; it is the reiterated word in fresh forms that causes it at last to prick up its ears and give heed. But no prophet who brings an earnest message, learned out of his own soul, and delivers it in a way that is his very own, has ever yet failed to make some impress, if only on a small portion of the "remnant that saves." This being true, we boldly and publicly bid Mr. Robinson to be of good courage, which, however, he appears disposed to be without our bidding.

A little paper edition printed by the author a year ago, containing the greater part of what the present bound volume contains, met with small notice and that hardly of an adequate quality. The most prominent of these notices dismissed Mr. Robinson as a pessimist; but the critic(?) must have had a curious idea of pessimism, or else he read superficially. There is undoubtedly a tinge of sadness in nearly everything this young poet writes—what we might call a New England sadness, arising from deep thought experience, never from despair. There is nowhere discernible to one who reads him thoroughly any faith in "hell's fulfillment of the end of things"—to quote a line of his own. It is Heaven's fulfillment that he looks for, nay, actually sees with those far-piercing poet's eyes. Hear him again, O dispassionate reader, and say if there is any lack of a right brave hope in him:

Forebodings are the fiends of Recreance;
The master of the moment, the clean seer
Of ages, too securely scans what is,
Ever to be appalled at what is not;
He sees beyond the groaning borough lines
Of Hell, God's highways gleaming, and he knows
That Love's complete communion is the end
Of anguish to the liberated man.

Elsewhere he sings of:

Life's all-purposeful
And all-triumphant sailing,

of:

Man's unconjectured godliness—

can any despair for the race be extracted out of this?

of:

indissoluble Truth,
Wherein redress reveals itself divine,
Transitional, transcendent.

of:

the glorifying light
That screens itself with knowledge,—

as if the much-valued earthly learning were less for our immediate enlightenment, than for a merciful shade to eyes now spiritually too dim to endure real Truth's bright shining. That we shall some day be strong-sighted enough to endure it, there is no doubt in our poet's mind, though he gives us small hope in this direction so long as we continue to pursue knowledge only for knowledge's sake; for he has the bard's true scorn for the shell without the meat; for:

> Songs without souls, that flicker for a day,
> To vanish in irrevocable night.

for:

> altars where we kneel
> To consecrate the flicker, not the flame—

and for:

> The prophet of dead words

who, he tells us, "defeats himself."

Not for a moment will he tolerate the laziness or the cowardice of soul that makes men to dawdle around the outside of things, indifferent if there be any inside, or unfaithfully fearful of the consequences of investigation. Never to such are the spiritual secrets of the material universe unfolded. "Never," he says:

> Never until our souls are strong enough
> To plunge into the crater of the Scheme—
> . . . are we to get
> Where atoms and the ages are one stuff.
>
> Nor ever shall we know the cursed waste
> Of life in the beneficence divine
> Of starlight and of sunlight and soul-shine
> That we have squandered in sin's frail distress,
> Till we have drunk, and trembled at the taste,
> The mead of Thought's prophetic endlessness.

That mead, terrible draught though it be, concentrated essence of the ages, oppressing weak spirits almost to death, is to him God's philter, the veritable love-potion of Divine Truth. He believes with Pater that "for man, in proportion as man thinks truly, thought and being are identical."

But this view is not to be interpreted as indicating that all of life—this present life—is in pure, inactive thought. Such thought is not God's, the Creator's. Man too, rejoicing in "The glory of eternal partnership," must create. The poet, nearest partner of God in his preeminent capacity of Seer—the man who most clearly sees the underlying meaning of things—must make, nor ever cease from making, and thus working faithfully, will he perhaps be able to show to others something of what he sees. And in proportion to this ability will he be Lord of the world, but at the same time the world's servant.

The master and the slave go hand in hand,
Though touch be lost. The poet is a slave,
And there be kings do sorrowfully crave
The joyance that a scullion may command.
But, ah, the sonnet-slave must understand
The mission of his bondage, or the grave
May clasp his bones, or ever he shall save
The perfect word that is the poet's wand!

The sonnet is a crown, whereof the rhymes
Are for Thought's purest gold the jewel-stones;
But shapes and echoes that are never done
Will haunt the workshop, as regret sometimes
Will bring with human yearning to sad thrones
The crash of battles that are never won.

And so the poor poet is a slave to himself as well as to the world, but he will work on, knowing well that:

There is one battle-field whereon we fall
Triumphant and unconquered.

The sonnets on Zola, Verlaine, Thomas Hood, Crabbe, and the short poem on Walt Whitman furnish what never fails to be interesting: A poet's characterization and estimate of poets. In "Cliff Klingenhagen," "Aaron Stark," "Charles Carville's Eyes," "Fleming Helphenstine," and "Reuben Bright," we find the sonnet form put to an entirely new use: That of a lightly touched, yet seriously conceived character study. These studies—seemingly of the fictitious order—remind us, in their quick, concentrated treatment of a single incident or trait, of the typical short story in prose, which par excellence, is "brief as woman's love" yet contains the essence of a life.

Upon "Luke Havergal," a little poem of four double stanzas, Mr. Robinson might rest his reputation for the pure poetical gift. Doubtless, a delicate spiritual discernment is needed to penetrate the supernatural atmosphere suffusing it, and to read under the paradoxes of its uncannily suggestive situation the true mystery of Love and Death; yet the lines have in themselves a weird attractiveness, whether they be meaningless or meaningful to the reader. The entire piece shall be given here to show the poet in a different mood from his usual one;—not less serious, for he is always that, but less oppressed by his sense of his mission, and indulging for the moment in the romance of poetry. Possibly he needs what Lowell attempted to teach himself in his "Fable for Critics":—to "learn the distinction twixt singing and preaching";—not that he should cease preaching, but that he should sing more, remembering that the "lyric cry" reaches souls that are beyond being touched by "strong songs" however "fearlessly" made. But the following is a strong song too, though it does not preach:

Go to the western gate, Luke Havergal,—
There where the vines cling crimson on the wall,—
And in the twilight wait for what will come.
The wind will moan, the leaves will whisper some—
Whisper of her, and strike you as they fall;
But go, and if you trust her she will call.
Go to the western gate, Luke Havergal—
Luke Havergal.

No, there is not a dawn in eastern skies
To rift the fiery night that's in your eyes;
But there, where western glooms are gathering,
The dark will end the dark, if anything:
God slays Himself with every leaf that flies,
And hell is more than half of paradise.
No, there is not a dawn in eastern skies—
In eastern skies.

Out of a grave I come to tell you this,—
Out of a grave I come to quench the kiss
That flames upon your forehead with a glow
That blinds you to the way that you must go.
Yes, there is yet one way to where she is,—
Bitter, but one that faith can never miss.
Out of a grave I come to tell you this—
To tell you this.

There is the western gate, Luke Havergal,
There are the crimson leaves upon the wall.
Go,—for the winds are tearing them away,—
Nor think to riddle the dead words they say,
Nor any more to feel them as they fall;
But go! and if you trust her she will call.
There is the western gate, Luke Havergal—
Luke Havergal.

"The Night Before," the only long poem in the book, can be little more than referred to here. Not to refer to it would be absurd in any review of this collection of poems, yet the foundations are laid almost too broad and deep for a touch-and-go comment. It is the very innermost history of a crime related by the criminal himself on the eve of his execution. A simple enough tale and all too common:—Love, the murder of love, and then murder of love's murderer. The telling of a tale is the thing;—not the mere narration of facts, but "That reality, that substance, that precious and eternal treasure—the Meaning, the Object, the Gist of all we know as fact; this is the reality of revelation—spiritual and material—and more, Divinely Natural."

It is the Divinely Natural quality of the narration in "The Night Before," which makes it worth the reading.

This article, insufficient though it be as a criticism, aims to offer for the benefit of any who may care to use it, a key to what would seem the real intent of the little book under consideration. It does not aim to fix the standing of the author as a poet. Whatever that standing may be, is already fixed and unalterable, and will be known when the time comes for knowing. But even as the poet has felt compelled to speak out to the world what was given him to utter, so has one of his readers been urged from within to reinforce, by calling attention to it, his message which seems to her full of help, comfort and stimulus—help which does not emasculate; comfort which is not coddling; stimulus that is not a stimulant producing temporary excitement, but that reaches to the very roots of soul-activities and stirs the eternal life that is there.

Let the last word here be his, as it is also the last in his book:

Now in a thought, now in a shadowed word,
Now in a voice that thrills eternity,
Ever there comes an onward phrase to me

Of some transcendent music I have heard;
No piteous thing by soft hands dulcimered,
No trumpet crash of blood-sick victory,
But a glad strain of some still symphony
That no proud mortal touch has ever stirred.

There is no music in the world like this,
No character wherewith to set it down,
No kind of instrument to make it sing,
No kind of instrument? Ah, yes there is!
And after time and place are overthrown,
God's touch will keep its one chord quivering.

Appendix III
BOOKS BY EDWIN ARLINGTON ROBINSON

1896 *The Torrent and the Night Before.* Gardiner, Maine: privately printed. (Riverside Press, Cambridge, Mass.)
1897 *The Children of the Night.* Boston: Richard G. Badger & Co.
1902 *Captain Craig.* Boston: Houghton, Mifflin & Co. (Riverside Press, Cambridge, Mass.)
——— London: A. P. Watt & Son.
1903 ——— Second Edition. Boston: Houghton, Mifflin & Co. (Riverside Press, Cambridge, Mass.)
1905 *The Children of the Night.* New York: Charles Scribner's Sons.
1910 *The Town Down the River.* New York: Charles Scribner's Sons.
1914 *Van Zorn.* New York: Macmillan Co.
1915 *The Porcupine.* New York: Macmillan Co.
Captain Craig. Revised Edition. New York, Macmillan Co.
1916 *The Man Against the Sky.* New York: Macmillan Co.
1917 *Merlin.* New York: Macmillan Co.
1920 *Lancelot.* New York: Thomas Seltzer.
The Three Taverns. New York: Macmillan Co.
1921 *Avon's Harvest.* New York: Macmillan Co.
Collected Poems. New York: Macmillan Co.
——— New York: Brick Row Book Shop. 2 vols.
1922 ——— London: Cecil Palmer.
1923 *Roman Bartholow.* New York: Macmillan Co.
——— London: Cecil Palmer.
1924 *The Man Who Died Twice.* New York: Macmillan Co.
——— London: Cecil Palmer.
1925 *Dionysus in Doubt.* New York: Macmillan Co.
1927 *Tristram.* New York: Macmillan Co.
——— New York: The Literary Guild of America.
Collected Poems. New York: Macmillan Co. 5 vols.
——— Cambridge, Mass.: Dunster House. 5 vols.
1928 *Tristram.* London: Victor Gollancz, Ltd.
The Torrent and the Night Before. New York: Brick Row Book Shop.

Fortunatus. Reno: Slide Mountain Press.
Sonnets, 1889–1927. New York: Crosby Gaige.
——— New York: Macmillan Co.

1929 *Modred*. New York: Brick Row Book Shop.
Cavender's House. New York: Macmillan Co.
Collected Poems. New York: Macmillan Co.

1930 *Cavender's House*. London: Hogarth Press.
The Glory of the Nightingales. New York: Macmillan Co.

1931 *Selected Poems*. New York: Macmillan Co.
Matthias at the Door. New York: Macmillan Co.

1932 *Nicodemus*. New York: Macmillan Co.

1933 *Talifer*. New York: Macmillan Co.

1934 *Amaranth*. New York: Macmillan Co.

1935 *King Jasper*. New York: Macmillan Co.

1937 *Collected Poems*. New York: Macmillan Co.

Index